Praise for
Tax Me I'm Canadian

The essence of government is coercion. Faceless others over whom we have little control tell us how to spend much of our time and money. The silent and deadly coercive tool of choice is taxation. Government revenues constitute 43 cents out of every dollar in Canada. How to get a handle on this? Knowledge is the starting point for those who would be free. Mark Milke does us a huge service in this second book devoted to the great enemy of big government—truth. It will illuminate, outrage and hopefully motivate us to keep throwing the rascals out for as long as it takes. British Columbia (the subject of his first book) has made that happen. Why not Canada?

Gordon Gibson, columnist, author, and former B.C. Liberal leader

I don't know which is more distressing about the devastation this book reveals: the loss of the potential of two generations of Canadians, or the carnage that has been effected in the private market in Canada by thirty years of meddlesome bureaucrats with an authoritarian agenda and the power to tax. In either case, the Canadian people have been the victims of theft and this book explains, in the simplest of language, slowly, methodically, and sanely, why and how.

How did we arrive at this crossroads? This book explains it, with searing clarity. When you read it, remember to breathe. Then do something.

Elizabeth Nickson, columnist for the *National Post*

A brilliant, enlightening book that shows the heavy hand of the taxman in Canada. This book takes us from the first tax on moose and beaver pelts in 1650, to the 'temporary' income tax in 1917, to the hated GST in the 1990s. The title is *so* fitting.

Linda Leatherdale, Money Editor, *The Toronto Sun*

Also by Mark Milke
Barbarians in the Garden City - The BC NDP in Power (2001)

Thomas & Black Publishers
Calgary

Cover illustrations used by permission of Don Kew and Graeme MacKay

Printed in Canada by Friesen's

Retailers: Distributed by Sandhill Book Marketing
www.sandhillbooks.com
1-800-667-3848

National Library of Canada Cataloguing in Publication Data

Milke, Mark, 1967-
Tax me I'm Canadian : your money and how politicians spend it / Mark Milke and the staff of the Canadian Taxpayers Federation ; foreword by Elizabeth Nickson.

Includes bibliographical references and index.
ISBN 0-9687915-1-4

1. Taxation—Canada. 2. Fiscal policy—Canada. I. Canadian Taxpayers Federation. II. Title.
HJ2449.M54 2002 336.2'00971 C2002-911293-1

Contents

At the trough

Nice intentions, too bad about the results

Choices

Acknowledgements

I need to thank a small army of people for what the reader now holds in their hand. At the Canadian Taxpayers Federation: Ken Azzopardi for taking the risk; Troy Lanigan for proofing my verbose early drafts; Bruce Winchester for his research; Walter Robinson whose work on corporate welfare and health care reform is second to none (I have summarized much of Walter's work in the chapter on business subsidies); Tanis Fiss and Richard Truscott for their research; and Lois Wilkie for help with data entry. Dean Smith, who formatted and laid out the book and created the cover, deserves special mention. Thanks also to John Carpay and Victor Vrsnik.

Thanks to Elizabeth Nickson for the foreword and Gordon Gibson and Linda Leatherdale for your kind words. Other helpful people include Faith Farthing, Nancy Wise, Jason Clemens, Joel Emes, Peter Foster, Desiree Bukowski, Fred McMahon, Bill Robson and Finn Poschmann. Thanks to David Perry at the Canadian Tax Foundation for alerting me to the excellent works of tax historians J. Harvey Perry, Milton Moore, and W. Irwin Gillespie—their work helped immensely to provide context for the country's taxation and spending policies in Canada's early years. James Gauthier at the Public Institutions Division at Statistics Canada explained some of the finer details of the agency's information and how it differed from other data collected in other departments.

Cartoonist Adrian Raeside provided some of his very fine past work. The cover figures are courtesy of Graeme MacKay (who drew Paul Martin) and Don Kew (who drew Pierre Trudeau, Brian Mulroney and Jean Chretien).

Although the above people contributed to this project, their work and information should not be construed as an endorsement of what is contained herein. Also, while past research, studies and information requests conducted by the Canadian Taxpayers Federation were used in this book, any interpretation, opinions, and errors expressed are my sole responsibility.

Canadian Income Tax

THE INCOME WAR TAX ACT, 1917

WITH EXPLANATIONS BY THE MINISTER OF FINANCE

(AS REPORTED IN HANSARD)

AND

INSTRUCTIONS OF FINANCE DEPARTMENT

TABLE OF TAX PAYABLE BY INDIVIDUALS AND COMPANIES

FULLY INDEXED

BRYAN PONTIFEX

Chartered Accountant

TORONTO

THE CARSWELL COMPANY, LIMITED

19 DUNCAN ST., TORONTO

(The Compiler's profits will be donated to the Navy League of Canada)

Foreword

I don't know which is more distressing about the devastation this book reveals: the loss of the potential of two generations of Canadians, or the carnage that has been effected in the private market in Canada by thirty years of meddlesome bureaucrats with an authoritarian agenda and the power to tax. In either case, the Canadian people have been the victims of theft and this book explains, in the simplest of language, slowly, methodically, and sanely, why and how.

The social cost too is made plain. We have great unused capacity that is going stagnant. Remove the countless barriers to growth, and Canada could be a world leader. But right now, there is, in every sector, an incentive not to work, not to try, not to produce. The black economy is huge, no doubt greater than any measure yet devised can calculate. Many people, with great gifts and energy, rather than give their lives to Ottawa, have chosen to simply opt out or leave their home for another country. Why try? Why bother?

In ten years, the largest generational cohort in human history will begin to retire. They will begin to display the expensive diseases of aging; many have not been able to save enough for retirement. Because of the irresponsible fiscal policies of the liberal bureaucracy in Ottawa, we will not be able to pay the bills. We will face a Hobson's choice: additional tax hikes for the Canada Pension Plan, or huge borrowing, or large cuts to senior citizens' retirement benefits. Forty-five percent of every federal personal income tax dollar already goes to pay interest on the national debt. By 2025, 100 percent of the tax revenues of Alberta and B.C. will go to pay for health care.

How did we arrive at this crossroads? This book explains it, with searing clarity. When you read it, remember to breathe.

It's our money. We pay for everything. Here's a list: $50,000 to a UBC professor to study strippers. $250,000 to millionaire Moses Znaimer for his extremely successful monopoly station, MuchMusic. $6.5 billion a year, federally, to First Nations, who still live in poverty and despair, ruled with no accountability, and in authoritarian fashion, often by corrupt and predatory Native "chiefs." Billions of dollars over time to inefficient and dying corporations from coast to coast. Tens of billions of dollars in equalization payments to have-not provinces which provide incentives to citizens not to work.

In the most incendiary chapters, Mark Milke outlines just how many corporations and advocacy groups, non-profits, and charities receive tax money, which they then, in some cases, do not have to account for, even in the most rudimentary of ways. This funding creates a massive distortion in the democratic process, because the funding of these groups depends upon the whim or, in what is more likely, the tenaciously held political belief of bureaucrats who, when they distribute public money, our money, should be fiercely neutral. This open hand, with business, with environmental action groups, with anti-globalization protesters—who, in a fiendish set of contradictions, we pay to destroy public property, which we initially paid for and which we then pay to fix—is entirely destructive. Advocacy groups must compete for dollars in a free market. It is the only way they can know their supporters are whole-heartedly behind them. I resent the fact that I pay 18-year-olds to fight globalization, because I believe globalization and free markets are the only way to lift the poor in the Third World out of despair.

I resent the fact that I pay to advance the lesbian agenda in the public schools—not because I disapprove of lesbians, but because I disapprove of non-family members teaching about lesbian sex to children. I disapprove of my tax dollars going to prop up Bombardier in Quebec because, if the firm is so successful, they don't need public funding.

Over ten years, the Canadian Labour Congress received $41 million dollars from the Canadian government. I resent that fruits of some of my labour went to fund that, because I believe that, while trade unions once had a strong case, now they act, largely, as a drag upon the wages of ordinary men and women, the very clients they assert they protect. Do I have a choice in any of these funding decisions? No. Not only do I not have a choice but there is little accountability—if I refused to fund them, I would go to jail. This is not democracy in action; in fact, it is decidedly not democratic. Yet, in Canada, it is epidemic.

The government is stitched into every industry in such intimate ways that it acts like a cancer itself, feeding on and destroying the competitive market, which, as everyone reading this book knows, or should know, is the best, easiest, most efficient, and most moral way to bring goods to market, and execute almost all the basic functions of human life. Adam Smith's invisible hand is no myth.

Every businessman and woman knows that. No bureaucrat does. Why? Because they have never had to earn a living and sell something people actually want and need, which is a bracing lesson, and one everybody must sooner or later learn.

Read this book. Then do something. Let's unleash Canada's potential, and end the bias against work, saving, and investment. Let's stop our smartest, most ambitious, most mobile kids from leaving the country. We can do that by one simple act: increase the after-tax rate of return on productive activities. If we do that one thing—begin to surgically unpick the tentacles and stranglehold the vast bureaucracy has on our economy—tax revenues will rise sharply, and we will be able to pay our bills. Raising the after-tax reward for work, saving and investment will spur entrepreneurial risk-taking, increase new business starts, spur expansion of existing businesses, and raise the equity value of investments. It will increase real after-tax wages, therefore increasing the standard of living and the capacity to save for retirement.

In your hand you hold the defence for every argument you must make. Consider yourself called.

If not you, then who?

Elizabeth Nickson,
Salt Spring Island, October 2002.
Columnist for *The National Post*

Author's introduction

Every year, the federal government transfers $900 million to the Canadian Broadcasting Corporation but spends only half that amount ($437 million) on all of Canada's national parks system. On average over the last several years, Ottawa spent between $113 million and $290 million annually on Canada's roads—or between two and six percent of what it collects in gasoline taxes every year. Over the last decade, $700 million was expended on a gun registry that critics argue will not do much, if anything, to reduce crime. The $60 million spent every year on that program could put an extra 850 full-time cops on the street instead. The $100 million spent on two new planes for the prime minister or the other $100 million spent to set up a scholarship fund in Pierre Trudeau's memory—something private money usually accomplishes for politicians in other countries—could have gone to give our troops in Afghanistan proper uniforms for their surroundings or, at home, MRI machines for our hospitals.

The art of politics and the art of governing are both about making choices. No matter how much wealth a country creates, and whether its tax rates are 10 percent or 90 percent of its economy, choices will still have to be made about how to apportion the resulting tax revenue.

This book is all about choices, and it is meant to inform the reader about some of the choices made by our political class in the past, present, and what may confront them in the future. Speaking of choices, they were also made about this book. Much of the information herein pertains mainly to federal taxation and spending, though not all. Also, a volume 20 times as large on such issues could be written but that would require Auditor General report-type lengths. Instead, the reader will see snapshots of current political priorities: for example, special interest group funding. In other areas, history is helpful. Canadians should know that our country was not always enamoured with government for its own sake, but once believed that a limited state was preferable to the overtaxed, over-governed rebel colonies south of the border.

While Canada's size of government in 2010 should not resemble the Dominion's in 1890, neither is government as it exists now ideal. Many governments attempt too much and as a result waste tremendous amounts of time and money; auditor general reports testify to such on an annual basis.

In addition to the historical look at our tax and spending levels, the moral and philosophical arguments for taxing and spending for their own sake are examined and, arguably, are found wanting. States with governments of a medium size are every bit as peaceful and prosperous and healthy—sometimes more so—than nations with large governments vis-à-vis the economy.

In terms of solutions, I do not attempt to provide an "answer" for every problem. Sometimes a proper remedy is for a government *not* to do something it currently does. "Do no harm" is not a bad motto to live by. For example, governments should quit giving cash to corporate Canada. They may wish to reduce business tax rates in exchange, but enough empirical evidence exists to show that business subsidies are a failure and counter-productive; their elimination is long overdue. In other cases, politicians should rethink the relationship between the citizen and the state and how incentives and long-term trends matter—medical savings accounts and the reform of health care, for example. That said, while solutions are occasionally discussed in these pages, *Tax Me I'm Canadian* is meant to be expository and to introduce the general reader to ideas perhaps not yet considered, to point in the direction of possible solutions, including those suggested by others, but not to serve as a textbook or last word on any one issue.

Some parts of this book will entertain; others will irritate. (It is perhaps best not to read the chapter on boondoggles just before turning in for the night.) Hopefully it will also serve as a reference. But whether the reader chuckles or clenches, no one should think Canada cannot be changed and for the better. One can be realistic about politics without being cynical; that's the lazy way out. If that sounds unreasonably optimistic, it is not; it is based on my experience of pushing, pulling and cajoling governments and politicians on issues of accountability, sensible spending and tax relief.

In fact, I think politics is a noble calling and the blind cynicism that thinks all politicians or all governments are the same and that nothing will change is wrong. On that note, some will mistake the critiques in this book of certain political decisions as a slight against the institution of government itself or even as an attack on politicians in general. Wrong. Governments are necessary and desirable when limited in scope and modest in aim. But civil society thrives when governments respect the foundational elements of such: the rule of law, the protection of property, and the ability to provide for one's family and give to one's friends. Left alone, most people, families and friendships will bloom quite well with those minimums.

There will always be those in need, and one should be neither callous nor romantic about that. Compassionate societies and the politicians who govern should attempt to combat poverty, but there is a vast difference, for example, between an able-bodied male who can work and a handicapped mother who cannot; in terms of government policy, taxpayers and politicians should always make proper distinctions between the two.

But thinking that change is possible is not the same as thinking it is automatic or easy. Democracy requires vigilance and to ignore that duty is to show the greatest possible contempt for democracy itself. In five years with the Canadian Taxpayers Federation, I regularly came across stories, files, and documents about government priorities that made me wonder if progress was possible.

But then, on occasion, governments would get religion. When Alberta's Conservatives outlawed business subsidies in 1996, they did it after the public was mighty fed up with dishing out taxpayer cash to corporations. When the federal government proposed $20 million in subsidies for the National Hockey League in 2000, it was quickly bodychecked by taxpayers and the idea was dropped. One of the most recent and important victories for taxpayers over the past decade came in 2000, when the federal government and most provincial governments ended the practice of "bracket creep" taxation. Taxpayers were pushed into higher tax brackets simply by inflation and that ruse by governments cost taxpayers an extra $90 billion over fourteen years. By 2000, a $40,000 income had paid about $9,000 extra over that period compared to what that taxpayer would have paid had brackets been properly indexed for inflation.

Victories happened because some of us at the Canadian Taxpayers Federation researched, wrote, published studies and commentaries, sent out news releases to the media, did literally hundreds of interviews on those topics and tried to inform our supporters and the public at large. In the end though, when taxpayers picked up the phone and called their member of Parliament and told them hockey subsidies were a bad idea, that policy balloon popped in short order.

So tax relief and progress on spending priorities is possible. You *can* fight city hall, as well as your provincial capital and Ottawa. It is not always easy, it is not always successful, but it is always worth it. That said, I often must remind people who think the Canadian Taxpayers Federation and its staff or anyone else can solve something on their behalf, such sentiments are a retreat to the default position that many Canadians possess: i.e., "Let someone else (often government) take care of the problem or issue. They will solve it."

Part of the reward of limited government is a lower tax bill; part of the responsibility (as well as the path to that end) requires that people, wherever possible, take matters into their *own* hands. That includes not expecting government to provide every service and every good; it also, on the proactive side of things, requires citizens to press their politicians directly, write a letter to the newspaper or call a talk-show and express an opinion, or become involved politically. At the Federation, we often try and get information into the hands of our supporters and everyone else precisely so *they* can lobby the politicians and argue for change. Citizens working together can accomplish much. Canadians have more clout than they think.

So citizens, if they indeed prefer less funding for the CBC and more for parks, a better-equipped military, road and transit improvements as opposed to patronage spending, or sensible health care (as opposed to political) spending, and tax relief as opposed to corporate welfare, must communicate such priorities to their parliamentarians and legislators. Difficult or easy, in times of deficit or surplus, choices will always be made.

I reject the notion that Canada is merely a sorry, collectivist, groupthink nation, a second-rate country the identity of which is based on one-part anti-American political rhetoric and two-parts collective poverty vis-à-vis our neighbour to the south. More attention to individual responsibility and initiative is not the opposite of a civil society as some assume; it is in fact the foundation for it. There are other countries—Taiwan and Switzerland, for example—that are smaller than their respective neighbours (China and Germany or France) but exceed them in per capita wealth, health and other indicators. Canada too could exceed the United States on every indicator, but that will require correct choices and priorities.

Some define their Canada through a government program, subsidy, or Crown corporation that developed in the last 50 years. But this country has too proud a history—from the robust self-sufficiency of the first settlers on this continent long before Europeans arrived, to the beaches in Europe in two World Wars—to base its identity on something as uninspiring as a government bureaucracy or program. Personally, I feel much more Canadian when I hike through Banff National Park than when I watch another navel-gazing CBC documentary. If it were up to me, I know which one I would fund.

Mark Milke
October 2002

1

In the beginning...
The early origins of tax

All taxation is a loss *per se*. It is the sacred duty of the
government to take only from the people what is necessary to
the proper discharge of the public service; and that taxation in
any other mode, is simply in one shape or another, legalized
robbery.

Sir Richard Cartwright
Dominion Minister of Finance, Budget Speech, 1878[1]

The first tax

To find the origins of tax, one has to travel back in time to the ancient
world and to a fertile plain between the Tigris and Euphrates rivers, now
modern Iraq. History's first recorded tax was brought to mankind in
Sumer, six thousand years ago. It is there, inscribed on clay stones
excavated at Lagash that we learn of the first taxes, instituted to fight a
ferocious war. But as has often been the case throughout history, when
the battles ceased, the taxes stayed—a cause of no small discontent on
the part of the locals, who complained that taxes filled up the land from
one end to the other.[2]

Six millennia later, taxes have appeared, risen and fallen and are
intertwined with the history of peoples and states. When limited and
coupled with specific aims, taxes have helped some countries keep and
build empires. The case of the English income tax, first instituted in 1798
under Prime Minister William Pitt, is often cited as a key factor in
England's success in her war with France. (Napoleon refused to institute
a similar levy to prosecute his war.) The new tax provided a third of the
additional revenue needed to win the war with France.

Unsurprisingly though, Pitt's income tax was hardly popular. A naval
officer spoke for many in 1799 when he ventured: "It is a vile, Jacobin,

jumped up Jack-in-Office piece of impertinence—is a true Briton to have no privacy? Are the fruits of his labour and toil to be picked over, farthing by farthing, by the pimply minions of bureaucracy?"[3] Pitt's tax was repealed in 1802, and the modified version introduced by his successor was cancelled at the end of hostilities in 1815, and gave exception to the general rule that wars come and go but taxes stay.[a]

But if some taxes have been helpful to states and peoples, others have been injurious and fatal to freedom. In pre-Bolshevik Russia, serfdom evolved as overtaxed peasants could not fulfill their obligations to the state and accepted bondage to landowners in preference to taxation. In theory, the peasants could work off the debt they owed to wealthy landowners (incurred after the landowner paid taxes on their behalf); in practice, it rarely occurred. It was not the first time in history that the interests of a government in pursuit of tax and a special interest (i.e., landowners) coincided to penalize the very poor.[4]

Canada's first tax—on beaver pelts

In Canada, the first known instance of taxation was, with the view of history, rich with symbolism: an export duty on beaver pelts (at 50 percent) and moose pelts (at 10 percent) in what was then New France, in 1650.

And while the tax on beaver furs was soon reduced to 25 percent three years hence, by 1662, every import into the country was subject to a 10 percent tax for six years, necessary to help pay off colonial debt. (That levy stayed for *eight* years and was then replaced by equivalent duties on imported tobacco, wine and brandy.)

From there, the taxes of the colonial outpost multiplied. Excise taxes on both imports and exports sprouted as the European settlers grew in number and in geographic reach. The beaver pelt tax was abolished in 1707, but duties had already increased on tobacco and alcoholic imports. A new tax, on property, was instituted in Montreal in 1716, to pay for a stone wall built around the settlement.

Duties and excise taxes

Much of Canada's early and pre-Confederation governments relied heavily on duties and excise taxes applied to imports and exports as their main source of revenue. While other taxes existed, such as a land tax in Nova Scotia, most colonial governments used customs duties for

---

[a] The exception was itself temporary; another income tax introduced in 1842 in Britain remains to this day.

their revenues, applied in various ways. Ships that left Halifax, for example, were charged according to tonnage.

And it mattered little who the colonial master was; after the 1763 Treaty of Paris that gave the English formal control over French colonies, the existing tariff system was preserved and expanded. Over in Nova Scotia, import duties were applied to sugar, bricks, lumber, and billiard tables in 1764. One year later, excise taxes were levied on coffee and playing cards. Those were followed later that century by duties on chocolate and rum, and also a 10-percent tariff on American imports (with the exception of lumber, grain, and cattle).

From the end of the 18th century to Confederation, the average tariff rate rose from three percent to 12-15 percent,[5] which were increasingly joined by poll taxes[b] and property taxes as the main revenue providers for governments. Some were levied by cities, others by Upper Canada, Lower Canada, or the Atlantic colonies.[c] Provincial licences were necessary for peddlers in 1807 in Upper Canada. By 1882, New Brunswick required municipalities to levy poll and property taxes. In 1827, Upper Canada levied the first stumpage fees (the tax paid for cutting down trees on Crown land).[6]

Pre-Confederation income taxes: few, and levied by municipalities

While many Canadians might think the first income tax arrived in 1917 to help finance World War One, tax historian J. Harvey Perry speculates that the country's first income tax, at least in rudimentary form, may well have been in 1775. In that year, Nova Scotia instituted a temporary poll tax (for one year), which was graduated according to income.

Another more recognizable type of income tax to the modern citizen though was instituted in 1831 in the few New Brunswick municipalities then in existence. Perry notes that over in Nova Scotia, Halifax levied an income tax from its incorporation in 1849 and that tax continued for over three decades.[7]

With new governments came more taxes, and the establishment of a municipal system in Upper Canada in 1849 led to new levies exacted by elected municipal councils (as opposed to justices of the peace). After

---

[b] "Poll taxes" are uniform fees assessed on each person, usually as a prerequisite to voting.

[c] Prince Edward Island became a separate colony apart from Nova Scotia in 1769; New Brunswick followed by splitting off from Nova Scotia in 1784.

the 1850 *Assessment Act*, local taxes also included incomes, as long as the value of that income along with one's land and some other personal property exceeded £50.[8] Power to tax income was expanded again three years later. Meanwhile, over on the lightly populated West Coast colony of Vancouver Island, a "salaries tax" was imposed in the mid-1860s.[9]

Thus, while Upper and Lower Canada and the Atlantic colonies relied more on tariffs and duties for revenues, local governments relied on taxes applied to real estate, personal property and lightly on tax from incomes where it was included in the overall assessment of one's property.

The marginal nature of income tax in particular is evidenced by one of the earliest comprehensive records of municipal revenues. Total tax revenues to municipalities in Ontario in 1867 amounted to $3.2 million (based on a total assessed value of $244.7 million). Only *three percent* of that revenue came from the tax levied on incomes; the rest came from real estate taxes (87 percent) and taxes levied on personal property (10 percent).[10]

The Dominion of Canada in 1867

By 1867 and the founding of Canada, the colonies of Upper and Lower Canada had been the largest tax collectors, a position then abandoned as they relinquished most taxing power (of the type that was important at the time—duties and excise taxes) to the new Dominion government.

To gain an understanding of the makeup of federal revenues at Confederation, an examination of the revenues that flowed into the public treasury is most helpful. In 1867, total revenues to the Dominion government totalled $13.7 million. Almost two-thirds (62 percent) of the revenue came from customs,[d] while excise[e] taxes accounted for 22 percent of the revenues. Miscellaneous revenues and post-office money accounted for the other 14 percent.[10] At this point there were few of the taxes most modern Canadians are most familiar with, such as sales and income taxes.

In terms of what the new Dominion government spent money on in 1867, debt payments accounted for the largest share of federal expenses that year at $4.1 million (30 percent) of a $13.7-million budget. Transfers

---

[d] Webster's Dictionary defines "customs" as "duties imposed by law on imported, or less commonly, exported goods."

[e] Webster's Dictionary defines "excise" as "an inland tax or duty on certain commodities, such as spirits or tobacco, levied on their manufacture, sale or consumption within the country."

to provinces and municipalities accounted for $2.6 million; resource and development spending (on agriculture and surveying for example) accounted for $1.5 million.

General government outlays (policing, other law and order, justice and general administrative costs) accounted for $1.5 million. Defence expenditures totalled $800,000 while $300,000 was spent on other transfers including treaty payments. Another $1.1 million in spending is not listed under any particular category. Transportation and communication (for outlays mainly for public infrastructure such as railways for example) amounted to $1.8 million.[12]

With the addition of own-source revenues and expenditures from the provinces and municipalities, it is estimated that Dominion, provincial and local government revenues and expenditures would not have amounted to much more than $25 million in the Dominion's first year.[13]

Dominion Government Revenues and Expenditures in 1867
(millions of dollars)

Revenues

Excise Duties	Customs Import Duties	Post Office	Other	Misc.*				Total Budgetary Revenue
3.0	8.6	0.5	0.2	1.4				13.7

Expenditures

Defence	Other	Transport & Comm	Resources and Devel't	Public Debt Charges	General	Payments to Provinces and Municipalities	Not Classified	Total Budgetary Expenditure
0.8	0.3	1.8	1.5	4.1	1.5	2.6	1.1	13.7

*Miscellaneous revenues includes revenue from bullion and coinage, licences and permits, sales, and receipts for services.   Source: Urquhart and Buckley, Historical Statistics of Canada.

Keep us away from those high-tax Yankees

In Canada today, it is often assumed that our identity rests upon a higher tax burden vis-à-vis the United States. High taxes are justified as compassionate by those who equate effective government and compassion as the exclusive or primary domain of government intervention in the economy, with its requisite high levels of taxation.

There are problems with such an assumption, not least of which is the existence of other countries with higher standards of living—including longer life expectancies and an educated populace equal to our own—but with lower levels of taxation relative to the economy.[f] While some government is necessary for the rule of law, the security of property, defence of the nation and other foundational elements to a civilized society, a government that expands for its own sake is subject to the law of diminishing returns and *diminished* returns once it grows so large that it inhibits prosperity.

The curious attachment to high taxes on the part of some Canadians is questionable in its means to prosperity and in its moral assumption about what makes a country compassionate, i.e., that it is *government* spending and not personal charity or voluntary co-operation or non-government activities and attitudes that nurture and define compassion. But debates over the proper size of government aside, the historical record is that Canada's early identity was partly found in its attachment to limited government, lower taxes and more robust desire for liberty in *contrast* to the United States in the 19th century. At Canada's founding, and for at least 50 years after Confederation, Canada's leaders argued that such policies were necessary for the country's well-being.

Welcome to low-tax Canada: Love it so you won't leave it

For our earliest founders and Finance ministers, attracting immigrants and investment to Canada through the promotion of a low-tax regime was the stated goal for at least the first 50 years of our country's existence. The Dominion's leading politicians trumpeted Canada's lower taxes compared to the tax-happy Americans, an advantage they argued was needed to ensure citizens and would-be immigrants were not lost to the Yanks.

The idea that citizens existed as vassals for the state, to be emptied of money at the whim of a government that wanted revenue for higher purposes, was largely absent from Canada's founders. Theirs was a classic liberal world, in which the role of the state was to protect the citizen *from* government and to provide basic services, defined rather narrowly at that time, to be sure.[g]

This view was true as it concerned taxes in general, but was also held by the Liberal party of the day as it concerned one main revenue source of the day: tariffs. That tax, unlike most, had political appeal, as it could be used to stoke protectionist sentiment where a politician thought it

---

[f] For more on this, see Chapter 15.

[g] For more on this, see the excerpt at the end of this chapter on the debates between Canada's founders about whether they should enter Confederation. Some legislators believed such a move would lead to a crushing tax burden and, for that and other reasons, opposed relinquishing the sovereignty of their colonial legislature.

would win votes. The Liberals, who in that age understood themselves as disciples of Adam Smith and thus stood in the tradition of English free-traders and economic liberals, thought higher tariffs were not only uneconomical but also morally questionable.

At the time, while the Conservatives were generally more sympathetic to higher tariffs (the protectionist element was more politically tempting to them), both parties attempted to renew a reciprocity treaty even after the Americans opted out of the previous pact in 1866. The implicit foundation of such a treaty was, of course, fewer and lower tariffs. Even after the abrogation, Canadian governments continued to allow many American products in for free or at a low tariff while it attempted to sign another agreement on the issue.[14]

In 1876, the first post-Confederation Finance minister for the Liberals, Sir Richard Cartwright,[h] responded critically to the call for higher tariffs. He pointed out that such a hike would be injurious to most Canadians, as it transferred wealth from the many (in rural Canada) who bought a good, to the few (in the cities) who might manufacture or import the product:

> To enrich a very few and seriously impoverish the great mass of the people ... is not to add to any great extent to the population of the country, but to promote an artificial transference from the rural districts to the towns and cities at the expense of the agricultural interests...[15]

Cartwright's attitude to tariff hikes was buttressed by his philosophy towards taxes in general, which was in line with the classic liberal thought of the late 19th century, which by default favoured free markets. It was notably distinct from liberalism one century later in Canada and the U.S., where "liberal" and "socialist" were at times nearly interchangeable. That was not the liberalism of Cartwright's time, as his 1878 budget speech makes clear:

> All taxation is a loss *per se*. It is the sacred duty of the government to take only from the people what is necessary to the proper discharge of the public service; and that taxation in any other mode, is simply in one shape or another, legalized robbery.[16]

Another Liberal expressed much the same sentiment in the closing decade of the 19th century. In his 1894 campaign swing through Winnipeg in 1894, Liberal Opposition leader, Sir Wilfred Laurier (soon-to-be

---

[h] Cartwright was the Liberal's first Finance minister (1874-1878), but the new country's fourth. The other three, Conservative all, were: Honourable John Rose (1867-1869), Sir Francis Hincks (1870-1872), and Honourable S.L. Tilley (1873).

prime minister in 1896) attacked the protectionist policies of the Conservative government and emphasized freedom in a manner that today might be equated with modern American political rhetoric.

> The good Saxon word, freedom; freedom in every sense of the term, freedom of speech, freedom of action, freedom in religious life and civil life and last but not least, freedom in commercial life.[17]

For the 50 years between Confederation and the introduction of the wartime income tax in 1917, Canada's budget speeches had two central themes: Attract people to Canada and build the country. As Irwin Gillespie has written, our Confederation-era politicians assumed a policy of taxes lower than the U.S. as crucial to filling the country with immigrants and with investment, as both were the natural conditions necessary for prosperity:

> Dominion governments feared losing potential immigrants, as well as those immigrants who were newly settled in Canada, to the United States. Thus the principle applied to numerous tax rate changes was that they should not exceed the tax levels in the United States. Competition for those mobile human resources, not to mention the capital with which these immigrants (be they farmers or businessmen) arrived, was fierce. Consequently, all Dominion governments were determined to keep tax rates low.[18]

And the preference went beyond just lower taxes in general; in the specific case of an income tax, Canadian politicians between 1867 and 1917 routinely dismissed any call for such a tax as a political deathwish, as it was undesired by Canadians. George Foster, the Conservative Finance minister between 1889 and 1896, remarked in 1893 that he "would like to see the man who could be elected in any constituency on a policy of direct taxation."[19]

And besides, many politicians noted that such a tax would constitute interference with the taxing jurisdiction of the provinces and urban areas that already levied such a tax. As late as 1915, the federal Finance minister, also a Tory, noted the fact of income taxation in many municipalities and two provinces as one more reason why the Dominion government should not impose an additional income tax.[20]

Canada's modern taxes: Thank the USA

So what changed? A combination of events and American policy, actually. World War One and the federal income tax is the most obvious example of how an event propelled the introduction of that previously forbidden levy. But while events provided the context, new American policy often provided the justification. When Canadian politicians imposed additional and higher taxes in the late 19th and early 20th century, they invariably did so only after the Americans acted first. As well, there were direct legislative influences on Canadian tax laws both federally and provincially. Think of almost any modern Canadian tax: federal income tax, gasoline taxes, property taxes, and corporate taxes; almost all have American origins.

For example, the first provincial corporate tax in Quebec in 1882 came from an American precedent. The taxation of personal property, common in many Canadian municipalities at Confederation, was also American in origin, not British, as that country abandoned such taxes centuries before.[21] When Ontario and the other provinces introduced succession duty levies (known also as estate taxes or more bluntly as "death taxes"), the influence of American legislation in the Canadian versions was clear. As tax historian J. Harvey Perry writes:

> The Canadian provincial legislation was inspired by and modelled after legislation of the American states. Clear testimony to this fact is given in the work of R.A. Bayly (1902). Bayly said this about the original Ontario Succession Duty Act, on which many of the other provincial acts were based: "That the New York and Pennsylvania Acts in force at the time were copied in principle and detail must be at once apparent to anyone who compares them with the Ontario Act of 1892."[22]

At another point he writes:

> "The first Canadian Act was drafted in the office of the Attorney General for Ontario and was modelled upon the Acts of New York passed in 1887.... The Ontario Act of 1892 was purely American in its origin."[23]

The pattern established in the last twenty years of the 19th century—where Canadian governments copied the taxing habits and also the legislation of American governments—continued unabated into the new century.

Canada's federal income tax, introduced in 1917 and three years after the American federal income tax, bore the mark of U.S. legislative influence. Canada's first federal income tax,[i] brought into being by the

---

[i] The Americans brought in a federal income tax briefly in the 19th century, during the Civil War, abandoned it afterward and then, after a skirmish in the country's Supreme Court in the 1890s and then a constitutional amendment, introduced it again in 1913.

Tax Fact
How much would the 1917 basic personal exemption be worth in today's dollars?

Back in 1917 when income tax was first instituted, Canadians could earn $1,500 before federal tax began to take effect. Given inflation, that $1,500 basic personal exemption would now be worth $19,088.

How does that compare to today's exemption? As of 2002, the federal exemption for Canadians was $7,700, while provincial basic exemptions ranged from a generous $13,339 in Alberta to a meagre $6,213 in Quebec.

Dominion Income War Tax Act of 1917 "bore an unmistakable resemblance to the similar 1913 American legislation," wrote one historian.[24]

The combination of events and American influence can be seen in the incidence of Canada's first gasoline taxes. With the provinces responsible for road construction during this period, the burgeoning growth in vehicle ownership in Canada necessitated new taxes to pay for the additional roads. In 1905, the number of registered passenger cars in all of Canada had totalled just 553. That jumped to over 60,000 ten years later, and then to over one million by 1930.[25]

The first gasoline tax in Canada was levied by Alberta in 1922 at a rate of two cents per gallon. But Alberta was hardly the first North American jurisdiction; the Americans already taxed fuel in Oregon, Colorado and North Dakota by 1919; in Kentucky in 1920, and in 15 other U.S. states in 1921. In all, 19 states placed a tax on gasoline before Alberta. But once the "wild rose province" taxed gasoline, other Canadian provinces soon followed with only Saskatchewan holding out until 1928 and taking pride in having waited that long.[26]

In terms of revenues, the automobile was an ever-increasing component of provincial revenues. Minimal in 1920 (when revenues for vehicles came solely from registration), by 1930 gasoline taxes and vehicle licensing accounted for 26 percent of all provincial revenues.[27]

The American precedent was also there for other taxes. When Canadian provinces introduced sales taxes over the course of several decades, beginning with Alberta in 1936 under the *Ultimate*

Henry Ford and his Model T in Buffalo, New York, 1921. Ford's invention of the assembly line was a boon to provincial governments in Canada. By the end of the 1920s, the revenues from automobile licences and gasoline taxes accounted for one-quarter of all provincial revenues. (From the Collections of the Henry Ford Historical Museum.)

Purchasers Act[28] (though the province yanked the tax just one year later), American states had already ventured into that territory.

After the Americans: The Great Depression and World War Two

While World War One and new and easily taxed inventions such as the automobile boosted government taxation and spending in the first several decades of the 20th century, the Great Depression (and later World War Two) propelled government intervention and taxation to new heights. But while the upheaval of the Depression resulted in government and taxes unheard of to citizens of that period, the burden was small by today's measure. Nonetheless, it was judged by what people were familiar with to that point and the Depression sent Canadian governments in search of more revenues and every tax lever at hand was soon pumped in the attempt. Once again, Perry:

> In the scramble for tax revenues, corporate and personal incomes were particularly the subject of attack. Only the Dominion, British Columbia and Prince Edward Island taxed corporate profits in 1930; a decade later all provinces were in the field. Similarly, the number of provinces levying personal income taxes increased from three to seven. While these new provincial taxes were being imposed the federal income tax rates approximately doubled. The federal sales tax was increased from a rate of one percent to eight percent and many new excise taxes were introduced. Provincial gasoline taxes were raised 50 percent on average; retail sales taxes were introduced in the provinces of Saskatchewan and Quebec and in the cities of Montreal and Quebec, succession duty rates were raised, exemptions lowered and enforcement stiffened. New flat rate taxes were introduced and old ones increased. In terms of increased rates and new levies, the onslaught on the taxpayer was comparable to that of World War II, but in addition the hidden burden in the form of double or triple taxation, overlapping administration, multiple accounting and multifarious forms was also onerous.[29]

One clear measure of the increased tax burden is in the ratio of taxes relative to the economy. In 1929, taxes amounted to just over 15 percent of Gross Domestic Product (GDP). As the onslaught of the Depression deepened, the combination of a shrunken economy and new and higher taxes meant that by 1932, taxes as a percentage of the economy climbed to over 25 percent. That ratio declined slightly during the ensuing years but was broached again by 1941. And that height was soon surpassed again. The necessity of revenues for the war effort resulted in taxes equal to 48 percent of all economic output in 1944.

One measure of the tax burden for individuals is shown in the decreased personal exemption and higher rates; mid-war in 1942, the basic exemption was lowered to just $660, significantly less than the original $1,500 allowed when income tax was introduced in 1917. Thus, 25 years later and despite inflation, more personal income than ever was subject to taxation. And marginal federal tax rates, which ranged from four percent to 29 percent in 1917, hit a 1944 wartime marginal rate peak of between 33 and 98 percent.

Post-World War Two, taxes (as well as spending) were consistently reduced both in actual rates on people and business and also relative to the growing economy, and by 1950 taxes amounted to just 21 percent of the economy. The tradeoff was slower debt reduction, but as Liberal Finance minister D.C. Abbott remarked at mid-century, "the present level of personal income taxes is regarded as excessive by a large proportion of the public."[30] Indeed.

Retrospective: Was the federal income tax intended to be permanent?

It is assumed that the federal income tax introduced in 1917 was meant to be temporary. Certainly it seems that way from a reading of budget speeches of the period, and the federal government made every effort to avoid levying an income tax. Sir Thomas White, the Conservative Finance minister who eventually brought in the income tax, first attempted to finance the war effort via increases in existing duties and tariffs.

In the 1914 budget, tariffs were increased on coffee, sugar, spirits, and tobacco and excise duties were also upped. In 1915, additional tariff increases were applied once again to most consumable goods. "The chief source and mainstay of our revenue is the tariff and it is to this we look principally for relief of our present financial condition,"[31] noted White, who was also forced to borrow heavily to finance the war effort. (It is estimated that in the second year of the war effort, $166 million would be required for that purpose; the tax increases were meant to bring in between $28 million and $35 million.)

In 1915, White still resisted an imposition of an income tax. His chief objection was that the provinces had very few taxes that they could levy under the constitution, and thus, because several provinces already did so, it was his view that "the Dominion should not enter upon the domain to which they [the provinces] are confined to a greater degree than is necessary in the national interest."[32]

By 1916, however, the war had lasted longer than anyone had foreseen in 1914, and the reality of wartime needs forced a change in policy. Public opinion and the sacrifices imposed by a wartime economy had also been critical of the appearance of some firms making large profits during wartime. Thus, in the budget, Sir Thomas White introduced a tax upon business war profits. Some thought he did not go far enough but he later cautioned such critics in this manner:

> During the war there has been considerable criticism to the effect that the Business Profits Tax was not sufficiently heavy. In my view this criticism is not sound and fails to take into consideration many vital aspects of the subject. A Business Profits Tax is justifiable during a prolonged war, because money is urgently needed and it is a ready method of obtaining it in large amounts. There is also a justification in the fact that public opinion is offended at the sight of abnormal profits in a period of great suffering and privation. On principle, however, the tax is not sound and tends to produce much economic evil in the State. It is really a tax upon business success, and consequently tends to discourage business enterprise and administrative efficiency....[33]

White also took exception to the view that a tax on business was in some way neutral to the average citizen. He noted that taxation costs, like any other, are built into the price of products and thus transferred to the public.

> There is no doubt in my mind that the taxation of business profits in England, United States and Canada has had much to do with increased prices of commodities. Taxation always tends to transfer itself to the consuming public, no matter what its immediate incidence may be.... It is not difficult to see the national disadvantage of such a tax beyond the abnormal war period.[34]

Taxes become personal

As late as April 1917, and despite increases in the Business Profits Tax, the Finance minister still resisted introducing a personal income tax. But three months later, another 100,000 men were called to serve. This was to be an extra cost to the nation not only in dollars but of more obvious importance—potentially in blood. Thus, Thomas introduced the Dominion's first national income tax on July 25, 1917, in the *Income Tax War Act*. He noted that this was a reluctant action, given that several provinces already imposed such a tax (Prince Edward Island and British Columbia) and that municipalities also imposed an income tax, similar in measure to the amount the Dominion government was then poised to bring into force.

Was it meant to be permanent? White's reluctance to see a permanent business tax imposed was matched by his distaste for a tax on personal income, but he seemed to realize that the decision about its permanence was not likely to be his to make:

> I have placed no time limit upon this measure, but merely placed upon Hansard the suggestion that a year or two after the war is over, the measure should be definitely reviewed by the Minister of Finance and the Government of the day, with a view of judging whether it is suitable to the conditions which then prevail.[35]

Thus was Canada's first federal income tax born; the rate began at four percent for any income above $1,500 (then the basic exemption), or just above $19,000 in today's dollars.

Taxes and Canada's founding debates

Concerns about taxes and self-government (along with many other issues) featured prominently in 19th-century debates over whether British colonies should join the proposed Dominion of Canada.

Some legislators argued that their colonies should remain their own entity rather than join Canada and one day be taxed and governed in a manner not to their liking.

Not everyone at the time agreed with such sentiments, but they do reveal one aspect of the debate about whether or not Confederation was entirely desirable. Here are some excerpts from *Canada's Founding Debates,* edited by Janet Ajzenstat.

It was idle to suppose that if we joined this Confederation, we should be exempt from an increase of taxes. How were an army and navy for the Confederation to be supported? In four or five years hence we would have as much increased taxation as we received from Canada.

John Casey, House of Assembly, Newfoundland, January 27, 1865[36]

As far as I can see, there is no chance of gaining anything, but there are many chances to lose. I think the offer is something like this: if we give up one-half of our revenue to the Canadians, and allow them to tax us as much as they please, they would then take charge of us. We fought hard and contended long for responsible government, and are we now going to give up our constitution and say we are not able to govern ourselves? I do not think that any man or any body of men in Canada can know the wishes or wants of the people of this island as well as we do ourselves.

Alexander Anderson, Prince Edward Island Legislative Council, April 1, 1865[37]

The expenses of this scheme would have been enormous, inasmuch as we would have had to have kept our own legislature and a union of all the legislatures in Canada, and we give them the power to tax us as much as they please; if there was any necessity for this union it would be much better to have one parliament for all; by this means we would save a great deal of expense.

Robert Thomson, New Brunswick, House of Assembly, June 1, 1865[38]

This Confederation scheme cannot benefit our trade. We have not a single article we can send to Canada… We would soon have all our offices filled with employees of the Canadian government, while we would have to pay three times the taxes in proportion to our numbers…

Robert Thomson, New Brunswick, House of Assembly, June 1, 1865[39]

If we are confederated with Canada we become its tributary, and in all that concerns us chiefly Canada has to act for us. In all our chief concerns—commerce, shipping, and mercantile laws, agriculture, trade, navigation, fisheries, currency, banking—Canada rules. She may tax us to any extent and in any manner she pleases, so that it is quite possible we may have export duties on gold and coal. All such things as require money for their performance are left for the colony to provide; those that require intellect are supplied by Canada. Is it necessary that we should pay for the intellect of Canada? Is not our own as good? Cannot we do all as well as they? Cannot we pay our colonial intellect to do our business well, instead of theirs to do it badly?

J.S. Helmcken, British Columbia Legislative Council, March 9, 1870[40]

At present we are legislating in the face of our constituents, having an election every four years; and if we oppress them or overtax them they can supply our places with those men worthy of their confidence. But if we united with Canada we would have no redress, for Canada would do with us as she pleased. What influence would eight men have to prevent our taxation being doubled?

John Haywood, Newfoundland House of Assembly, February 22, 1865[41]

I say that the power of regulating our own commerce is taken away and the only power left to us is that of raising taxes for municipal purposes. That is the difference between being a colony of Canada and a colony of England. The distance is so great between this colony and Ottawa, without any railway and without any telegraphic communication, that laws might be passed there which would ruin British Columbia, without our having any notice of them.

J.S. Helmcken, British Columbia Legislative Council, March 16, 1870[42]

Taxes in Canada: Confederation - present

Gov't	Customs	Excise	🪙 Personal Income	Poll	Natural Resource	Death
Federal	1867	1867	1917		1974	1941*
PE	&	&	1894	1877*	1971	1894*
NS	C	C	1962		1869	1892*
NB	C	C	1962		1901	1892*
NF	&	&	1917		1844	1914*
PQ	C	C	1939		1880	1892*
ON	C	C	1936		1826	1892*
MB	&	&	1923		1931	1893*
SK			1932	1919*	1931	1903*
AB			1932		1931	1903*
BC	&	&	1876	1869*	1871	1894*

* Asterisk indicates tax was later repealed. C indicates tax was repealed at Confederation. & indicates customs and excise taxes were repealed in Manitoba in 1870, PEI in 1873, in B.C. in 1871, in Newfoundland in 1949. Note that some provincial taxes, such as corporate income and business taxes, and personal income taxes, were suspended during part of World War Two (and also later depending on the province and its agreements with the federal government) in exchange for additional payments from the federal government.

Taxes in Canada: Confederation - present (continued)

Gov't	Corporate Income	Corporate	General Sales	Selected Excise Taxes on:		
				Alcohol	Autos	Gas
Federal	1918	1916	1920	1920	1918	1942
PE	1920	1894	1960	1918	1914	1924
NS	1939	1903	1959	1920	1912	1925
NB	1938	1892	1950	1920	1911	1926
NF	1917	1949	1950	1925	1906	1949
PQ	1932	1882	1940	1921	1906	1924
ON	1932	1899	1961	1918	1903	1925
MB	1931	1900	1967	1922	1908	1923
SK	1931	1907	1937	1915	1908	1928
AB	1932	1907	1936*	1918	1912	1922
BC	1901	1901	1948	1917	1914	1923

*Asterisk indicates tax was later repealed. Sources: W.I. Gillespie. (1991).*Tax, Borrow and Spend* and Milton Moore and J. Harvey Perry. (1966). *The Financing of Canadian Federation: The First Hundred Years*.

2

Plucking the goose
How taxes are collected and spent

The art of taxation consists in so plucking the goose as to obtain the largest amount of feathers with the least possible amount of hissing.

Jean Baptiste Colbert, Controller General to Louis XIV

How are you taxed? Let me count the ways

Personal income tax. Corporate income tax. Property tax. Goods and services tax. Provincial sales tax. Tobacco tax. Permit tax. Hotel tax. Employment Insurance tax. Canada Pension Plan tax. Royalty tax. Air conditioning tax. Airport security tax. Natural resource tax. Business tax. Toll taxes. Airport departure tax. Airport navigation tax. Duty taxes. Tire tax. Environmental tax. Fuel tax. School tax. Licence tax. Gun permit tax. User fee taxes. Tape tax. Excise tax. Personal surtax. Corporate capital tax. Personal capital gains tax. Financial institutions tax. Provincial payroll tax. Alcohol tax. Liquor mark-up tax. Customs tax. Import tax.

And now governments even tax you for the withdrawal of your own money at an Automatic Teller Machine (ATM).

And that's the short list. Add up all the taxes and (measured as a percentage of GDP) they equal 37.5 percent of the economy.[1]

But that's not the whole story. Add up all the *expenditures* by every level of government, and it equals 41.9 percent of the economy.[2] Add up all the *revenues* governments in Canada collect and the size of government in Canada equals 42.7 percent of the economy.[3]

Why the difference in the percentages? Several reasons: for one, think of the Crown corporations that do not collect taxes but may collect fees or charge for their services (the post office for example). If such extensions of government were a ministry instead of a Crown, their "taking" and "spending" would be counted in government budgets as regular revenues and expenditures.

As well, governments can and do spend more than they take in taxes; thus expenditures can and are often higher than government revenues. When governments run deficits, it does not show up in the tax burden—*this* year. But deficits reveal themselves later when the time comes to repay that borrowed money; taxes must then be higher than they otherwise would be. So, to grasp the size of government, one has to look at all its tentacles, which includes those agencies and corporations at arm's-length, as well as how much a government borrows.

Revenues—all levels of government

In total, Canadian governments collected over $463 billion in 2002 and spent $454 billion, eking out an overall Canada-wide government surplus of $9 billion. That includes all provinces, the federal government, municipalities, and Crown corporations.

The lion's share of that revenue came from income tax ($185 billion or 39.5 percent); consumption taxes contributed another $89 billion (19.2 percent). Property taxes—probably the second most "seen" and hated tax (after the goods and services tax) because most Canadians pay it in a large chunk once a year—contribute $41 billion or 8.9 percent every year to government bottom lines. Social security taxes such as the Canada Pension Plan and Employment Insurance throw almost $60 billion into the pot (13 percent). Never let it be said that governments are not active participants in business: Over $34 billion in government revenues comes from government-owned businesses.

Why your boss hasn't given you a raise: rising payroll taxes

Want to know why your boss hasn't given you a raise recently? Part of the answer is that your raise went to Ottawa in the form of increased payroll taxes (Canada Pension Plan and Employment Insurance premiums). Since 1992, payroll taxes for an employee who earns $41,000 have jumped by 40 percent to over $2,530 every year from $1,800—a $730 increase.[a]

Businesses must also remit payroll taxes on their employees' behalf. To use the same $41,000 example, that employer pays almost $630 more per year now compared to ten years ago.

---

[a] One often-misunderstood part of federal revenues is the Employment Insurance account "surplus." Some have called for the EI surplus (worth about $36 billion) to be refunded to workers and businesses, who both pay the payroll tax. There is only one problem: there is no actual surplus; it exists only on paper. The EI money collected has gone into general revenues and has already paid for health care, transfer payments to the provinces, as well as numerous other items and programs the federal government spends tax dollars on every year.

Taxes as a percentage of GDP
1965 - 2000

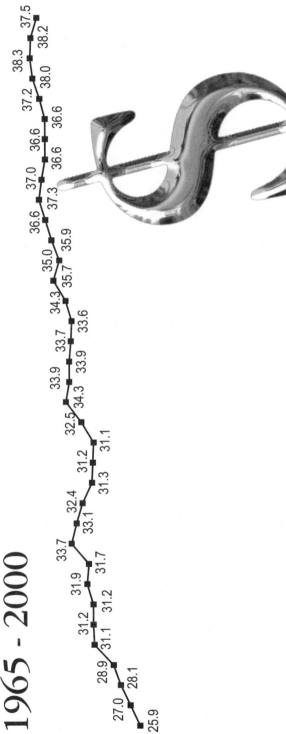

27.0 28.9 31.2 31.9 33.7 32.4 31.2 32.5 34.3 33.9 33.7 34.3 35.0 36.6 37.0 36.6 37.2 38.3 37.5
25.9 28.1 31.1 31.2 31.7 33.1 31.2 31.1 31.3 33.9 33.6 35.7 35.9 37.3 36.6 36.6 38.0 38.2

65 66 67 68 69 70 71 72 73 74 75 76 77 78 79 80 81 82 83 84 85 86 87 88 89 90 91 92 93 94 95 96 97 98 99 00

Source: Organization for
Economic Cooperation and
Development

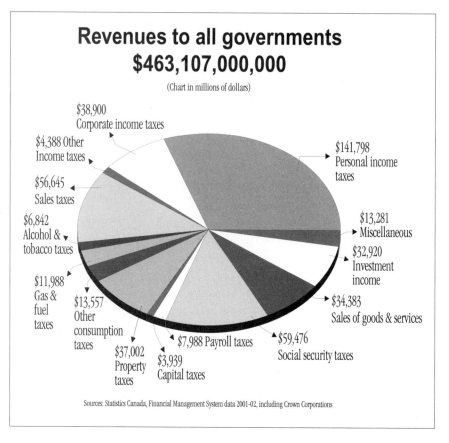

Revenues to all governments
$463,107,000,000

(Chart in millions of dollars)

$38,900
Corporate income taxes

$4,388 Other
Income taxes

$56,645
Sales taxes

$6,842
Alcohol &
tobacco taxes

$11,988
Gas &
fuel
taxes

$13,557
Other
consumption
taxes

$37,002
Property
taxes

$3,939
Capital taxes

$7,988 Payroll taxes

$59,476
Social security taxes

$141,798
Personal income
taxes

$13,281
Miscellaneous

$32,920
Investment
income

$34,383
Sales of goods & services

Sources: Statistics Canada, Financial Management System data 2001-02, including Crown Corporations

Because payroll taxes are, literally, a tax on jobs, the possibility for new employment is also affected. For example, a company with 65 employees must pay almost $187,000 every year in payroll taxes, up from $146,000 ten years ago. At $41,000 per job, a full-time job could be created if payroll taxes were at 1992 levels, rather than lost to increased payroll taxes.[b]

One final note on payroll taxes. Despite the rise in overall payroll taxes in the 1990s under his tenure, former federal Finance minister Paul Martin once excoriated them. In 1994 he argued—correctly—that "there is nothing more ludicrous than a tax on hiring. But that's what high

---

[b] These statistics were based on 1992 versus 2002 comparisons, the latest data available at the time of writing. Canada Pension Plan premiums were again scheduled to rise as of January 1, 2003, so these calculations are conservative. If past government actions are any guide, Employment Insurance premium reductions (set in November of each year) will not cancel out the dramatic increase in CPP rates, thus the figures quoted above will be even higher as of 2003. The figure of $41,000 is chosen as it is just above the maximum income subject to Employment Insurance and Canada Pension Plan taxes.

payroll taxes are. They have grown dramatically over time. They affect lower wage earners much more than those at the high end."[4]

Ottawa's four-percent tax cut

But have income tax reductions offset rising payroll taxes? Only marginally. To start, analyse the "$103-billion tax cut" then-federal Finance minister Paul Martin talked about in Budget 2000. Media reports at the time gave the impression that Canadians received over $100 billion in tax cuts that year, an impression the Ministry of Finance did nothing to dispel. An analysis of that $103-billion figure shows the real tax cut was nowhere near that amount.

That $103 billion is the estimated tax reductions in *total* between 1997 and 2004. On an annual basis, the tax reduction is better described as worth $29.5 billion by 2004.

But there are problems with even that figure. For example, because the government cancelled automatic tax increases (where inflation pushed

How a $103-billion tax cut equals $8.8 billion	
Claimed cumulative tax reduction 1997-2004: $103 billion (Ministry of Finance)	
Annual tax reduction as of 2004	$29.5 billion
Minus	
Spending disguised as a tax cut (e.g., enhanced child tax benefit)	-2.8
Foregone revenues from a tax hike that never happened (indexation of basic personal exemption and brackets)	-6.2
Canada Pension Plan tax hike (what taxpayers will pay in 2004 over and above what they would have paid if 1996 rates were in effect)*	-11.3
Extra taxes in 2001 budget (net)	-.425
Total actual annual tax cut as of 2004	**$8.775 billion**
Tax cuts as a percentage of estimated federal revenues in 2004 (including CPP revenues)	4.4%

*When the federal government claimed $103 billion in tax cuts, it made the assumption compared to pre-1997 rates (i.e., 1996). Thus to compare tax increases in the Canada Pension Plan, the example shown also compares to 1996 rates.

taxpayers into higher tax brackets, also known as "bracket creep") that amount should be subtracted from the estimated tax relief ($6.2 billion).

Taxpayers should also subtract spending that Ottawa counts as a tax cut—a child tax benefit worth $2.8 billion. (If the government sends cheques out, it is *spending*; it is *not* a tax cut.)

Then subtract $11.3 billion to account for what Canada Pension Plan taxes will cost in 2004 as opposed to what they would have cost if 1996 rates were in effect. (If the federal government is going to count tax relief since 1997, it is only accurate to also count tax *increases* from that year.)

And then lop off another $425 million annually because of *other* tax hikes since 1997.

Grand total once the calculations are made? An annual tax cut worth $8.8 billion in 2004. That's not bad; it is preferable to an $8.8-billion increase in taxes. But it is not a $103-billion cut or a $29.5-billion reduction as federal politicians might like the public to believe.

And as a percentage of federal revenues, all the federal tax cuts announced since 1997 will amount to about 4.4% of the expected $200-billion revenues Ottawa will collect in 2004.[c]

Spending—all levels of government

Ask people what expense is the largest one for governments and many will answer "health." Wrong. Social services (welfare and other payments) accounted for the largest chunk of government-cut cheques—$140 billion, compared to second-place health, which accounted for almost $77 billion in spending in 2002. Third was education, at $64.1 billion, and fourth? Debt charges, at $53.4 billion.

An analysis of recent spending trends from 1998[d] onward shows a significant increase in health care spending, social services and, to a lesser extent, education.[e]

The fact that social service payments are the biggest expenditure helps explain why provincial governments have tried to pare down welfare rolls over the past decade. And with a glance to the future, health spending has also risen dramatically, which is why it looms as the biggest challenge for governments that want to balance their books over the next decade.

---

[c] CPP taxes are included in the estimate of 2004 revenues. While they are separated from the general revenue fund, taxpayers must of course pay CPP taxes and so, for the purpose of examining the entire tax burden, I include them in this calculation.

To look at just the last five years, in almost every province across the country, the spending increases in health care vastly eclipsed the rise in either revenues, or in spending in general by provincial governments. For example, in Canada's richest province per person—Alberta—revenue increases amounted to 21 percent between 1997 and 2002 and health care spending increased by 57 percent. No province can continue to increase its expenditures above and beyond its revenue growth. How provinces deal with the health care costs they now face will be their largest challenge in the next decade.

How many people work for government?

The question of how many Canadians work for a government in Canada calls for a lawyer's answer: "It depends." For example, Statistics Canada numbers exclude anyone who works on or for an Indian reserve government. As well, some Canadians who receive income from government do not receive a T-4 slip. In that category, think of doctors (most are technically self-employed and receive payment for services) and others who work on a contract basis for governments. Some Canadians work for companies that contract with government (a cleaning or catering service, for example); those people, although funded indirectly by taxpayers, are not considered government employees.

So the number of Canadians who receive money from government is significant and the breakdown of public sector versus private sector workers does not accurately reflect just how large government really is relative to the private sector. And that has ramifications for tax and spending policies.

At a minimum, Statistics Canada notes that 2.9 million people work full-time or part-time for governments in Canada (federal, provincial, municipal, and Crown corporations). Because about 15.4 million Canadians work (full-time and part-time), 19 percent or almost one out of five are directly employed by Canadian governments in some capacity.[6]

---

[d] As noted at the beginning of the book, the years referred to are fiscal years but the first part of the identification as normally found in government budget and statistical documents is omitted. "1998" then is the fiscal year that ended March 31, 1998, which is portrayed in most budget and statistical documents as 1997/98.

[e] Health is especially noteworthy as spending in that category jumped 36 percent in four years, by $20.3 billion from $56.7 billion (1998) to $77 billion (2002). Per capita, health spending hit $2,463 per person in 2002, up from $1,874 in 1998. If health spending had advanced only for population growth and inflation, it would have been $2,064 by 2002. Health care spending has advanced three times faster than inflation.

How much are government employees paid?

As with size-of-government queries, there are various answers as to how much government workers are paid vis-à-vis the private sector. One of the more comprehensive studies on the issue produced by the Canadian Policy Research Networks (which receives some funding from the federal government and was generally sympathetic to arguments for higher pay in government) noted that public sector salaries were on average 11.6 percent *higher* than those of the private sector.

After the authors accounted for unionization (much higher in the public sector than in the private sector), the public sector salaries were still higher by 7.6 percent. That was *after* the authors accounted for variables such as age, education and other factors that might explain the higher average wages paid to the government employees.[f]

The study, based on Labour Market Survey data from Statistics Canada, was limited in one important respect: the data did not include some health care workers as "public" but instead classified them as private. As the authors wrote:

> The narrow definition of the Labour Force Survey definition of the public sector does mean that some organizations in the broader public sectors of health, education, and transportation, communication, and utilities that are funded and controlled but not owned by the government are considered here as in the private sector.... The public-private wage gap here may thereby be biased downwards and could be considered a conservative estimate of the gap for that reason.[7]

So, the 11 percent (or 7.6 percent after unionization factors are looked at) is a *conservative* estimate of the wage advantage public-sector employees have over the private sector employees.

Unionization explains higher wages but it does not justify such disparities

One final note: What should readers think about the impact of unionization on the public sector? When, in statistical language, unionization is "controlled for," the average public-sector wage premium is 7.6 percent; it is 11.2 percent when "*not* controlled for."

Unionization is an explanation for higher average wages in the public sector vis-à-vis the private sector, which is not the same as a *justification* for higher average public-sector wages. Expressed differently, high unionization rates in government help *explain* the pay advantage government workers receive, but it is still the lower-paid private sector that must foot the bill for the government sector. (If the private sector did

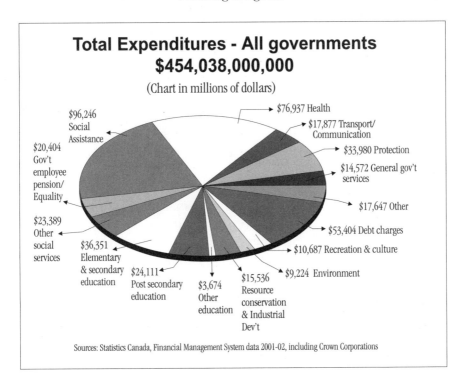

Total Expenditures - All governments
$454,038,000,000

(Chart in millions of dollars)

- $96,246 Social Assistance
- $20,404 Gov't employee pension/ Equality
- $23,389 Other social services
- $36,351 Elementary & secondary education
- $24,111 Post secondary education
- $3,674 Other education
- $15,536 Resource conservation & Industrial Dev't
- $9,224 Environment
- $10,687 Recreation & culture
- $53,404 Debt charges
- $17,647 Other
- $14,572 General gov't services
- $33,980 Protection
- $17,877 Transport/ Communication
- $76,937 Health

Sources: Statistics Canada, Financial Management System data 2001-02, including Crown Corporations

not put the money into the public treasury to begin with, public sector workers would not be paid.) One can argue that maybe private sector workers should be paid more but no magic wand will bring about this outcome. That government workers are more unionized is merely a technical explanation of the difference, not a justification for it.

Dependency on government

To go beyond the 2.9-million figure of those who work in some capacity for government to those who also receive money from government for other reasons—either through public service pensions, the Canada Pension Plan, welfare, unemployment, or other payments—it becomes easier to understand why changes to any government funding quickly become controversial.

Rightly or wrongly, and arguments over the efficiency of some government services vis-à-vis similar private services aside, a large number

---

[f] There are exceptions to every rule, such as computer programmers easily lured away from government with better pay in the private sector. But private sector taxpayers must still pay the bill for government workers, who on average, and after accounting for relevant factors, are paid more.

of Canadians receive some sort of cash transfer from government. Those
who receive some sort of cash transfer from government number over 10
million, or at least 82 percent of those who work in the private sector.
And that is a conservative estimate. For example, it does not include the
number of people who receive treaty payments nor does it include
doctors. In the chart below, they would be considered as within the
private sector, even though as noted earlier, most receive compensation
from government through fee-for-service arrangements and thus from
the public treasury.

Not all of the 10.3 million people receive all of their income from
government; for some it may only be partial. And despite the large
number of Canadians who receive some sort of transfer, that does not
necessarily equal a view on their part that government should provide
a particular service it now provides, even if they earn their living via a
current government transfer.

But precisely because so many people receive some cash transfer
from government, any change carries with it political ramifications. Any
change to a government service or program, even if it could be performed better and more effectively by the non-profit sector or private
sector is guaranteed to be controversial because any change, no matter
how well thought-out or beneficial, has the potential to affect a large
number of people.

Number of Canadians working in private sector *v.* those dependent on at least some government transfers		
Private sector workforce	12,480,400	
Public sector workforce		2,936,300
Social assistance		2,085,100
Employment assistance		1,027,220
Canada Pension Plan / Old Age Security		3,925,102
Canada student loans		343,000
Total		**10,316,722**
Canadians reliant on government for at least some income, as measured as a percentage of private sector employment.		82.6%
Sources: See endnote 8.		

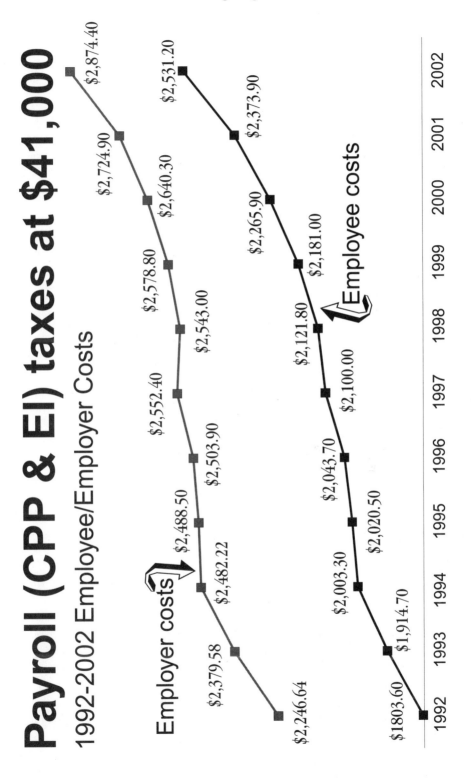

Payroll (CPP & EI) taxes at $41,000
1992-2002 Employee/Employer Costs

Employer costs

$2,874.40
$2,724.90
$2,640.30
$2,578.80
$2,552.40
$2,543.00
$2,503.90
$2,488.50
$2,482.22
$2,379.58
$2,246.64

Employee costs

$2,531.20
$2,373.90
$2,265.90
$2,181.00
$2,121.80
$2,100.00
$2,043.70
$2,020.50
$2,003.30
$1,914.70
$1803.60

1992 1993 1994 1995 1996 1997 1998 1999 2000 2001 2002

Canada's most ungrateful tax: The Chinese 'head' tax

There are few things more ugly than ungratefulness. In 1885, after the completion of the Canadian Pacific Railway across Canada, and to British Columbia where that portion was built mainly by Chinese labourers, thousands of whom died in the process, the Canadian government passed the *Canadian Immigration Act.*

The *Act* stipulated that most Chinese immigrants must pay a "capitation tax" before being granted the right to disembark. Certain occupational groups such as merchants and clergy were exempted (and later, teachers) but the "Chinese head tax," as it is more commonly known, was set at $50 in 1885, raised to $100 in 1890, and to $500 in 1903. Given the exemptions, it was mostly labourers who paid the head tax.

To understand how costly that was to workers of that period, a labourer in 1885 worked an average of 60 hours a week for an annual salary of $290. By 1905, when the tax bill was $500, the average annual earnings of a production worker in Canada were $375.[9] So, depending on the year, the head tax was equivalent to between two months' and 16 months' worth of an average labourer's salary.

The effect of the federal legislation was to restrict the flow of Chinese immigrants—not to exclude them entirely but even that restriction was not enough for some. At the time, labour leaders and politicians in B.C. lobbied repeatedly for the full exclusion of the Chinese, sentiments they said were grounded in "concern" over competition for jobs, but stark racism was also, clearly, a factor in the late 19th century. From the inception of the *Act* in 1885 until 1923, over 82,000 Chinese, mostly male, paid the tax, which contributed $18 million to federal coffers. A worse law—the *Chinese Exclusion Act*—that completely banned the entry of Chinese immigrants then replaced the earlier 1885 legislation.

In addition to the federal tax the British Columbia government also instituted a "Chinese tax" which collected over $7.7 million. The money was not insubstantial, either for those forced to pay it or for the government that collected it. At its revenue peak in British Columbia, the provincial tax brought in over $1.7 million in 1913— or about 18 percent of the total $9.6 million in provincial revenues that year. The provincial "Chinese tax" was the third largest revenue source behind mainly timber royalties (31 percent) and the sale of timber and land (24 percent).[10]

In addition to the obvious discrimination, the head taxes were tragic in other ways. The demographics of the Chinese who entered Canada (mostly male) meant there were limited opportunities for marriage given the relatively few single Chinese women (and the almost complete absence of interracial marriage). The high cost of the head tax also meant that many who were already married could not afford to send for their spouses.

Various Chinese associations have long pressed for redress and repayment through the courts and through Parliament, but the legal claim was rejected by the Ontario Superior Court in 2001 on the grounds that the 1982 constitution could not be applied retroactively. The judge did note that there was certainly no question about the inherent racism of the 1885 legislation.[11]

Parliament could refund the tax to Chinese descendants, but this brings up a dilemma for today's taxpayers. To refund a voluntary tax, even one as offensive as the Chinese head tax which began in 1885 and ended nearly eight decades ago, could open a Pandora's box where today's taxpayers might be required to compensate many for the sins of politicians of generations ago. And many of today's immigrants would pay for the policies enacted long before they or their ancestors arrived in Canada, some with equally tragic histories from the countries they fled.

Regardless of the legal and philosophical arguments for and against reimbursement, the Chinese head tax should always be remembered as Canada's most offensive tax. And, given the Chinese contribution to the country's first transcontinental railroad, it is also, tragically, Canada's most ungrateful tax.

3

Want a 45-percent tax break?
Be careful with the VISA

He who promises runs into debt.
The Talmud

How not to secure your future

Over the last 30 years, Canada's debt binge was justified under any number of higher sounding justifications: "Investing in the future," "Sharing the infrastructure burden with all generations," and "We only owe it (the debt) to ourselves so what's the big deal?" At base though, it is always the same pitch: Take the new car/fridge/stereo/highway home and no payments until at least 2050!

If Canadians need an example of why a chronic addiction to debt is bad for our fiscal health, consider this: interest on the federal debt (at $40.5 billion) now swallows up 45 percent of federal personal income taxes.[a] Expressed differently, if there was no federal debt and no interest to pay on it, every Canadian could slash their personal April tax bill by 45 percent and not a penny in program spending would be touched.

To examine provincial debt on average, provincial individual income tax bills could be slashed by 48 percent without touching program spending—*if* there was no debt. Consider another scenario: if the $25 billion now spent annually to service provincial debts was not necessary, government health care spending could increase by 34 percent.[b]

---

[a] In 2002, federal personal income tax collections amounted to $89.7 billion; interest on the federal debt was $40.5 billion, or 45 percent of all personal income tax collected.
[b] Total provincial debt payments amounted to $25.2 billion in 2002; health care spending across the country amounted to $74.5 billion. These examples are based on data from Statistics Canada, Financial Management System (FMS) Basis. For consistency, *Tax Me I'm Canadian* relies as much as possible on Statistics Canada FMS data.

However one cuts the fiscal cake, debt interest has made taxes higher and has restricted program spending options. It has been a lose-lose scenario for some time.[c]

To be sure, there are times when increasing Canada's debt was worth it. Winning the war against the Nazis in World War Two is the best example. But as much as war and rumours of war are understandable reasons for increasing a nation's debt, the justifications become distinctly weak when politicians borrow money for trinkets and goodies to buy votes from one generation only to leave the bill with the kids.

Increasing the debt to fund health care sounds compassionate, but to fund today's social programs through increased debt means that tomorrow's citizens will pay for not only their heart operations but for those of the previous generation. In essence, much debt financing reveals an unwillingness to pay up front or make difficult choices about which capital project will be built and which one will be delayed. It is understandable that politicians would wish to avoid hard choices; that costs votes. But citizens should make it less tempting for politicians and demand the available choices—and the bill—up front.

Why the debt issue is not (unfortunately) past history

Back in 1970, Canada's total government net debt amounted to 19.6 percent of the economy, peaked at 88 percent in 1996 and, due in part to a growing economy and some debt repayment, declined to 66 percent in 2000.[1] (In dollar terms, the federal debt grew from $19.3 billion in 1970 to a peak of $583.2 billion in 1997 and declined slightly to $547.4 billion by 2001. In the provinces, net public debt climbed from $18.8 billion in 1981 to $250.3 billion by 1999 and then declined slightly to $237.8 billion in 2001.[2]) An observer from another planet may be forgiven for wondering if they missed a major war during those three decades. The debt climbed to an extent that a historian who was oblivious to all context could examine only the increase in the debt during those years and think a major war had occurred.

Positive as the trend of the overall debt-to-GDP ratio was (finally) by 2000, by 2002 many provincial governments again ran deficits.[d] The

---

[c] It should be noted that governments receive much more than income tax revenues. As a percentage of their entire budgets then, the percentages noted above would obviously be smaller when compared to overall spending. But the illustration vis-à-vis personal tax is useful in that it demonstrates on a personal level how much of the income of Canadians is given over to government debt interest.

[d] Statistics Canada, in its Financial Management System Basis, reported that even Alberta ran a $1-billion deficit in the fiscal year ending March 31, 2002. The Alberta government, using a different measurement, disputes their analysis.

turn-of-the-century situation where virtually every province briefly ran surpluses is already ancient economic history.

Social programs, infrastructure, war, interest, or Pierre Trudeau: What caused the federal debt?

One debate over the federal debt (and the same arguments swirl around provincial debts) is what led to its 1998 peak of $583 billion before the government began to run surpluses and then pay it down. Did an explosion of social program spending cause it? Or infrastructure requirements such as the Trans-Canada Highway? Or escalating interest rates that hit highs of 21 percent in the early 1980s? And then of course, there were two World Wars as well as Korea.

1947-1977: Debt down, government up, as a percentage of GNP

Between 1946, when net public debt (for all Canadian governments) equalled 106.6 percent of GNP and 1975 when it hit a low of 16.8 percent of the domestic economy, government had grown dramatically.[3] Tax historian J. Harvey Perry, commenting on the work of economist Richard Bird explains:

> Government expenditures as a percentage of gross national expenditures (a different concept then GNP but the same total figure) rose from an average of 22.9 percent in 1947-51 to an average of 39.4 percent in 1973-77; the ratio in 1977 was 41.1 percent. Bird makes the point that government expenditures over the period 1947 to 1977 rose 71 percent faster than GNE.[4]

In other words, post-World War Two and up to the 1970s, and as it relates to the debt, two trends were in evidence: One, Canadian government spending increased much quicker than economic growth and thus took up a greater share of the economy. Two, even though the debts of Canada's governments also rose in actual dollars (for example, federally from $12.7 billion in 1947[5] to $40.5 billion in 1977[6]), the country's debts shrunk as a percentage of the economy. This was not a difficult task to accomplish as long as the economy (in percentage terms) grew faster than the debt.

But the continual expansion of government as a share of the economy was financed in part by annual deficits, which laid the groundwork for future problems. Again, to concentrate only on federal books, between 1947 and 1971, only five surplus years were recorded and three of those occurred in the 1950s.

Spending and debt both grew between World War Two and the 1970s, but the effect was of no great concern given that the economy expanded faster than the debt. And economically, until the mid-1970s recession, few would question the expansion of government as a percentage of the economy, given that the 1950s and 1960s were golden years. It seemed to work.

But once the slowdown of the 1970s hit, which then combined with rising interest rates, the government expansion relative to the economy (that was anyway on a collision sector with the relatively shrinking private sector) was financed in part with borrowed money. Thus, government finances were in a set-up position for a nasty shock. Canadian governments rarely lived within their means; they often borrowed money and it suddenly became much more expensive.

If interest rates had been lower in the 1970s, then interest payments and also the debt would naturally have been lower. But that is a "so what" point insofar as the debate over what led to the increase of the debt.

It follows logically that, if spending was 90 percent or 80 percent of what it actually turned out to be between World War Two and the 1970s, the debt—and interest on the debt—would be less and the growth in the debt itself would have been less dramatic.

Given the growth in borrowing as well as in government spending, it was inevitable once inflation started to rise that the debt was set for a dramatic explosion. High interest rates would have been less painful for the government's bottom line (and taxpayers who financed it) as rates would have been calculated on a smaller base.[e] But since spending beyond current tax receipts was desired, borrowing was the default choice, and that necessitated increasing debt interest payments.

Lenders cannot charge interest—low or high—on money that is never borrowed. Governments spend money either on programs or infrastructure; they only spend money on debt interest payments if money is first borrowed to pay for those programs or capital projects.

This is something every homeowner knows, which is why smarter ones don't borrow everything banks are willing to lend them. After all, if one mortgages a $300,000 house as opposed to a $150,000 house, it likewise is the case that higher interest rates will be more painful in the first case then the latter.

Hindsight is helpful, and given the view of the past from the present, it is a bit much for the current tax-and-spend crowd in Canada to argue that interest rates were the "cause" of Canada's debt explosion, as if there was never the spending that triggered the borrowing.

---

[e] For example, while governments would pay somewhat less than this, in August of 1981 the Bank of Canada overnight money market rate hit a high of 21.57 percent.

Predictably and ironically, groups that call for more government spending are often those ones that call for more inflation. The Canadian Labour Congress, which often lobbies for higher taxes and more government spending, still advises politicians that inflation should be allowed to rise.[7] It is an absurd suggestion since inflation hurts the poor and middle income earners more than the rich (who can withstand much inflation before it hurts their lifestyle). But inflation of course also translates into higher interest rates, which is problematic for annual payments on government debt.

Those who attempt to blame high interest rates for Canada's dramatic increase in the debt and accompanying high interest payments, have it backwards. Less spending, and expenditures that were paid for from current tax receipts would have made the debt that already existed far less punishing to the country's governments and taxpayers.

Avoiding future debt: Balanced-budget laws and taxpayer protection

If taxpayers want to avoid more of their money being drained away to interest payments instead of tax reductions or government programs, they and their governments will have to make a choice.

Given the recent ruminations from even the Alberta government about floating bonds to pay for highway construction, current signals are not encouraging on this front.[f] One can hope that that province does not reverse its fine record of debt repayment over the past decade in exchange for more wasted tax dollars (i.e., on interest). Here then are two legislative actions that have and will make a difference.

Tougher balanced-budget laws

A "balanced-budget law," simply defined and as the words imply, refers to legislation that requires a government to balance its revenues with its expenditures. It is a legal mechanism that binds governments to balance their books.

Models of such legislation can be found in jurisdictions around the world ranging from Switzerland to certain American states and also in some Canadian provinces. As of this writing, seven provinces and one territory have some form of balanced-budget legislation. The list in-

---

[f] It is worth noting that Alberta has fallen off the fiscally responsible wagon. Spending increased by 53 percent between 1997 and 2002, in contrast to inflation growth of 14 percent and population growth of 12 percent. Alberta's decisions on double-digit wage increases for nurses, for example, have also put increased pressure on other less wealthy provinces.

Debt interest as a % of federal personal income tax collection

In millions of $

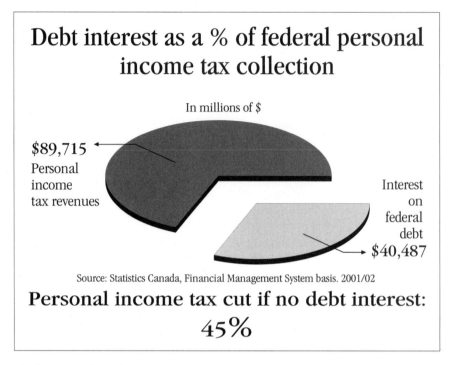

$89,715
Personal
income
tax revenues

Interest
on
federal
debt
$40,487

Source: Statistics Canada, Financial Management System basis. 2001/02

Personal income tax cut if no debt interest:
45%

cludes British Columbia,[g] Alberta, Saskatchewan, Manitoba, Ontario, Quebec, New Brunswick and the Yukon.

The strength of the legislation varies across the country.[h] For example, at present, Alberta's law requires a balanced budget every year. Depending on which statistics one wants to hold to though—Statistics Canada's or the Alberta government's—Alberta is already in technical violation of its own law. Thus, even Alberta's law can be strengthened (financial penalties for cabinet minister and MLAs in the event of non-compliance would be a start). That province's law should certainly not be weakened as is now being considered. The same holds true for other provinces; some attempt to skirt their balanced-budget requirements through a variety of measures that have more in common with Arthur Andersen and Enron than with frank and clear disclosures of their financial situation.

However, another problem has now appeared on the horizon as it concerns government budgets. Recent accounting changes across Canada mean that future debt may not be fully reflected in the annual budgets

---

[g] B.C.'s balanced-budget law becomes fully effective in 2004; as of that date, deficits are prohibited.

[h] Manitoba's legislation, based on a draft 1995 Canadian Taxpayers Federation submission, is probably the best in the country. It contains financial penalties for non-compliance, among other commendable elements.

of governments. It may be the case that annual budgets will appear balanced when, in fact, revenues will be less than expenditures as governments move slowly towards Generally Accepted Accounting Principles (GAAP). One aspect of such accounting for government is that instead of recording a capital expense all in one year, or recording the entire debt for a capital expense, it may be recorded over several budget years, much like a lease payment. Yet the obligation—the debt—exists in full, even though not fully recorded immediately.

The justification given is that this is how capital projects are recorded in the private sector. The problem is that, with government, debt obligations may then exist but not be recorded in their entirety, or in a way that lets taxpayers grasp the full liabilities. Thus, accounting changes that are now being enacted by governments are not necessarily all positive. Private business uses GAAP extensively, but that did not prevent the confusion and outright chicanery that occurred at Enron. Corporate scandals are a valuable reminder that accounting is still an art, not an exact science.[i] Balanced-budget laws may well need to be updated to try to catch these new concerns. It may be necessary for governments to produce more comprehensive reports on their debt, measured slightly differently than they would be under GAAP rules for example.

Taxpayer protection: Canada's first *Taxpayer Protection Act*

In addition to strengthened balanced-budget legislation, provinces and the federal government would serve taxpayers better—regardless of their priorities for tax dollars—if taxpayer protection legislation and expenditure limits are also put in place. The concept is as clear as it sounds: limits on the abilities of governments to raise taxes, and limits on the ability of governments to raise expenditures beyond inflation, population, or economic growth or some combination of the three.

As an example, here is what the British Columbia government proclaimed in early 1991. The *Taxpayer Protection Act* set out to accomplish three primary objectives:

1 Freeze taxes. Twelve specific taxes were frozen and the government was prevented from introducing any new taxes until March 31, 1994.

2 Place limits on expenditures. The government was required to submit a plan every year detailing how it would

---

[i] For more on effective components of balanced-budget laws, see: Protecting taxpayers— An analysis of balanced budget legislation in Canada, available at www.taxpayer.com.

balance the revenues and expenditures of the general fund over a five-year cycle. The rate of increase in forecast expenditures could not exceed a certain percentage determined by a formula that referred to the rate of increase in B.C.'s gross domestic product.

3 <u>Debt reduction</u>. The minister of Finance was required to prepare and present a debt reduction plan to the Legislative Assembly.

Unfortunately, shortly after Canada's first *Taxpayer Protection Act* was introduced, an election was called and the new government—the New Democrat government of Mike Harcourt—repealed the *Act* in short order.

However short-lived, the *Taxpayer Protection Act* was the first legislation of its kind in the country. By passing a provincial statute, the government of the day was prepared to provide more than rhetorical limits on its spending, taxing and borrowing habits. Governments across the country—especially Alberta in light of its recent spending spikes and tax hikes—should revisit the decade-old British Columbia proposal.[j] If budgets are to be balanced, a limitation on expenditures and taxes is an integral part of such a balancing act.

Objection

Should provinces with existing balanced-budget laws weaken instead of strengthen such legislation, citizens should object strenuously; Canadians have spent enough money on debt interest. And as for the federal government and its approach, it appears that Ottawa may well be the last jurisdiction to implement such legislation, if ever.

Far from the "quick fix" that some argue balanced-budget legislation or taxpayer protection laws are, such laws are a challenge to those who govern to *not* indulge in politically easy quick fixes. Had balanced-budget laws been in place in Canada over the past three decades, politicians would have had to choose between raising taxes or cutting spending (immediately or over a four-year period depending on the type of balanced-budget law assumed) to bring a government's finances into balance. (Even as useful and as needed as is tax relief, different types of tax relief measures help boost economic growth at various rates

---

[j] Ontario under Premier Mike Harris introduced a commendable version of taxpayer protection legislation in 1999. It helped that his signature and picture was on the 1995 pledge given to him by the Canadian Taxpayers Federation. His successor, alas, has weakened the legislation with 2002 budget tax increases that violate the spirit of the *Act*.

and none of them replace their own revenues overnight. Choices are always necessary, though obviously the medium to long-term should be kept in mind as it concerns taxation policy—which is to say lower and simpler is better.)

Instead, politicians chose to put off the difficult decision of balancing the books for decades. They chose to borrow, which inevitably led to higher taxes while the fundamental problem of unchecked spending was left untouched. The result was a quick fix for politicians who desired re-election while the bills were handed to future taxpayers.

Balanced-budget laws, expenditure limits, and taxpayer protection are three close cousins. For example, without taxpayer protection, a balanced-budget law may merely mean that taxes will be raised to balance the budget (at least temporarily before such taxes act as a deterrent to future growth). Without expenditure control legislation, prudent analysis of existing government spending and reallocation of such spending is elbowed aside in favour of overall and unthinking spending increases.

For those who want a limit on the ability of governments to repeat the last three decades in terms of taxes and debt, such measures are useful. Not coincidentally, the result would be a virtuous circle where fewer dollars would be lost in the future to interest payments; that frees up more choices for both tax reductions and spending priorities. Let's pay for the new car/fridge/stereo/highway up front this time.

Debt payments as a % of provincial income tax revenues
Provincial and Territorial Government Revenues and Expenditures (millions $)

Year	NF	PE	NS	NB	PQ	ON	MB	SK	AB	BC	YK	NWT	NT	All Prov
2001/02 personal income tax revenues	611	156	1,274	909	16,955	19,114	1,710	1,197	4,654	5,403	28	51	14	52,076
2001/02 debt interest	627	113	1,102	966	5,873	9,424	1,576	997	1,300	3,219	3	15	23	25,238
Income tax break if no debt interest	103%	72%	86%	106%	35%	49%	92%	83%	28%	60%	11%	29%	164%	48%

Source: Statistics Canada, Financial Management System Basis, 2001/02

Debt payments as a % of provincial health care expenditures
Provincial and Territorial Government Revenues and Expenditures

Year (Million)	NF	PE	NS	NB	PQ	ON	MB	SK	AB	BC	YK	NWT	NT	All Prov
2001/02 debt charges	627	113	1,102	966	5,873	9,424	1,576	997	1,300	3,219	3	15	23	25,238
2001/02 health care spending	1,574	366	2,269	1,719	17,070	27,938	2,973	2,370	7,381	10,717	84	225	154	74,840
Extra % to health care if no debt interest	40%	31%	49%	56%	34%	34%	53%	42%	18%	30%	4%	7%	15%	34%

Source: Statistics Canada, Financial Management System Basis, 2001/02

Who owns our debt?

The easiest way to stir up nationalist resentment in any country is to note how much money leaves the country to go to foreign bondholders. And many people are just curious about how much of our debt is held by those outside Canada. As it turns out, Canadians hold much of the money.

Out of the $547-billion federal debt, individual Canadians hold 64 percent. If you ever bought a Canada Savings Bond or a war bond in earlier decades (now likely long paid out) you helped finance Canada's federal debt. Twenty-eight percent of our debt is held by federal employee pension plans and the Canada Pension Plan. So how much is left for foreigners? Only eight percent.

Breakdown of who holds the federal debt

$547 billion

8% Foreign held

28% Pension Liability minus assets

64% Held in Canada

Who balanced the federal books?
Taxpayers.

Federal spending did decrease in the mid-1990s through a combination of reduced federal program expenditures and reduced transfers to the provinces. But higher revenues (mostly taxes) accounted for the largest share of the credit for the balanced books that occurred by 1997/98. The chart below contains numbers on federal revenues, debt charges, program expenditures and deficits/surpluses, from the federal government's Fiscal Reference Tables.

(millions of dollars)	1993/ 1994	1994/ 1995	1995/ 1996	1996/ 1997	1997/ 1998	1998/ 1999	1999/ 2000	2000/ 2001	2001/ 2002
Total Revenue - Fiscal Reference Tables	115,984	123,323	130,301	140,896	153,501	155,899	166,123	179,590	173,315
Debt Charges	37,982	42,046	46,905	44,973	40,931	41,394	41,647	42,094	37,735
Program Expenditures	120,014	118,739	112,013	104,820	108,753	111,393	111,763	119,348	126,673
Surplus (Deficit)	-42,012	-37,462	-28,617	-8,897	3,817	3,112	12,713	18,148	8,907

Source: Fiscal Reference Tables, October 2002. Totals may not add up due to rounding.

JEAN CHRETIEN KEEPS HIS PROMISE TO ARAFAT:
HEYYY... WE GOT AN HRDC GRANT.
RAESIDE
www.raesidecartoon.com
VICTORIA TIMES COLONIST-DIST. BY KOKO PRESS INC.

4

Enron, meet Canada's governments

If the headlines show us anything, it is that the greed and cooked books of the corporate world are no substitute for public services.

> Jack Layton, candidate for federal
> New Democrat leader, on the Enron scandal.[1]

Europe's taxpayers are being cheated on a massive scale.

> A British House of Lords report on
> European Union corruption.[2]

The politicians get lucky

If there was ever a case of a misplaced superiority complex, it is in recent crowing from politicians over the revelations of accounting shenanigans and fraud in the business world.

The revelation in late 2001 that Enron overstated (and fudged) over US$500 million in earnings, along with the multiple restatements from other companies by spring and summer 2002, gave politicians an excuse to bash business and trumpet the superiority of government regulation. It was back to the good old days of the early 20th century where politicians could make hay by crossing swords with pinstriped corporate

---

[a] In the popular view, the stock market crash "caused" the 1930s Depression. It has been a useful symbol of capitalism run amok ever since, and useful for the critics of free markets to bash business with as well. But the popular belief is incorrect. Nobel prize-winning economist, Milton Friedman, punctured this errant belief in his 1979 book, *Free to Choose*. Friedman points out that the New York Federal Reserve Bank loosened credit after the stock market crash only to be trumped by the Federal Reserve Board which tightened the money supply at a time when it should have enacted an opposite policy. The effect was to dry up capital markets and contract the money supply in the year following the market crash. That action, combined with moves by the Reserve on other fronts in 1930 and over the next two years, exacerbated the effects of the 1929 crash.

fatcats. Some politicians seem almost to drool for a replay of those years or the ones surrounding the 1929 stock market crash and the Great Depression.[a]

Those in Canada from the *government-can-manage-your-money-better-than-you-can* crowd were especially pleased at the scandals and the ensuing drop in stock markets. For them, it seemed to vindicate their faith in central planning. The reasoning was simple and attractive: greed had been discovered once again in corporate boardrooms and the public should be shocked—*shocked!*—that excesses could ever be found where the possibility for great material gain exists.

Quick! To the head of the parade!

That the embarrassment and prosecution of fraudulent CEOs and their accountants was deserved was self-evident. And that the shakeout, and accounting fudge-factory shutdowns were necessary and worthwhile is also a given, though it was cold comfort for the ripped-off shareholders and average employees of the defunct firms.

From Wall Street to Bay Street to Main Street and the smallest of investors, the calls for reform and for heads to roll proceeded apace with vicious market sentiment against the crooks and number-crunching swindlers and anyone even thought to have been less than scrupulous.

On the biggest scandal, Enron, with US$63.4 billion in assets, was forced into bankruptcy within six months of the first critical article that appeared in the business press about Enron's shoddy accounting practices. WorldCom, with US$103.8 billion in listed assets, filed for Chapter 11-bankruptcy protection within one month of admitting that earnings were overstated by US$3.8 billion.[3]

In other examples, Tyco, Bristol-Myers Squibb and Merck had historical results that looked quite impressive, but once equity markets became suspicious about their numbers, shares in those companies dropped by 50 percent in six months.[4]

But the irony of the corporate scandals was that once business books were shredded by outside analysts, market reaction was swift, damning and irreversible. By the time the politicians raced to the head of the "reform business ethics" parade, it had already been underway for some time. After all, the initial questions about the Enron books originated with *Barron's* and other Wall street analysts and publications, not with Washington, D.C., and certainly not with Canada's politicians, who had their own multiple Enron-like accounting shenanigans to answer for.

The political pot calling the corporate kettle black

The reaction of investors in specific and markets in general to shoddy corporate accounting was in sharp contrast to what some politicians have done over the decades and the rarity with which they have faced similar chastisement.

In recent memory, any observer of Canadian politics could come up with several examples of shoddy government accounting. There was the uncovering of the $1 billion in Human Resources Development Canada (HRDC) money where tracking of how the money was disbursed was loose and in some cases non-existent. (Never mind that some of the money should never have been given out no matter how closely tracked.) Then there was the double payment of money to a Quebec ad firm by the federal government, a "mistake" worth $3 million, which even the prime minister admitted might have been outright theft by the company. But Jean Chretien argued the offence paled in comparison to winning the 1995 Quebec referendum, as if an ad campaign by the federal government was the reason the nationalists lost in Quebec.

The markets punished questionable behaviour far quicker than any cabinet minister in Ottawa has ever suffered for the same: questionable patronage grants to Quebec companies by Liberal cabinet minister Alfonse Gagliano only meant he was sent to Denmark as "punishment."

Not that any of the recent boondoggles in Ottawa or in the provincial capitals over the past two decades stopped politicians from crowing about how superior government was in relation to the private sector. Jack Layton, a Toronto councillor and candidate for the leader of the federal New Democrats trumpeted "if the headlines show us anything, it is that the greed and cooked books of the corporate world are no substitute for public services."[5]

Layton must have missed the experience of New Democrats in British Columbia where the auditor general and other professional civil servants of that province ripped apart the accounting practices, estimates and budget controls of the NDP when they ran that province in the 1990s.

International Enron governments

But it was not only British Columbia or other Canadian provinces or the federal government that occasionally outdid Enron. In Europe, governments had their own "Enronic" behaviour. Countries that belong to the European Union are obligated to keep budget deficits below three percent of GDP or risk a huge fine from Brussels. Portugal reported a 2001 figure of only 2.2 percent and Eurostat, the EU's statistical agency, balked at it and demanded a restatement. That, as it turned out, was substantially higher at 4.1 percent.

The European Commission's comment on government accounting in Portugal? "There had clearly been serious omissions in the production of government data." Italy did a similar restating after the EU investigated and its budget deficit climbed from 1.6 percent to 2.2 percent. Apparently, misleading government books are not just a problem in Canada.[6]

Earlier in the decade, European Union auditors noted that out of a US$93.6-billion budget, $10 billion was wasted because of fraud and mismanagement. Examples? Money intended for training airline pilots disappeared; olive-oil producers claimed subsidies twice; and an EU office that promoted tourism was accused of setting up shell companies to transfer kickbacks to their staff (the office was later raided by police). The British House of Lords concluded, "Europe's taxpayers are being cheated on a massive scale." A deputy of the French National Assembly and author of a book on EU fraud, Francois D'Aubert, concluded that the core of the problem was that taxpayer dollars given to the European Union came to be considered by bureaucrats as "money without nationality, which means that it's anyone's to take."[7]

And if European governments were not models of numerical accuracy on occasion, the prospect of aid money given to Palestinian authorities only to be allegedly ripped off by PLO Chairman Yasser Arafat was even more proof that governments can hardly claim to track money better than the private sector. Governments in Europe, America, and Canada who themselves sometimes keep shoddy books, gave money to the Palestinian government, only to perhaps see US$12.5 million transferred to Arafat's own personal account, this according to a former PLO treasurer and Arafat aide.[8]

Big labour's Enron accounting and fraud

Even big labour had Enronitis. In the United States, ULLICO, a financial services company run by union leaders that invested union pension funds, is being investigated by a U.S. grand jury, for possible shenanigans.

When, after the markets started to melt, the union bosses voted to have their fund buy back shares from shareholders at prices much higher than the shares were then worth, those with large holdings were restricted in how much they could sell back to ULLICO. That meant large entities, such as union pension funds, were restricted in how much they could sell while small shareholders (such as ULLICO officers and board members) could trade in their shares at a vastly higher price than they would receive on the open market. The bounty for the union bosses—

which included the heads of communications, plumbers, asbestos, iron-workers, and carpenters unions across the U.S.—came at the expense of rank and file union members.[9]

In another case of possible union fraud and corruption, three United Auto Workers (UAW) officials were indicted in 2002 by the U.S. Justice Department for forcing a costly strike on workers and General Motors. The three UAW representatives are accused of extorting GM for bogus overtime pay and jobs for family and friends in exchange for ending the 1987 strike. One defendant, William Coffey, a UAW committeeman, received $40,000, according to the indictment. UAW Local 594 chair Jay Douglas was accused of garnering $60,000. The 87-day strike cost 5,000 GM employees $10,000 to $20,000 each in lost wages.[10]

Voter punishment *versus* market punishment

The key difference between government fraud and mismanagement on a national or international scale is that retribution for incompetence and outright fraud in the business sector is dealt with swiftly once known. In Canadian politics as well as international affairs *a la* Arafat, politicians can mismanage finances for years before they are held to account in an election. Even then, voters may well take a pass.

Unlike the stock markets, which executed errant companies and their chief executive officers and chief financial officers with the zeal of French revolutionaries in the late 18th century, voters have rarely shown such zeal with politicians who cook the public books.

Maybe that's because a four-year lag exists between what politicians and their political staff can do and when they have to account for it. Perhaps it is because the public is too cynical and thus accepts lower standards in political life than they would from a CEO. Whatever the reason, some politicians in Canada (not all) can massage or overlook numbers in the public books and be assured that they will rarely be held to account by voters in the way shareholders now trash widely held companies.

Selected examples from Canada's governments

In Canada, provincial and federal auditors general routinely excoriate the governments they report on, sometimes to good effect and also, on occasion, to no avail.

It would take a whole book to list the malfeasance, missing and questionable grants, and outright pork-barrelling practised by some, to say nothing of the torturous accounting often practised under the public radar (and sometimes in full view). Here are just some examples on the issues raised by the corporate accounting scandal and parallels in Canada's political world.

Issue: Optimistic and unsupportable revenue projections
Case study: British Columbia's 1996 "fudge-it" budget

In 1996, the governing New Democrats pumped optimistic assumptions into their pre-election budget. The NDP government predicted substantial growth in revenues while private sector analysts forecast a downturn in the same. Much of the budget optimism resulted after the ascension of Glen Clark to the helm of the NDP and the premier's office earlier that year. Mysteriously, after Clark took control, budget forecasts were revised upward despite all inside and outside advice that such forecasts were wrong.

Unlike the private sector where companies took massive hits to their share prices when such activities were revealed and sometimes forced into bankruptcy, it took three years before a commission reported on how to provide more transparent government books. It was another full year before the government accepted some of the recommendations. It also took a similar length of time before the province's auditor general reported on the mess, which was damning when it finally appeared:

> Crucial information was missing from the budget forecasts and for all of these reasons, prescribing arbitrary optimism to improve the budget forecast had no merit.[11]

And other recommendations were to be phased in over several years. Unlike Enron or WorldCom or others, the people responsible for the overly optimistic and false forecasts remained in power for almost a half-decade before they were punished; the books took years to clean up.

Issue: Poor bookkeeping and poor corporate control
Case study: Prince Edward Island's Business Development Agency

Prince Edward Island, as is the case with most provinces with the exception of Alberta (as of 1996) and British Columbia (as of 2002), gives financial assistance to business. The Crown agency that performs this task, PEI Business Development Inc. (BDI), disburses grants, contributions, equity investments, loans, and loan guarantees, and owns eight subsidiaries with expenditures of approximately $50 million.

In 2002, the province's auditor general looked into grants and contributions at BDI that totalled $26 million during the fiscal year 2001/02 and found the following[12]:

- Despite the amount of money involved, the Board of BDI met only three times between 1999 (the inception of the Crown agency) and March 2001. (The Board began to meet regularly subsequent to the auditor general's initial report on the matter.)[13]

- On corporate control: "The Board did not have a role in the strategic planning process nor did it approve the corporate plan. In addition, authorization was received from Treasury Board for BDI to purchase a building for approximately $2.5 million and relocate its offices but there is no record in the Board minutes where authorization was requested or provided for this major undertaking."[14]

- The Board was to approve any assistance over $1 million. In practice, any assistance above that was approved by the provincial Cabinet and without first being recommended by the Board of Directors.[15]

- Most grant programs (there are 12) have eligibility criteria and guidelines, but two of the largest programs—the Infrastructure Program and the Sectoral Development Fund—do not have any criteria or eligibility requirements. The Infrastructure Fund disbursed $8.5 million in 2001 and the Sectoral Development Fund gave out $3.5 million.

- $26 million in grants was disbursed in 2001; many of the grants were given on the justification of job creation. Said the auditor general: "We noted however, that for the projects we examined, involving $26 million in grants, we saw no evidence of specific verification of jobs created."[16]

Issue: Poor governance and missing documentation
Case study: Manitoba government

In 2001, looking back over five years, the Manitoba auditor general had this to say about some of his work:

> Too often during the past five years, our audit work was hampered by inadequacies in, or absence of, documentation supporting key decisions. It is important to keep in mind that this is not just an audit issue. It is fundamentally a threat to the effective operation of our democratic accountability processes.[17]

Issue: Restricting auditor access to key financial documents
Case study: Ontario Ministry of Transportation

In 2001, the Ontario auditor general reported that his staff was not given proper access to key files.

The auditor general's comments:

> For the first time since being appointed Provincial Auditor, I have to report an instance where my office did not receive all the information and explanations we required. During our value-for-money audit of the Ministry of Transportation's Road User Safety Program, contrary to Section 10 of the *Audit Act*, the then-senior management of the Ministry hindered the audit process by not giving my staff full access to pertinent files, not providing all information requested, and deleting parts of pertinent documents they provided. As well, certain restrictions were placed on ministry staff such that they may have been inhibited from speaking freely with my staff.[18]

Issue: Large off-book transactions
Case study: Saskatchewan budgets

Over 40 percent of Saskatchewan's budget is not accounted for in the main set of books, the provincial budget.

The most cogent analysis of this situation was in an editorial entitled "Look south, Eric" in the *Saskatoon Star Phoenix*:

> Saskatchewan residents are shareholders who don't have an option to dump their equity in the enterprise operated by Cline and CEO Lorne Calvert. However, what people —becoming painfully aware of the consequences of fudged books—can do is to dump the executives at first chance. It's something "Enron Eric" and "WorldCom Calvert" should bear in mind as they tout the province's 'balanced' books.[19]

Enronitis in the federal government

Accounting practices and standards vary widely across the provinces, as well as the degree of accountability and transparency and the time frame in which offending departments/governments comply with auditor's recommendations. As for the federal government, it is, alas, too easy to find questionable accounting of the type that would make Arthur Andersen executives blush.

Here are some examples of accounting irregularities and occasionally questionable tracking and reporting of public money from recent federal auditor general reports:

General comment on erosion of parliamentary control over finances:

> Canadians have the right to control how public funds are collected and used, and ultimately it is the members of Parliament we elect who carry out this control on our behalf. That is why I am concerned about recent examples of the erosion of parliamentary control, involving billions of dollars of revenue and expenditure.[20]

On poor management of $16 billion worth of annual grant and contribution programs:

> In 1998, we reported that two decades of audits of grant and contribution programs had sent a consistent message: there are serious and chronic problems in the way they are managed. A lack of diligence in designing programs, assessing applications, and monitoring recipients' performance meant that public funds were placed at risk.... The Treasury Board Secretariat recently released a revised and improved policy framework for managing these types of programs. But the attention paid to grants and contributions has not yet been translated into overall improvement in the way they are managed across the federal government.[21]

On program evaluations of grants and contributions:

> Where they existed, program evaluations were often limited in scope and did not provide a clear picture of whether programs were achieving value for money.

> Many of the programs had not been evaluated for more than five years.[22]

On the $7 billion allocated to foundations and largely out of the public's and Parliament's view and control, and the possibility that the government books money now to make budget balance sheets look better later:

> Since 1997, the government has created a number of new organizations to support, for example, research and development, students in post-secondary education, and Aboriginal healing. It has allocated more than $7 billion to nine of these foundations and recorded the amount as spending by the federal government. Most of the funds

however, are still in the foundations' bank accounts and investments.

While the foundations will support worthy causes, **I am concerned that a prime motivator for funding them in advance is the accounting impact on the government's bottom line: showing larger expenditures today and smaller ones tomorrow reduces the size of current surpluses.** (Author emphasis.) I am also concerned that Parliament has only limited means of holding the government to account for the public policy functions performed by these foundations.[23]

On incomplete applications for $9 million in funding from the Department of Canadian Heritage under the Promotion of Official Languages Program:

In the Department's assessment of applications that we estimate accounted for $9 million (or 33 percent) of the $27 million in expenditures we audited for 2000-01, we found the following shortcomings:

The general application forms were not filled out and the applications were incomplete.[24]

The auditor general noted that applications did not state the expected results of the proposed projects, as required by the terms of the program. Furthermore, applications generally did not include a plan to evaluate the progress of the activities towards goals of established objectives.

Also, according to the auditor general there was nothing in the file to show that the Department had considered the eligibility criteria in deciding to fund activities. Internal audits raised the same issue in 36 percent of the cases it reviewed in 1999-2000.[25]

Stuff that walked away

Thefts (and accidents) in the federal government that cost you money

Like any large organization, there are good apples and there are bad apples. The *bad* ones that work for the federal government, or found their way into federal offices and ripped items off their desks, have cost taxpayers at least $78 million since 1992.

The federal Public Accounts of Canada catalogues the losses of public money and property due to an offence, illegal act or accident. Some of the items lost or stolen make one wonder why one would even think of taking such items—such as a $5 license plate from a Nova Scotia office. Then there were the items that are most popular to steal, such as laptop computers.

While theft and loss is a problem, the biggest loss of money to the public treasury (excluding billion-dollar political errors, neglect, and incompetence where grants, loans and disbursements are not tracked properly, or corporate or special interest welfare are at issue) occurs not through stolen taxi chits or $100 snowshoes from Parks Canada, but through $723 million in Employment Insurance fraud.

In any event, here are just a *few* of the more interesting examples of equipment and money that have gone missing over the last several years.

Favorites: Sony, Toshiba, IBM, and Dell

Laptops walked away more often than desktop computers, naturally, given that the former are easier to run with. So which department was most embarrassed? Public Works, which saw $140,876 stolen and recovered only $8,100.

Call me a cab:

- Theft of taxi chits from the department of Finance, 2001: $100.
- Loss of taxi-chit booklets from the department of Natural Resources, 2001: $350.

Canadian heritage, stolen.

- There was a break-in at Fort Walsh in 2001, not to be confused with Fort Knox, given the lax security. The department of Canadian Heritage lost $10,000, none of which was expected to be recovered.

- A deposit bag containing $5,870 went missing from the safe at the Lake Louise Visitor Reception Centre. Neither the bag or money were ever recovered. (Canadian Heritage 2001)

- Theft of snowshoes: $100. (Parks Canada, 2001)

Souvenir?

- Theft of a license plate in Nova Scotia: $5. (Human Resources Development, 2001)

Hard up?

- Theft of a mouse (the computer kind): $20. (Foreign Affairs, 2001)

Military mischief: Stolen from National Defence

- Theft of a bayonet: $24
- Theft of military kits (384 cases): $117,596
- Theft of computers and laptops: $117,069

It's a riot

- Five inmate riots in 2001 cost $49,542 in 2001. (Solicitor General, 2001)

Foreign Affairs and International Trade

- Theft was the reason for three briefcases of missing embassy funds worth almost $1 million ($935,794). Nothing has been recovered yet the government says it will only lose $85,794 and expects to recoup $850,000, or about 91 percent.

- Taxpayers can hope, but the record is otherwise. Between 1992 and 2000, the government lost almost $1.5 million in embassies, consulars and missions due to theft or negligence, and by 2001, recovered only about $310,000, or 21 percent. Keep your fingers crossed.

The big picture

Overall, $765 million in public property, cash, or money due, was lost, stolen or filched from taxpayers according to records kept by the auditor general.

That figure though does not reveal the entire story. In some cases, some departments report data back to the early 1990s on losses of public money or property; others since 1996 or even later.

On the other hand, the department of Transport, which lost $42,806 back in 1963(!) due to the alteration of deposit slips, has recouped $20,723, but insists—at least according to the public accounts—that it will still retrieve another $22,083 on a 40-year debt.

Overall, the government's books have recouped $508 million, have written off $78 million, but still plan to recover $179 million.

Who's the biggest crook? Umm, maybe citizens

So who is the biggest offender? Canadians. As much as some federal employees have stolen, lost or misplaced public cash and property, some Canadians milked the taxpayer cow and then some.

For example, between 1996 and 2000, Ottawa caught enough Canadians filing fraudulent unemployment insurance claims ($723 million) to *almost* pay for Prince Edward Island's program spending for a full budget year ($873 million). By far, and in terms of program spending, fraudulent unemployment insurance claims were the biggest cost to taxpayers over the years (excluding corporate welfare and political boondoggles).

Ottawa recovered half a billion dollars, hopes to recover another $164 million, but will still write off almost $64 million. And this is the fraud and theft that was discovered. Presumably, some undiscovered fraud occurred.

Q: WHICH IS MORE PAINFUL?

A: GETTING A ROOT CANAL:

B: DOING YOUR INCOME TAX:

C: WATCHING THE DEBATE:

5

Think like a serf
Canada's election gag laws

It is time to remember that the first thing we belong to is humanity. And humanity is separated from the animal world by thought and speech and they should naturally be free. If they are fettered, we go back to being animals.

Alexander Solzhenitsyn[1]

Stay out of our sandbox

There are few signs that better reveal a politician's true opinion of her constituents than whether or not she muzzles voters. Tragic then that not only are most federal politicians happy to pass gag laws that prevent anyone but political parties and their candidates from voicing an opinion during elections, the same people also force citizens to finance political parties.[a]

And has the restriction made elections more substantive? When politicians ban free speech by those bothersome labour unions, environmental lobbies, citizens' groups, taxpayer lobbies and individuals—who work, vote, remit taxes, and pay the salaries of MPs—has the gag led to better, more informative and intellectually stimulating elections? Where ideas of philosophy and grave matters of state are discussed with the utmost of sobriety, without cheap political shots and fluffy party advertising that insults the intelligence of voters? To ask the question is to answer it.

Exhibit A on this one is the 2000 federal election, where taxpayers were forced to hand over $23 million to political parties and their candidates, entities that already benefited from generous tax credits that

---

[a] The exception to this recently has been the Reform party and its successor, the Canadian Alliance. The Progressive Conservatives have reversed their earlier position and voted against the latest incarnation of the gag law.

pump tens of millions of dollars into party coffers.[b] Substantive issues were not discussed, as demonstrated by the leader's debate where Jean Chretien, Stockwell Day, Alexa McDonough, Joe Clark and Gilles Duceppe all outdid each other to prove that original thinking about health care policy would never occur if *their* party were in charge.

Advocacy group advertising might have pried open the idea box by broadcasting fresh ideas on that and other issues, but that was effectively banned by a law that restricted "third party" spending to minuscule amounts per riding. So the election was left solely in the hands of the play-it-safe professional political consultants whose philosophical, economic and historical horizons are either short-term or non-existent.

A short history of gag laws

The restriction on free speech is relatively recent. For over a century since Confederation, no federal government enacted restrictions on election-time speech,[2] a situation that lasted until 1974, when Pierre Trudeau's Liberals introduced amendments to the country's *Elections Act*, which also first regulated political party finances. While the 1974 law technically banned citizens' groups, unions and others from election advertising, the law made an exception that "allowed" Canadians to advance support (or not) for issues of public policy.

That exception lasted until 1983 when federal political parties figured their generosity on free speech lasted long enough, and in only 40 minutes of parliamentary debate voted to remove the free speech exception. All three parties then in Parliament—the governing Liberals, and opposition Progressive Conservatives and New Democrats—voted to restrict election-time advertising for politicians only. A Tory MP in 1983 was at least honest about the purpose of the law: it would, he said, make elections "easier to police."[3]

The comment betrayed an elitist and tyrannical view of the source of political power and legitimacy: that power emanates from rulers who, should they care, may on occasion deign to share it with the peasantry. That it came from a Conservative, who presumably should be more suspicious of state power, revealed the intellectual rot within Canadian conservatism in the early 1980s where there was little difference between any major party and their views on the role of the state vis-à-vis citizens.

---

[b] In the 2000 general election, and *not* including the value of political tax credits, taxpayers reimbursed political parties for almost $7.7 million. Candidates across the country who received more than 15 percent of the vote in their riding were also reimbursed; that amounted to an *additional* $15.5 million.

Fortunately not all Canadians agreed with the top-down consensus. David Sommerville, then head of the National Citizens' Coalition, went to court to have the law quashed, was successful, and thus for the 1984 and 1988 elections, freedom of speech was in play.

Gag-free elections = substantive debates

The result was that in 1988 the most memorable election in recent Canadian history was fought over an actual issue as opposed to the usual uninformative political party pulp. As a free trade agreement with the United States was due to be signed if Brian Mulroney and the Tories were re-elected, would-be MPs, business and labour groups and voters themselves argued about free trade in newspapers, on talk shows and in coffee shops. By one estimate, advocacy groups that supported free trade spent $4 million advertising in 14 newspapers.[4] That figure was equivalent to roughly 40 percent of what the major parties spent on advertising that year. Anti-free-trade groups spent $1.7 million.[5]

The pro-gag law argument then was that the unequal spending meant pro-free-trade groups influenced the 1988 election more than anti-free-trade groups. But on examination, it was a baseless claim: the two anti-free-trade parties (the Liberals and New Democrats) won a majority of the votes, which, as one journalist noted "must also mean a majority voted for the side that spent *less* on third-party advertising."[6]

The empire strikes back: the Lortie Commission

Not that the facts would stand in the way of more restrictions: Barely three years after a robust, issues-based campaign, the federally appointed Lortie Commission urged Ottawa to impose another gag law. This time, the proposal was for a $1,000 limit (just over *three dollars* per riding) on election expenses for third parties.

The 1992 recommendations were predictable; the Commission was made up of like-minded groups that preferred restrictions on free speech. And there was no mystery as to why; after all, if one is in power or is connected with those that are, the status quo is fine, even if on occasion existing policy might be deleterious for the country at large. For those with influence, tempted by power that inflates one's perception of their place in the world, the temptation to silence potential critics is constant. Add to that an actual vacuum of ideas, where, if all one has to offer in terms of policy is vague homilies and meaningless assertions, then actual fresh thinking on defence, taxation, social policy and other policy areas represent a real threat. Better to smother fresh ideas and voices.

That the politicians and bureaucrats who drafted the 1991 law were touchy about their status and ready to defend their turf became evident in a later interview with a witness who appeared before the Lortie Commission. Economist Dr. Filip Palda appeared before the committee only to be berated for two hours and told by committee members, "politicians are not respected, they are under attack and need protection."[7] The same committee later lectured media witnesses and threatened to impose new rules on what reporters could write about during elections. As further evidence that the committee was power tripping, 80 percent of the committee's 31 sessions were held in private (*in camera*) with no records kept of their deliberations.[8]

Unsurprisingly, fresh thinking was not on the menu when the committee emerged to give its recommendations; instead, party hacks and bureaucrats helped deliver the politically desired result. As further evidence that open debate was not high on the list of priorities in 1992, out of the six major objectives listed by the 1992 Royal Commission on Electoral Reform and Party Financing, not one mentioned freedom of speech. The Commission was more concerned with "strengthening political parties as primary political organizations."[9] Translation: pesky citizens' groups should hit the road. Pierre Lortie, chair of the committee, confirmed the intent of the proposed legislation when he smugly observed that "$1,000 doesn't buy a lot of TV."[10]

Ignore the facts

The Lortie Commission, as with other proponents of gagging citizens at election time, assumed that money spent on advertising sways helpless voters who cannot be trusted to parse through election time rhetoric from a party or a citizens' group, and make up their own mind about it all.

But there is little proof for this belief. Even if one thought the 1988 election results were murky (not all who voted Liberal necessarily opposed free trade), another example of independent voters revealed itself in the early 1990s to puncture the claim that political advertising necessarily sways citizens.

In 1992, after an earlier attempt to amend the Constitution failed, the Conservative government put a new package of amendments directly to the Canadian public. The Charlottetown accord was perhaps the worst piece of constitutional committee work in the history of the country, and a perfectly modern example of what happens when too many special interests and politicians are placed in a room together and deprived of fresh air. Moreover, much of it was vague and a mishmash of special interest grievances writ large; it also possessed the predictable nanny-state solutions for Canada's ills.[c]

But the proposed amendments had the support of most of the country's talking heads and pundits, to say nothing of the federal and provincial governments. Also weighing in heavily on the "yes" side was the cheerleading state-owned radio and television network, the CBC. In addition to overwhelming elite support for the constitutional fix, the "yes" forces outspent the "no" side by a measure of *thirteen to one*. Given the theory about how easily political ads influenced Canadians and combined with the pundit advantage on the "yes" side, approval of the Charlottetown constitutional amendments should have been easy.

Despite the favourable odds for the "yes" side, Canadians could and did make up their own minds. They rejected the package with the "no" side winning, 54.2 percent to 44.8 percent.[11] Insofar as the theory that Canadians were mindless sheep that needed protection from advertising in the form of gag laws, citizens were given the opportunity in 1992 to follow the money and the politicians. They took a pass.

MPs, sheep, and Animal Farm

But there were some Canadians who did not think for themselves and take account of facts. Thus it was that a majority of members of Parliament brought in yet another gag law in 1993, this time with a $1,000 limit as recommended by the Lortie Commission.

Ironically, if politicians needed yet another demonstration that political ads do not always sway voters, shortly after the 1993 gag law was passed, the governing Progressive Conservatives spent $10.4 million in their re-election attempt (more than any other party) and elected just two members of Parliament.[12] So much for the theory that money buys votes.

Meanwhile, the National Citizens' Coalition sued and the Alberta Court of Queen's Bench agreed that the revised *Canada Elections Act* violated the Charter of Rights and Freedoms. The federal government appealed again, and lost, again. Mr. Justice Roger Kerans and two other justices almost laughed the government lawyers out of their courtroom.

---

[c] They ranged from guaranteed special status for Quebec and 25 percent of all seats in Parliament regardless of its population relative to the rest of the country, to a guarantee of all manner of social programs including "full employment," as if governments could wave a wand and make this magically come about. Among other ludicrous proposals, regional economic development programs (read: political pork) were to be permanently entrenched in the Constitution.

The federal government lawyer, James Shaw, argued the restrictions merely attempted to create a "level playing field" during elections, to prevent big spenders from twisting the public debate by buying what the federal government argued was "excessive" advertising. The judges were having none of it. Judge Kerans noted that the law could be seen as perhaps having another purpose: "to shut out people who disagree [with the political parties]. That's the other interpretation."[13] He labelled the $1,000 limit a joke, said it amounted to "absolute prohibition" and that it smacked of George Orwell's novel *Animal Farm*, where "everyone's equal as long as everyone's not able to speak."[14]

In striking down the law, the court made this argument:

> Insofar as these impugned provisions severely limit the ability of third parties to participate in the very communicative process which allows a citizen's vote to be 'informed,' they undermine the rights of citizens to vote. Thus, this is the antithesis of an informed vote in a free and democratic country.[15]

The court noted that the government presented no evidence that advertising by third parties has ever in Canadian history convinced any significant number of people to vote one way or another. And the judge noted:

> In any event, I have great difficulty accepting that an opposite finding would justify suppression of expression... there can be no pressing and substantial need to suppress that input merely because it might have an impact.[16]

Writing the judgment, Madame Justice Carole Conrad found that:

> The spending restrictions... force those who wish to participate by advertising in any meaningful way to do so through political parties and candidates. As such, the sections interfere with an individual's freedom of association to accomplish not only very legitimate, but essential objectives in a democratic country. [The result was] legislation which ironically purports to protect the democratic process, by means of infringing the very rights which are fundamental to democracy.[17]

The federal government never appealed it to the Supreme Court of Canada and so gave up, temporarily.

It's Groundhog Day, *again*

Similar to the movie, *Groundhog Day*, voters woke up only to relive the same events. Despite the court rulings, politicians tried again to kick voters out of the election-time sandbox. In the latest attempt, they were aided by a 1997 Supreme Court of Canada ruling that threw out a

Quebec law that banned amounts higher than $600 spent to support or oppose separation in the 1995 Quebec referendum on separation. (The law only allowed for amounts higher than $600 to be spent by the official "yes" or "no" camps.)

While the Supreme Court struck down the $600 limit as too low, the Court hinted that perhaps *$1,000* might be an acceptable limit. It also suggested that the federal government should have appealed the Alberta Court of Appeal ruling (in the earlier gag law case initiated by the National Citizens' Coalition). Apparently the difference between an unconstitutional law and one to be stamped "OK" by the court was $400.

Encouraged by the judicial tip-off, the federal government changed the *Elections Act* to decree that no entity other than politicians and their party could spend more than $152,000 nationally, or about $500 per riding.[d] Spent all at once, the nationwide limit might buy one full-page ad in ten major dailies across the country for a single day. If used in each riding, groups could, after they paid for the printing, paste flyers to telephone poles. The penalty for busting the third-party limit was a jail term of up to five years. In a riding with tens of thousands of voters and in a country with 30 million people, $500 per riding for everyone else save political parties was a joke. Any attempt to communicate with a majority of the country's voting age public is not inexpensive.

Political parties knew that which is why politicians gave themselves generous limits. For example, the largest political party in the country (the federal Liberals) under the law could spend over $12.7 million; the Alliance, New Democrats and Tories were allowed similar amounts if they fielded a full slate of candidates. On average, political parties could spend $42,226 per riding, not including what candidates spent in addition. Thus, political parties could spend their millions to blanket the newspapers, mailboxes, radio and television viewers with their message.[e]

The National Citizens' Coalition once again attacked the law in an Alberta court during the 2000 election, had it suspended, only to have the Court of Appeal restore the law for the election period. Two years later, Alberta courts dumped the expense limits on third parties but the Court of Appeal preserved sections of the law that required individuals and groups to register with Elections Canada and disclose their donors.

---

[d] If advocacy groups (or anyone else) wanted to, they could spend up to $3,000 per riding, as long as the national limit of $152,000 was not breached. Thus, the average per riding was just over $500.

[e] In total, all the registered political parties could collectively spend over $74.1 million; (they spent $35 million). And the 49 "third parties" that registered with Elections Canada (given their individual limit of $152,000 each) could collectively spend $7.5 million; in the end, they spent just $666,000.

Both the NCC and the federal government appealed sections of the ruling; it is expected the case will end up in the Supreme Court.

Meanwhile, other court battles continued. Elections Canada charged several people with violations of the law, including an elderly Nova Scotia man and B.C. libertarian Paul Bryan (both posted results of election returns in eastern Canada before polls closed in western Canada). An anti-gun control lobby that posted signs decrying the federal gun registry was also targeted. By May 2001, Ottawa spent over $525,000 in taxpayer money to defend its restriction on the very taxpayers who were being muzzled by the law,[18] an amount almost as much as all third parties together spent in the 2000 election.

Pay us and keep quiet: The thinking of gag law proponents

Naturally, politicians who vote in favour of gag laws (Liberals, New Democrats and the Bloc Quebecois voted for the most recent free speech restriction) always have reasons. Forget for a moment that taxpayers pay members of Parliament $131,400 every year, plus extra if the MP is a cabinet minister (+$63,240) or the prime minister (+$131,588).

Ignore as well that Canadians send $190 billion to Ottawa every year in taxes and have a right to say how that money is spent when politicians feel most vulnerable: at election time. For those who want to pipe up about taxes, environment, union or business issues, sorry. During elections, the opinion bar is closed.

It was the same for the 1983 law. Then, members of Parliament justified the free speech gag this way: politicians were "particularly concerned about single-issue groups pushing a very emotional issue to the extent that it clouds the *real* issues of a campaign."[19] Harvie Andre, the Progressive Conservative MP responsible for the 1991 gag law earlier opposed such laws but flip-flopped: "I certainly recognize there are real benefits to me and everybody else in the system having limits…. The third parties can't come in."[20]

That was rich. In effect, Andre argued that Canadians (voters) should never be allowed to: a) define the "real" issues (that was reserved for politicians), and b) become upset over an issue and make life difficult for a politician who does not share the same passion. It was condescending, undemocratic, and specious logic. Historical campaigns for the emancipation of slaves, suffrage for women, and an end to discriminatory laws against Aboriginal, Chinese and Japanese Canadians were all based on at least some outrage about the indignity of their respective situations and the unfairness of it all.

Passion is part of life and of politics. If a parolee murdered someone's child and relatives wanted a change to Canada's lax parole system, their outrage would be entirely understandable and justified. If citizens are upset and want changed laws or policies, it is their right to demand the same, and without permission from the very people they pay to govern on their behalf. It is not for voters to crawl to politicians to beg for the right to express their opinion. If citizens channel their anger and frustration through democratic and non-violent channels, it is not the place of politicians to instruct voters as to when they may or may not speak, as if such voters were children.

But similar to Harvie Andre's line of thinking, Ed Broadbent, former federal NDP leader, has argued that he is delighted with such restrictive laws. In fact, Mr. Broadbent argues they do not go nearly far enough. England, he noted, does not allow political advertising on television.

> It meant that mindless and malicious political advertising, so typical in American elections and increasingly used in Canada (witness Reform's anti-Quebecois commercials), was absent from British television. Another benefit was that the policy saved all parties millions of pounds in election expenses.[21]

This is a fascinating justification. Canadians might think *Mr. Broadbent's* party, with its constant attack on free markets, has been the mindless and malicious force in Canada over the years, attacking as it does wealth creation and greater freedom for individuals to live their lives as they— not government—see fit. But, in his opinion piece, Mr. Broadbent argues the same line that many nanny-statists set out as it concerns gag laws and third parties:

> Once the role of money is restricted, political parties are compelled to rely more on the voluntary efforts of their own members and other citizens. Parties—left, right or centre— which are most successful in winning individual citizens deserve to have greater impact. In a democracy, people and ideas, not money and power, should count. The same reasoning also holds for maintaining serious restrictions on "third-party" advertising during an election campaign.[22]

Note Mr. Broadbent's pre-occupation with political parties and his *a priori* assumption that political parties deserve to have greater impact on elections. Depending on the year, about one to two percent of Canadians belong to political parties. What Broadbent and others who peddle this line ignore is the fact that many people no longer want to advance their ideas through political parties; in fact, some feel they cannot do so. They may be correct or wrong about that, but it is entirely the right of individuals to make such a choice.

The gag law pushers see a decline in political party affiliation as unhealthy, but the opposite can just as easily be argued. Instead of contributing to a political party, Canadians may give to and work on behalf of advocacy groups as another avenue to express their convictions. This method also allows people to reconcile their desire to support diverse causes that may not be found within one political party.

For example, what if one takes a greener view of the environment than does the Alliance but is also more fiscally conservative than a federal Liberal or New Democrat? Maybe a Canadian cares to send their money to the World Wildlife Fund *and* the Fraser Institute. Another person might support the Liberals on their policy of subsidies to Quebec companies but not care for their foreign policy.

In any above example, individuals can write a cheque to associations that represent both concerns in a manner a particular party might not or perhaps could not, given the tendency of parties to reduce platforms to the lowest and most non-controversial common denominator.[f] The assumption that Canadians must work primarily through political parties for the greater public good reveals much about those who hold such assumptions. It reveals a preoccupation with party politics as the preferred means to most ends—not a particularly deep or broad view of what contributes to a healthy civilization.

Lortie's faulty foundations

The main justification for gag laws over the past decade is the 1991 *Lortie Report*, which itself relies on a study written by Richard Johnston, a professor at the University of British Columbia. Johnston's work on third-party advertising in the 1988 federal election purported to show that third-party spending affected voter intentions. But inconveniently for the gag law proponents, Johnston later testified in a British Columbia court about a provincial gag law brought in by that province's New Democrats. He disavowed his conclusions and said they were incorrect.

By extension then, so too was the Lortie Commission and so were government lawyers and anyone else who argued from that report as a justification for free speech restrictions.[g] Richard Johnston's new conclusion was never challenged by other witnesses at the trial or by any other empirical study.[23]

---

[f] This is desirable. The common complaint that "political parties don't represent me" is narcissistic. No one group or entity entirely represents one person's will or thinking or politics, nor should they. Political parties are useful in that compromise is hammered out in their platforms and in their governing if elected; such compromises are laudable and necessary in a democratic country. But the necessity of compromise in the art of governing or in seeking votes does not also require that political parties and politicians have a monopoly in the debate over ideas and policies at election time.

Another provincial attempt, with a twist

Another argument for gag laws as of late comes from New Democrat changes to Manitoba's election law in 2001. There, party fundraising from unions and businesses was banned as was advertising by third parties during elections.[h] While on the surface it is justified as the creation of a level playing field, what the law does in reality is ignore the advantage some parties have with their reliance on labour unions to supply a steady and large supply of union volunteers and easily channelled donations from the same during elections.[i] Given the government in power in Manitoba, this is not coincidental.

Meanwhile, citizens who do not belong to a union and do not share a government union's bias for tax and spending cannot flex their muscles except by joining advocacy groups who oppose such policies. Ban advocacy groups at election time as Manitoba's NDP government did, and the playing field is restricted to the major political parties in terms of advertising, and to government unions who have an on-the-ground advantage. Perhaps that is why some politicians like gag laws so much.[j]

The argument that Canadians should stay silent or join a political party if they want to "influence" an election is mistaken for another reason. In a country with thirty million people, $507 per riding means that citizens' groups are limited to 19th-century technology to communicate with other citizens, i.e., waybills on bulletin boards. Meanwhile,

---

[g] One reason advocacy groups and others may not have had a discernible effect on elections is due to the small amount of money spent by those groups. Even if they were to spend large amounts of money and have an effect, there would still be no justification for restrictions. People ought to have an effect upon ideas and elections; this country belongs to its citizens, not to its politicians or political parties.

[h] As of writing, the Manitoba government had, in law, banned business and union donations to parties in that province but had not yet proclaimed the section of the legislation dealing with advertising by citizen groups. If that section was proclaimed then it could be subject to a court challenge and possibly struck down in court prior to an election. If the government waits to proclaim it until just before an election, then a court may not strike it down in time for the campaign itself, thus barring any involvement during the election by so-called third parties no matter how unconstitutional the Manitoba legislation may be.

[i] The votes of labour union members are anything but uniform. Many more private sector union members supported the Liberals and the Alliance in the 2000 general election, while the New Democrats received only a small fraction of the labour vote. Unfortunately, many unions still push policies that would do irreparable harm to their members, such as the anti-free-trade stance which, if ever enacted, would be to Canada's disadvantage as a nation that relies heavily on free access to markets in other countries.

[j] In addition, there is also another advantage for left-wing political parties; many unions allow members to automatically contribute to the New Democratic Party via their paycheques, which allows unions to help the NDP receive "individual" contributions while restricting the flow of business money to the Manitoba Conservative party.

subsidized political parties will use tax dollars to advertise on TV, radio, newspaper and the Internet—in other words, to communicate with Canadians via 21st-century methods.

Blow-dried candidates

The argument that only political parties and their leaders can debate issues with the utmost of seriousness and appropriate gravitas is laughable. Elections are often run *by* politicians *for* politicians, especially those at the top. Ideas are mostly absent. Prospective MPs must stick to script and dutifully mouth non-controversial statements.

Political parties kill multiple trees to produce oft-meaningless motherhood-and-apple pie brochures that tell voters they are in favour of—what else—motherhood and apple pie, and it usually rolls out according to plan. Governments pray to coast back into power while opposition parties hope the prime minister utters something questionable that might garner them extra votes. Understandably, that is the primary motivation: winning votes; but it comes at the expense of clarity for citizens who might well prefer some politicians be forced to explain their intentions before the ballots are cast.

This is not blind cynicism. One cannot be too critical of attempts by political parties to monopolize speech. Moreover, when politicians talk about "third parties," it is a tip-off that they want the election-time sandbox to themselves. "Third party" really means someone without a central interest in a dispute. So voters who will not play in the "political sandbox" according to the dictates set down by politicians—no messy divisive issues the politicians cannot spin away—are assumed to be merely "third parties." This pejorative term turns the core assumption of representative and accountable government on its head. From this view, no longer does power flow from citizens to their government, but the other way around; and those who disagree at election time can keep quiet or talk to the judge. Such a view, enforced by the power of government, is injurious to freedom and to a fairly fought battle over ideas.

What the former NDP leader and others who hold such assumptions fail to consider is that ideas may be advanced better—and primarily—through vigorous debates at election time (as well as others) by not only politicians but by every Canadian in every conceivable manner, including public debates sparked by a rainbow of various interests who fight it out on the airwaves and in the newspapers. Often, ideas are advanced and thought through on that terrain much more often than by those who contest for political office; their understandable desire to get elected often smothers a frank discussion of issues.

Party limits?

Some might concede that political parties should not have an advantage, but still argue for limits on citizens' groups equal to that of political parties. It is a reasonable argument, except that political parties once in power also have unlimited access to taxpayer cash and never hesitate to use it. Before the last federal election, members of Parliament promoted themselves and their policies through advertising at taxpayer expense, including a last minute MP "mailer," dropped into the post office right before the election call at a cost of $3,000 per riding.[24] In addition, the federal government alone spends untold millions every year on advertising, on ads that are never restricted by election-time gag laws.

The argument about limits on election advertising, for parties or citizens' groups, also misses the river of money that flows to favoured ridings, companies and candidates in the form of grants and "loans." Stephen Harper, then head of the National Citizens' Coalition, noted this in an open letter to the prime minister in 1999 as the NCC pursued the gag law in court:

> One bigger example: your own riding. It seems that through various agencies and programs, more than $12 million in grants and loans found their way to Shawinigate in time for the last election.[25]

The corruption argument

Often the very donation of money by anyone, and the spending of it by a political party, is thought to be a "corrupting influence" in politics which must be limited. The limits, ironically, are put in place by the very people who stand to be corrupted, i.e., political representatives themselves. But the "corruption" argument is based on conjecture more than on a real analysis of the effect money has in Canadian politics. Election-time advertising is actually small relative to the amount spent annually on advertising in Canada (including the pre-production aspect of the industry).

As for corruption itself, the distinction in donations to political parties must be made with this in mind. As long as governments regulate business, unions, or ordinary citizens in any manner, all of those will be affected by government policies and laws; it is only reasonable that they will want a say on how such policies are formulated. That is hardly corruption; it is self-preservation, especially if the government may enact a measure that could threaten one's livelihood or one's environment.

Thus, Canadians, either individually or through associations, fund parties, or engage in advocacy and lobbying to represent their interests, as they well should, given that the state will not wither away any time soon.

For example, suppose a group of residents in northern Ontario are concerned about a proposed mine and its possible effect on their environment. If they lobby the government directly to ban mining, no matter how much money those same citizens gave to the government of the day in past elections, if the decision is made to ban mining and their past donations were openly disclosed (as is required under current law), there is nothing corrupt about such a process if it is transparent.[k]

Similarly, if a mining company made donations to the political party in power, and a decision to allow mining is made, that also is not in and of itself evidence of corruption. What occurs is that various interests—from the mining side and from the environmental side—fight for their self-interest as they see it. Both sides argue their case; both sides make contributions to political parties or advocacy groups that reflect their interests in an attempt to have laws and policies reflect their priorities.

That is not corruption; it is the stuff of democratic politics. To seek any other result in politics is to create a "pure" world of politics where government decisions are made free from any outside influence, i.e., the influence of voters themselves. That is a bizarre definition of democratic politics. No matter the decision a government makes—*for* mining or *against* mining or for *partial* mining—someone's interests, real or perceived, will be compromised to some degree. As such, the same people have the right to be heard, to lobby, to fund candidates and causes that they believe reflect their interests.

So where is corruption a potential problem? When those who seek favours from government do so without having to compete for contracts, when politicians are directly influenced by way of a bribe, or when donations to politicians or parties are not made in the open.

Beyond that, a donation to a political party is not in and of itself "corrupt" or indicative of a tendency to corruption. And to equate donations with corruption is to water down the term and empty it of meaning; the term should be reserved for what it plainly is: vote-buying by bribing and the awarding of government contracts on political or nepotistic grounds instead of on merit.

Those who argue that money should be "kept out of politics" in effect argue that the people most affected by a particular government policy—

---

[k] For the sake of a simple example, I am ignoring the other arguments that may come into play, such as property rights and how they would affect such a decision.

whether the multinational corporation with 50,000 employees or Joe's Stereo shop or the residents of a neighbourhood concerned about pollution—should have no ability to enter into the public discussion on that very issue: not directly via their own efforts and advertising, not through a union, advocacy group or business lobby or through donations to a political party.

In that scenario, elections would occur without the input of citizens and with the only voices being those of politicians, their parties, and the media. Evening television newscasts reach millions of viewers, many of whom receive their only dose of news from the same. Election-time restrictions create a playing field tilted heavily to the advantage of producers, newspaper editors, columnists, talk-show hosts, and political insiders who direct political parties. This is not equality of expression; it is enforced segregation of political opinion. To ban the public from an open debate about an issue is to treat the majority of citizens not affiliated with parties or unions, and those not employed by media organizations as inconvenient spectators, whose interests and voices should count for nothing. The premise of such an assumption is chilling.

The attempt to limit what advocacy groups or unions or parties spend to propagate their message is a bizarre way to make elections "fair."[1] Fair compared to what? Canadians spend at least $800 million every year just to feed their pets. Over $4.8 billion is spent to advertise everything from McCain french fries to Tim Horton's donuts. An expenditure of $35 million once every four years by political parties (perhaps double that if one counts provincial election expenses) is a minute amount in comparison to other ad money that sloshes around Canada.

Rather than limit how much parties spend, and enact *de facto* bans on everyone else, Canada's governments should scrap election-time limits, require the disclosure of donations, and throw open the idea contest.

---

[1] There are even more bizarre measures in Canada's election law that favour political parties at the expense of the private sector. For example, during an election, radio stations must give preferred and cheaper rates to those advertising during an election for such purposes. Obviously this makes advertising cheaper for such advertisers, primarily political parties and their candidates. And stations must even bump lucrative ads that may have been contracted long before the election to someone else and sold at a higher price. In effect, it would be as if the federal government passed a law that told hardware stores to price their products cheaper if a worker from a political campaign walks into the store to buy a product, and that the store must sell it to that worker even if they had already arranged to sell the same item to a regular buyer at a higher price. In essence, private industry is forced to subsidize political parties.

Spending comparisons

	Amount spent per riding, or riding average in selected examples $	Total allowed or spent nationally $
Allowed to each citizens' groups under the *Elections Act*	507	152,550
Allowed to a political party with a full candidate list under the *Elections Act*	42,226	12,710,074
Amount spent every year by Canadians on pet food	2,600,000	800,000,000
Amount spent in 2000 on advertising in general in Canada	15,946,684	4,800,000,000

Sources: Elections Canada and Statistics Canada. Calculations by author.

Actual election spending in 2000 election

	Average amount spent per riding $	Total spent nationally $
Advocacy groups/individuals: total	2,212	666,051
Political parties: total	116,186	34,972,236

Sources: Elections Canada. Calculations by author.

Who pays federal income tax?

Taxpayers | Income | Taxes Paid

Source: Tax Statistics On Individuals,
Canada Customs and Revenue Service, 2002 edition
(2000 tax year) (unedited)

	0 to $50,000	$50,000 to $100,000	$100,000 to $150,000	$150,000 to $250,000	$250,000 +
Taxpayers	83.0%	14.2%	1.6%	0.7%	0.5%
Income	50.5%	30.1%	6.2%	4.3%	9.0%
Taxes Paid	34.0%	34.9%	8.6%	6.6%	15.9%

6

Vice dressed up as virtue
Why more redistribution won't pay the bills

They imagine that our flourishing state in England is owing to
that bank-paper and not the bank-paper to the flourishing
condition of our commerce.

Edmund Burke
Reflections on the Revolution in France[1]

I have two choices; I can distribute poverty, or I can distribute
wealth.

Deng Xiaoping[2]

Since at least the French Revolution, advocates of state intervention
for its own sake often believe their cause to be noble and just. On the
extremes over the past century, this was a constant theme of Canadian
as well as international adherents of state intervention. Worldwide, the
bloody body count of 100 million that resulted from extreme command
and control regimes around the world provoked little modesty on the
part of fellow travellers.[a] In international politics over the past century,
what mattered to some, apparently, was the language and talk of liberation and justice, no matter how little of that prosperity and freedom was
ever produced under such regimes.

But one need not look at extreme arguments for state intervention to
wonder why lovers of state become giddy when the prospect of more taxes
and higher spending arises. In Canada, the tax-and-spend crowd continually assume that large government is equal to compassion and that its

---

[a] See *The Black Book of Communism: Crimes, Terror, Repression* from Harvard University Press, 1999, authored by prominent French intellectuals, some of whom were in their
earlier years either communists themselves or fellow travellers. It, like Alexander
Solzhenitsyn's *Gulag Archipelago*, lays bare the tragic blood-soaked historical fact of
communist theory when practised.

corollary, high taxes, are conducive to and responsible for a sense of community. Examine the rhetoric from those who think state power is somehow inherently friendly to those most vulnerable, and the assumption is that values such as compassion are somehow state-derived.

Values and morality, compassion and caring

Thus, *Maclean's* columnist Charles Gordon asserts that "Canada's tax hell" is a "myth" and argues that "while government spending does contribute to high taxation, it also pays for a way of life that most Canadians value."[3] He implicitly makes the link between a large government and the values that many Canadians believe to be distinctly Canadian, or at least, are primarily the domain of heavily taxed countries.[b]

Bill Phipps, onetime moderator of the United Church of Canada and later New Democrat candidate for Parliament, revealed this line of thought when, in 1999, he famously said, "as you fill out your tax return, you should be joyful," referencing the various activities government performs with tax dollars.[4]

> We've got to come back, even more so than we ever have, to caring for the common good and the things we hold in common. The planet is not private property. This whole neo-liberal agenda is to get people thinking only in terms of themselves; as long as I can make my million dollars, it doesn't matter what happens to you. That's what we're creating.[5]

Lorne Nystrom, a New Democrat member of Parliament from Saskatchewan also reinforced this link when he proudly pointed out the NDP's draft platform calls for a millionaires' tax, an "excess" corporate profits tax, and a tax on what he asserted was "rampant" currency speculation.[6]

The two core assumptions in all three men's arguments is first, that compassion in Canada is most helped by high taxes, much regulation, and a large role for government; and second, entrepreneurs and profit must be watched, regulated, and to some extent discouraged, as it is the antithesis of a decent, caring, and civilized society.

Undoubtedly, some who hold that belief are sincere, and as with any statement there is the question of balance.[c] But intensely believed or not, it is a chronic fault of modern intellectuals to think that any ill can

---

[b] The notion that high-tax states have better social indicators on lifespan, health care, and environmental indicators is false. There is a difference between developing economies and moderately and high taxed states on such measurements, but there is no difference between moderately and high taxed states. Some countries with less government involvement as a percentage of their economy have better indicators than Canada. For more on this comparison, see Chapter 15.

be solved if enough tax dollars and smart people are combined together in one room. Along with the sincere but mistaken, are those who desire to impose order on what they see as chaos in the private sector, sometimes from a fear of change, and occasionally from an urge to control the economic lives of others.

Results anyone?

"People before profits," "communities before corporations," and other slogans are the buzzwords of the new redistributionists. The words are attractive and compelling; after all, who would *not* prefer their local butcher, baker or candlestick maker to large faceless corporations? And who would not think that people are always, intrinsically, of more value than mere lucre?

But slogans are of little help in determining government policy about the proper level of tax rates and redistribution. And they are silly as regards one's attitude towards business. After all, when does a successful small business cross the line between the much-loved little guy and become the mythical and hated "corporation," the supposed fount of all evil? When Starbucks was a lone Seattle coffee outlet in the early 1970s, no doubt some of the same people who might now protest free trade and throw a brick through its window would have patronized it three decades ago and lavished praise on its "local" ambience. But let the world find pleasure in the same brew and expand to a couple of thousand locations? At what point did a successful small company cross the line? When it opened store number five, 78, or 356?

Of course, there is no easily discernible dividing line between the small business David and corporate Goliath and any attempt to define one only reveals the economic and intellectual hollowness of what is essentially a political slogan, not an economic analysis based on objective facts. After all, large companies (unionized or not) pay much better salaries than does small business and also provide better benefit packages, usually because they can afford to. But the anti-business/anti-globalization crowd is not likely to throw a brick through the minimum-wage local coffee shop or overpriced corner store; that's reserved for Microsoft and McDonald's.

The illogic of each slogan aside, there are several reasons why the "high taxes=compassion" crowd usurps the language of compassion to push redistribution for its own sake. One reason, as already noted, is

---

[c] For more on the argument about the proper role of the state and an examination of the balance necessary as it concerns civilization, see Chapter 15.

that some that favour redistribution (above all else) think it is indeed the route to a more decent world. Slogans about caring and compassion appeal (as they should) because such people genuinely care about others and think redistribution by government is the best way to achieve noble and desired ends, such as less poverty.

But excellent intentions are never enough. While some wrongly assume that only those who agree with government-as-agent-of-redistribution are compassionate, the reality is that many Canadians are no less concerned for the poor and about other social ills; they just refuse to buy into the simplistic notion that every private problem has a government-run, taxpayer-funded solution.

Instead, there are often market-based solutions that governments promote to better effect. For example, the federal government could hector everyone to save for their retirement or tax even more than they do to fund the Canada Pension Plan. Instead, the use of the market combined with tax breaks—tax-deductible Registered Retirement Savings Plans for example—has spurred Canadians to voluntarily save more for their own retirement. It has also made capital available for companies, which helps wealth creation and employment creation.

Another reason Canada's tax-and-spend crowd resorts to "values-talk" is because it must. Given the disastrous incentives created when redistribution is emphasized at the expense of opportunity and wealth creation, the real world record of rampant redistribution has been disastrous. Whether it is Cuba that plunged from the fourth richest state per capita in Latin America four decades ago to the fourth poorest today, or the contrasting examples of Singapore, Hong Kong and Taiwan over the last half-century versus China (which only took wealth creation seriously starting two decades ago), there are multiple examples where the over-concentration on redistribution has failed, continually.[d]

Thus, those who resort to values-talk about the "unjust" and "unequal" distribution of income do so because their real world policies have failed to produce much in the way of *new* wealth. In British

---

[d] Some would argue that Cuba's economic policies are not as much at fault for its poverty as the American embargo. This is a fascinating line of defence. In essence, the defenders of Fidel Castro's Cuba argue that its poverty has been caused by a lack of trade, an argument with which any good capitalist could agree. But that is just the point: those who think countries can develop without competition, free markets, and trade should be happy to have the example of Cuba to demonstrate the superiority of their preferred model. According to the defenders of Cuba's economic program, it should have been a smashing success without trade with the United States. Of course, nothing about Cuba's model is superior. It is a centrally controlled dictatorship that impoverished its citizens. Naturally, the only defenders left for that country's system are a few hard-core ideologues in Canada along with some political science professors.

Columbia for example, real, per person income dropped in the 1990s when anti-wealth creation policies were enacted by that province's government, a government that focused overmuch on redistribution. In 1992, British Columbians earned $500 more on average than other Canadians; after just seven years of anti-wealth creation policies, inhabitants of that province earned $700 *less* on average than other Canadians. That, after a decade when some of the world experienced the best economic boom since the 1920s.[7]

Envy in virtuous drag

When governments make such a mistake, there is often more "equality" if by that one means less distance from the top income earners to those at the bottom, but that is often the result of an equality based on greater poverty for most. It is curious that many socialists seem to prefer a poor society where there is less of a difference between the earnings of people, to a society where everyone is better off but the difference between incomes is greater. Such a motivation is envy dressed up in the drag of virtue. And in the end, given the record, redistributionist policies for their own sake—instead of for necessary redistribution—are anything but virtuous when they constantly limit opportunity for all.

Tragically, the worst off under extreme schemes of anti-wealth creation are the most vulnerable in society. Such policies result in lower investment, fewer jobs and thus less competition for workers, which in turn puts downward pressure on wages, among other negative effects. Whenever economic growth is downgraded by a ruling class, it is the people on the margins—society's poorest—who pay the price. After all, they will be the first to lose their jobs, not CEOs of corporations or armchair critics of free markets. The much-quoted quip[e] that a rising (economic) tide lifts all boats is as true as ever; its parallel truth is that a receding ocean certainly does leave most people more "equal," but stranded on the shore and without much hope for upward movement, essentially an equality of poverty.

---

[e] A good example of the success of redistributionist rhetoric at the expense of the poor is in the constant anti-"big box" tirades. Think for example of chronic attempts to keep Wal-Mart from some cities. It is in fact those big box stores that the "community not corporations" crowd so hates, that have been most helpful for competition and thus for the poorest Canadians. The rich will never care if their four litres of milk is $2.60 or $4.00 but the poor do, which is why cutthroat competition between grocery stores is so very positive for lower-income Canadians who spend most of their income on the necessities of life. Those who oppose such open competition argue against the real benefits that it brings; it is another example of where the anti-free-market crowd has not thought through an issue to its logical end.

Wealth creation or wealth redistribution

Instead of asking how to raise incomes across the board in a sustainable (i.e., economically grounded) manner, the nanny-state adherents look at the existing pie and constantly devise new ways to divide it up. And any critical question of whether excessive redistribution might in fact harm the creation of jobs and thus undermine Canadian families is beyond the interest of the rampant redistributionists. They look at such questions and critiques as misguided at best or immoral at worst.

In this view, the guiding assumption is that whatever was performed by government over the last several decades is simply assumed to be the natural right of governments and, conveniently, the bureaucrats and their unions that have a natural self-interest in running and controlling as much as possible. But merely dividing existing wealth cannot create more of it—an absolute necessity in a world with a growing population.

Community is voluntary and spontaneous, not coerced

As well, the idea that only government fosters co-operation or community, or in fact is the primary motivation of such, is nonsense. The entire insurance industry is predicated on the desire of people to minimize the risk to their well being, and that, without much government involvement. People co-operatively pool their resources to guard against the after-effects of tragedy (bankruptcy and loss of income) and they do so voluntarily.

In addition, the claim that community and a healthy civic life are the result of government ignores the historical and present-day record. Charitable societies and activities, churches and synagogues, amateur sports teams, bird watchers and bowlers and countless other voluntary associations, are all the result of voluntary choices made by people who join together without coercion for a spiritual, charitable, social or other purpose. Volunteerism is part of civic duty and responsibility. If anything, governments run the risk of damaging such "little platoons" of civilized life (as Edmund Burke called such voluntary efforts) when governments take over activities formerly carried out by volunteers and charitable organizations.

Those who assume that government should be a critical "partner" (beyond basic elements of a necessary state such as preserving the rule of law for example) with such little platoons mistakenly assume that much in life is political, and has or should have a political link. That is both erroneous and narrow; many people live their lives with their families and friends far removed from politics. That, far from being unhealthy as some suggest, is the most positive thing one can say about a society; that people are free to live without concern that a government will politicize every area of life.[f]

Moreover, it is curious that one argument used against those who prefer free markets for reasons of opportunity, wealth creation, and voluntary co-operation between peoples is that such a preference is naïve and that free markets cannot solve every problem. Moreover, opponents of free markets insist money is not a solution to every problem.

And they are correct; free markets cannot solve every problem though that is most often a straw man argument set up to easily knock down.[g]

Nor should money be the sum total of life. The 20th-century debate was about which economic system could deliver the goods.

The fact that free markets can deliver the goods to most people and that it helps the cause of freedom is not to say that what people do with such freedom is always wise or morally commendable. Nor is it to assume that money should be worshipped. Sometimes free choices are also unwise ones. But the preference for free markets is merely for a

---

[f] The former U.S. ambassador to the United Nations once noted how revolutionary regimes were different and worse than "normal" autocracies. Normal dictatorships were bad enough, but at least in those societies governments did not try and uproot every element of civilized life such as religion or family. Jeane Kirkpatrick noted that those dictators were satisfied with the maintenance of their power. In contrast, revolutionary regimes by virtue of their attachment to utopian ends (she was then writing of communism) demanded the overturn of the very roots of society: such uprooting was integral to the "success" of their revolution. Mere power was never enough; everyone had to conform to the revolutionary ends.

[g] The argument is that the preference for free markets, free trade, and limited government allows for competition to act as the guard against one entity having too much power. When governments possess not only military and political power, but also economic power, (as when they own industries directly or regulate to such an extent that there is little difference between government and private ownership), they possess a vial that no company, acting in a competitive marketplace, could ever possess. Thus, when governments control not only political and military levers of power, but also economic ones, the tragic results of such concentrated power should not come as a surprise.

Moreover, free markets allow people to use their creativity and ingenuity to solve problems, while preserving diverse choices—nothing less and nothing more. Those who read into that process a claim that it will "solve" a particular problem, never mind all societal ills, miss the central point: Markets allow more individual choice than in restricted economies, and in that choice-based environment, ingenuity and creativity flourishes more readily and may solve some problems. Markets expand choices in goods, services, jobs, and thus ultimately in lifestyles. What people do with such choices is up to them. Also, it is often overlooked that one benefit of open trade and commerce is that people from various backgrounds, creeds and nations co-operate voluntarily and, in so doing, help their own countries better understand other nations and cultures. Commerce thus acts as an aid to oil the more difficult political relationships between states.

method where people have the maximum amount of opportunity and liberty to decide for themselves what road they wish to pursue; the economic system is simply the engine, which in the case of lightly regulated buying and selling between free men and women, happens to be superior for providing opportunity.

It is also important to note that free markets help remove (some of) the opportunity for political coercion of jobs and salaries. For example, who would wish to be subject to the whim of a politician or a bureaucrat for their career or paycheque? While the business world is also rarely "fair," at least one has choices, and if there are competitors, one can most often go to another workplace. When governments exert undue influence, economically sensible decisions (including whom to hire) can often be and *are* often overridden by political considerations. That is most frustrating for individuals who might otherwise have a shot at a job but, in a political world, lack the connections.

As to the argument that dollars alone cannot solve all ills, those most likely to fling that charge are themselves the ones most guilty of such assumptions. Those on the Left argue hypocritically when they say money cannot solve every problem, only to then use the levers of state to extract as much wealth as possible from citizens. Thus, in a vain and ironic effort, the redistributionists attempt to demonstrate that money *can* solve every problem—so long as it is channelled through government.

Why redistribution is of limited value

As long as there are taxes, there will be redistribution of income; that is what taxes do. But too much of a focus on income redistribution as opposed to wealth creation can obscure the real benefits of an expanding economy. Consider these three examples.

Example One: Who pays the tax?

The claim that Canadians, any Canadian, should be taxed more is curious. As a percentage of GDP, taxes have rarely been so high even with the recent reductions. And taxes were barely cut before provincial and federal governments began to raise them once again.[h]

Canada's taxes are certainly "progressive," if by that it is meant that a Canadian pays more as she moves up the income scale. For example, with federal income taxes, Canadians that earn under $50,000 constitute 83 percent of all tax filers in the country; their income is equal to 50 percent of all income reported, and their share of federal taxes payable is 34 percent. Thus, those who earn under $50,000 (most of us) constitute the vast part of tax filers, we earn about half of the income reported, but are responsible for only a third of the share of federal tax. In contrast, those who earn more than $50,000 (17 percent of all tax filers) are responsible for paying *two-thirds* of federal income tax.

When Conservative Finance Minister Michael Wilson once remarked that what Canada needed was more millionaires, it is this distribution of income-to-taxes-paid that he had in mind. And he was correct.

Example Two: Grow the national economy or redistribute?

In 'Country A,' the average taxable income is $10,000 and the average tax rate per person is 45 percent, or $4,500.

---

[h] In B.C. and Alberta, health insurance premiums (taxes) were raised in 2002; federally, the government instituted a new security tax despite the surplus it already enjoyed.

In 'Country B,' the average taxable income is $25,000 but the average tax rate per person is 25 percent, or $6,250 per person. In this latter case, the government's take per person is higher *even though the tax rate is lower.*

Country A could increase its tax rates in an attempt to garner the same amount of revenue per person as Country B, or it could attempt to grow the economy over time. Growing the economy may include a number of measures ranging from tax reductions to labour market changes or attracting more foreign investment.

Has this ever happened? Yes. Quite often over the past half-century.

For example, shortly before Canadian soldiers fought a war on the Korean peninsula, the average Korean's "share" of their national economy was worth $770 (all figures adjusted for inflation to 1990 dollars). In comparison, Canada's per person economy in 1950 amounted to almost ten times that at $7,437 (again, in 1990 inflation-adjusted dollars). And while Korea's economy was small, other have-not countries in 1950 were similarly tiny. The average per capita share of GDP in the Congo, for example, was not much better, at $1,289.

Fast forward to 1998 and South Koreans were prosperous to a degree unimaginable one half-century before. Per capita income grew, in real terms, 17-fold since 1950 to stand at over $13,317 in 1999—or about two-thirds of the $20,000-per-person income in Canada in that year. Alas, during the same 50 years, the Congolese did not see even a doubling in their wealth. Fifty years on, the per-person economy of the Congo was worth just $2,239.

And there are examples of countries that went in reverse. Cuba, the fourth richest out of 15 countries in Latin America in 1950 with a per capita GDP of $3,390 that year, dropped to $2,164 by 1998 and was by then the fourth *poorest* country.[8]

Governments are always faced with the choice of growing the economy, growing the "pie," or merely redistributing the existing tax base; the nations that grow in all areas focus on wealth creation even as they debate how to divvy up existing tax revenues.

Example Three: Tax away everything over $60,000?

Arguments are sometimes made that if we just "taxed the rich" more, a lot more money would be available for government services or for redistribution to the poor.

Unfortunately for that argument, only about eight percent of all tax filers make over $60,000 in Canada. So, to use federal tax as an example, suppose that government did tax away all the income over $60,000. That would equal about $25 billion in more revenue for the federal government. And that assumes that taxing away all money above $60,000 would have zero effect on people's behaviour and thus economic output—not a serious or credible assumption, but assume it for the example anyway.

Imagine that the $25 billion was given to everyone below $60,000 in income; thus, every Canadian who earns less than $60,000 would get a cheque of about $1,300 every year. The same $1,300 increase in below-$60,000 incomes could also be accomplished by a 3.5-percent rise in income for everyone.[9] Still like redistribution for its own sake?

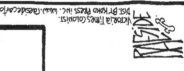

7

Sorry Virginia, income taxes are legal
(and constitutional)

To be forced by desire into any unwarrantable belief is a calamity.

- I.A. Richards

Don't you know? Income taxes are illegal…

If I had a buck for every time someone e-mailed, called, or wrote to insist that "the federal government cannot legally collect income tax," I would have long ago retired to sip red wine in an expensive villa in southern Italy. Out of any question (or assertion) that directors at the Canadian Taxpayers Federation receive, the bizarre claim that taxes are illegal or unconstitutional tops the list.

To be fair, it is a measure of Canadian's frustration with the tax burden that some people would buy the snake oil claim that income tax is illegal. Ottawa in particular has no end to the money it could waste without much of a penalty from voters. But want to give a lawyer plenty of work (and money) in the years ahead? Try not paying income tax for a season or two; the courts will not come to your aid.

The myth of illegal/unconstitutional income tax: It started down south

Like any conspiracy theory, it is impossible to track every strand of the origin of the belief that income tax is unconstitutional. But it appears that Canadian myths are mutations of similar American tales. South of the border, the myth that taxes are voluntary or a violation of the American Constitution has existed since the 16th Amendment to the U.S. Constitution was passed in 1913. That amendment cleared up any confusion and explicitly provided for federal income taxes to be levied, an opening quickly exploited by Congress that same year.[a]

Before 1913, the ability of the federal government to uniformly tax incomes throughout the United States was in doubt due to an 1895 Supreme Court decision. In Pollock *v*. Farmers Loan & Trust Company, a divided court found that the previous year's attempt by Congress to tax incomes (derived from property) was unconstitutional. *Some* forms of income tax were constitutional, for example, that which came from labour as opposed to income derived from property (i.e., rent). But the court voided the entire 1894 law on the grounds that Congress never intended to permit the entire "burden of the tax to be borne by professions, trades, employments, or vocations" after real estate and personal property were exempted.[1]

Oddly, just 15 years earlier, the court unanimously upheld the right of Congress to levy a similar tax during the American civil war.[2] Regardless, after 1913, the federal government could levy a tax on income anywhere in the United States of America and promptly did so.

Despite the 16th Amendment, some Americans who wished to lighten their tax load have variously argued that to pay tax is voluntary, or that federal reserve notes (i.e., U.S. currency) do not count as income, that the *actual* U.S. consists only of the District of Columbia and federal territories (such as Puerto Rico and Guam) and therefore only those areas are subject to federal tax. And then there is the claim that a taxpayer is not a "person" as defined by the Internal Revenue Code and thus not subject to federal tax laws.

All of the above errant beliefs have been defeated in U.S. courts, but similar to the Energizer bunny, the income-tax-is-illegal myth just keeps on going. And if some of those claims sound familiar, it is because a mini-industry mushroomed in Canada with similar tall tales.

Canadian myths

In Canada, the myth that income tax is illegal and unconstitutional likely originated with the American tales and then grew unique Canadian versions. Every few years the myth is reborn, aided by frustration with a tax burden that rarely declines. The latest wave began in the mid- to late-1990s in Alberta and British Columbia when various "de-taxers"

---

[a] The 16th Amendment to the U.S. Constitution: "The Congress shall have power to lay and collect taxes on incomes, from whatever source derived, without apportionment among the several States, and without regard to any census or enumeration."

as they are known, held seminars to teach people the "secrets of Revenue Canada." Errant beliefs about the legality of taxes are not restricted to the Wild West though. A Quebec-based publication entitled the *Michael Journal* also proclaimed that "Canada's Federal Income Tax is Unconstitutional."

One of the more famous de-taxers, Calgary-based Eldon Warman, has a website with a litany of bizarre claims and *ad hominem* attacks. For example, judges, according to Warman's website, are "sleazebag racketeering thugs." Warman claims that if a court spells a defendant's name in upper-case letters instead of lower-case script, it has no authority. As we shall shortly see, the courts are not exactly frozen in their tracks by this argument.

One reason that the income-tax-is-illegal myth took on new life in the late 1990s is because peacetime taxes had never been higher. Another is that there is great money to be made in selling such snake oil cures to high taxes; most of the myth-makers charge people for their de-tax manuals or seminars. One pamphlet lists a $25 fee for the first night climbing to $100 by the third evening. Those who want an entire seminar and guide can fork over $700. Another de-tax organization offers a swell deal for information on how to "cut your tax bill by 50%!" The price is $600 payable via a money order.

De-tax seminars associated with Vancouver-area de-taxers Bruce Stellar, Byrun Fox, and Sir Lawrence Leupol (or, known by their real names as Ken McMordie, Phil Naudi, and William Glen Kennay, respectively) claim to have taught 30,000 people how to "de-tax."[3] If so, they make a decent living at it. The Canadian De-Tax Group, as they call themselves, charge $250 for a home study kit, and $900 if a taxpayer wants to become a "corporation sole," which they claim would make people exempt from income taxes. Seminars appear to have been well attended in western Canada where they ripped through like prairie wildfire in the late 1990s. Seminars were also held in the Toronto area.[4]

A tour through conspiracies

Many groups that promote the extreme tax avoidance methods offer to "expose" secrets of Revenue Canada. If participants received innocuous and perhaps potentially useful tips when dealing with federal tax collectors, it would be nothing more than any good accountant or tax lawyer might offer.

But the de-taxers also offer services straight from the twilight zone. Some promoters promise to reveal "Who really owns Canada?" (several good jokes could result from such a question); "Who really issues birth certificates?"; or the apparently important question: "What do your birth certificate, income tax and international banking cartels have in common?"

The back of one de-tax booklet displays a chart illustrating who *really* controls the United States and Great Britain. At the top: the "Order of the Illuminati" followed by the Council of Thirteen, the Grand Druid Council and the Bilderbergers. Arrows also point to the Central Committee Communist Party of the Soviet Union. (The author apparently was unaware of the 1991 implosion of the Soviet Union.) Similarly, the KGB, the repressive Soviet-era secret police and intelligence agency are still listed in the "who's who" of who really controls the planet.

Others in on the world-wide conspiracy are the Order of Yale, House of Rockefellers, the U.S. Central Intelligence Agency, Rand Corporation, Trilateral Commission, National Students Association, U.S. Federal Reserve, United Nations, European Common Market, Club of Rome, British Labour party, World Bank, B.E.A.S.T. Computer, British Psychic Research and the London School of Economics. The National Lawyers Guild and the Maoist Progressive Labour party are also listed for good measure.

Closer readers might wonder how the KGB and the CIA co-operated so fabulously for years while their respective governments aimed nuclear-tipped weapons at each other. But then, conspiracy theories by definition do not have to make sense; they need only string together a few disparate strands and combine it with some all-encompassing theory that seems to explain a complex world.

The problem with conspiracy theories

Life is rarely so neat. On occasion, conspiracies exist and are tried; a few even succeed. For example, businesses that are supposed to compete have on occasion been convicted of conspiring to fix prices. Back in the 1950s, some U.S. radio stations and record labels were convicted in "payola" scandals where program managers were paid to play specific songs.

Almost anyone can "conspire" to control small events especially if the people involved are few in number. (People "conspire" all the time to get their favourite political candidates elected; it's called electioneering.) But the larger a conspiracy is, the more impossible it is to pull off. Acts of God, human foibles and plain bad luck are usually enough to disrupt any attempt at large conspiracy. In fact, given what is at stake—usually money and power—the less likely that any conspiracy can hold together. Such schemes often easily break apart on the rock of ambition and greed.

Charles Colson, a Richard Nixon adviser in the early 1970s, once noted that the code of silence agreed to the president's advisers as regards Watergate broke apart after only a few days. And those men had an immense motivation to maintain the conspiracy: power was at stake and, as it turned out, jail. Despite that, the conspiracy was quickly dashed.

In addition, conspiracy theories which assume mass participation—say, all tax lawyers, accountants, judges, and the entire federal bureaucracy—miss the rather key point that people with integrity in those fields value their own ethics and judgment and would not consent to the perpetration of a constitutional fraud.

But, of course, given the devotion with which some believe that income tax is illegal or unconstitutional, the only true explanation for my analysis is that this writer must also be part of the conspiracy.

The bizarre strategies offered by the various myth-makers is a mixture of wishful thinking, misrepresentation and a misunderstanding of Canada's laws and Constitution, in addition to a woeful confusion about how government works. Throw in paranoia and conspiracy theories, and a dime paid to the income-tax-is-illegal advocates is a worse investment than old Bre-X shares. At best, those Canadians who shell out cash for the various courses and materials waste their time and money; at worst, some de-tax followers have and will end up in court to face stiff fines and jail sentences.

By 2002, it appeared interest in the de-tax groups petered out, and civil war broke out between various factions (not surprising, given the money at stake). Some groups argued that *their* de-tax method is the "true" one. A survey of their literature reveals almost a religious-like passion about the issue and the purity of the de-taxing doctrine.

In addition, de-tax claims showed up in court and the results were not pretty for those taken in by the ridiculous claims. Various spokespeople from de-tax organizations still claim they do not file tax returns and that, because the federal government never prosecutes them for non-compliance, their de-tax advice works. The government's public response is that de-taxers can claim whatever they care to; the Canadian Customs and Revenue Agency (CCRA), due to the federal privacy law, does not comment about ongoing investigations of anyone's personal tax file.[b]

---

[b] The Canadian Customs and Revenue Agency (CCRA) is now what was formerly called Revenue Canada.

Some common claims

There are too many false claims about the status of income tax to list them all, but here are the claims most often heard.

"Federal income tax is unconstitutional."

This belief stems from the misunderstanding over what is written in the Constitution. A relevant section:

> **91.**
>
> It shall be lawful for the Queen, by and with the Advice and consent of the Senate and House of Commons, to make Laws for the Peace, Order, and good Government of Canada, in relation to all matters not coming within the Classes of Subjects by this Act assigned exclusively to the Legislatures of the Provinces; and for greater Certainty, but not so as to restrict the Generality of the foregoing Terms of this Section, it is hereby declared that (notwithstanding anything in this Act) the *exclusive Legislative Authority of the Parliament of Canada extends to all Matters* (emphasis added) coming within the Classes of Subjects next hereinafter enumerated; that is to say...

And section 92, sub-section 2, which applies to the provinces and concerns direct taxation:

> **92.**
>
> In each Province the Legislature may exclusively make Laws in relation to Matters coming within the Classes of Subjects next hereinafter enumerated; that is to say,
>
> **2**. Direct Taxation within the Province in order to the raising of Revenue for Provincial Purposes.

Section 91 of the Constitution makes clear that any power not specifically delegated to the provinces by the Constitution belongs to the federal government ("The Queen"). So where is the confusion? Some argue that because Section 92 of the Constitution gives the power of "Direct Taxation within the Province in order to the raising of Revenue for Provincial Purposes," then *only* the province can levy direct income tax.

The error in that argument is best deconstructed by the constitutional adviser to four British Columbia premiers, the late Mel Smith, Q.C., who noted that people misread the Constitution on this point:

> The argument saying the federal income tax is illegal goes something like this. Since each level of government is afforded

under the constitution exclusive jurisdiction on the subject matter listed to the exclusion of the other (true) and since income tax is direct taxation (true), then only provinces can impose income tax (false).

The fallacy lies in not reading fully what the provincial taxing powers section says. It does not say the provinces have the exclusive right to impose direct taxation. What it *does* say is that the provinces have exclusive right to impose direct taxation to raise "revenues for provincial purposes." By contrast, when the federal government imposes an income tax it does so for federal purposes (obviously) and therefore it cannot be said to be infringing upon the provincial taxing power.... It means the federal government cannot impose direct taxation (including income tax) "for provincial purposes," but why would it want to?[5]

Tax historian J. Harvey Perry took much the same view of the issue in his look at the subject:

It was early established in *Bank of Toronto* v. *Lambe,* and confirmed in *Caron* v. *the King,* that the existence of overlapping powers of direct taxation did not impede the use of this tax by the federal government.[6]

Beside the legal points noted above, the courts have heard the income-tax-is-unconstitutional shtick and thumped it in court. But those who make such claims at least provide entertainment for bored court clerks.

In 1999, Richard and Denise Rosenberg challenged the validity of the *Income Tax Act* and claimed that under common law "Canadians have control of their own affairs and the federal government has no authority to collect taxes."[7] Revenue Canada seized the couple's Winnipeg house, cabin, and even their canned food and toys due to an unpaid $1.2-million bill in back taxes. The judge refused to allow two friends—a millwright and an aviation maintenance worker—to act as the Rosenbergs' lawyers.

In 2001, Sir Daniel Lear, whose real name was Ralph Swim, was convicted in the largest case of tax evasion in Manitoba history. With over $8.4 million in income from various pyramid schemes, and $2.4 million in taxes evaded, Swim accumulated a sprawling estate on the Red River complete with luxury cars, and antique furniture. In his defence, he cited the King James Bible, the "doctrine of Philadelphia," the "Tokyo rules," the constitution of Ceylon, and the *British North America Act* to support his claim that the laws of Canada and the *Income Tax Act* did not apply to him.

God, he asserted, allowed him to create wealth without paying tax. Swim also claimed not to be a legal person, called the judge treasonous and noted that "destiny has brought flesh against the infidel." The infidel judge didn't buy it, and instead fined him $2.4 million and sentenced Sir Lear to five years and eight months in prison.[8]

In 2002, David Butterfield of Penticton, B.C., was fined $1,000 for failing to file a tax return. Butterfield held seminars in Okanagan area in 1999 and claimed that income tax was unconstitutional. He repeated the story that court cases prove this.[9] The judge ordered him to file his 1997 and 1998 tax returns.[10]

"Income tax is voluntary."

This is also a variation of the constitutional arguments. When governments note that filing income tax returns and reporting income is voluntary, it only means that citizens are free to file without *advance* coercion and that honesty is assumed: i.e., that the tax-filer is truthful about the amounts recorded as income, expenses, and deductions.

If the tax authorities have any reason to suspect that someone who did not file actually earned income, it is a different story, and that taxpayer should get ready to face an auditor and then the judge.

The Lord Nelson Myth

The Lord Nelson myth has become the Holy Grail of the income-tax-is-illegal crowd. The late Mel Smith also analysed the spurious logic behind the bizarre claim that the federal government cannot tax income.

> The case concerns an attempt by the government of Nova Scotia to provide by enabling legislation the delegation of certain of its exclusive legislative powers to Parliament in Ottawa and also to provide Ottawa the power to delegate certain of its powers to the legislature of Nova Scotia.
>
> The bill was passed in 1947 and because doubts immediately arose as to its constitutionality it was referred to the courts for an opinion. Both the Supreme Court of Nova Scotia *en banc* and the Supreme Court of Canada found that legislation to be unconstitutional on the grounds that one level of government could not delegate its power to legislate on matters within its jurisdiction to other levels of government and vice versa. The subject matters over which Nova Scotia sought inter-government delegation dealt with employment in industries,

works and undertakings. The legislation also attempted to delegate certain indirect taxation power to Nova Scotia.

Those claiming federal income taxes are illegal state that this case decided that one level of government cannot delegate its law-making power to the other (true). They then take a giant leap by declaring that since only the provincial government can impose direct taxes (false, because of reasons previously cited) it is unconstitutional for the federal government to impose the ultimate direct tax—income tax (false).

The Lord Nelson Case is one of the leading authorities on the question of interdelegation of legislative powers between the two levels of government, but it has absolutely no application to the question of whether the federal government can impose income tax. The power of the federal government to impose income tax for federal purposes is firmly grounded in Clause 3 of Section 91 of the Constitution referred to above. It does not depend on any interdelegation of legislative powers from the provinces.

The hoary mythology of misinterpretation that attaches itself to the Lord Nelson Hotel case has produced more barnacles than Nova Scotia's famous bluenose, a scant few miles away. Let's once and for all sink the myth and give it the burial it deserves.[11]

"You can pay your Canadian taxes in pesos because the $ sign is the recognized symbol for pesos as well as the Canadian dollar."

Nice try. In 2000, Calgarian James Weber tried to pay a $110,650 tax bill with 110,650 Columbian pesos—worth about CAN$75. The judge congratulated Weber on raising an intriguing argument but had this to say:

> The whole exercise may be summed up by saying that neither the Canadian tax system nor indeed, the Canadian economy, ought to be held hostage to a typesetter's selection, at any given time, of what is considered a pleasing and useful typeface for a dollar sign. Were Mr. Weber's gambit to have been successful, one might, in April, expect a high demand in Canada for Colombian pesos, pushing the Columbian peso far beyond the present worth of less than a thousandth of a cent. As it is, taxpayers, including [Mr. Weber] will have to pay taxes this year in Canadian dollars.

The court then seized Weber's BMW motorcycle along with his helmet and pants.[12]

"You should request that tax auditors from CCRA show you an official *Income Tax Act* and not merely a privately printed copy, and if they cannot, they have no legal standing."

This is another argument that misunderstands how laws are created and updated. Some Acts of Parliament are relatively simple, rarely changed and may only run to a few pages. Others, such as the *Income Tax Act*, constantly evolve over time. For example, if the government changes the corporate or personal tax rates in a budget, an amendment to legislation is required. If the government creates or abolishes a tax deduction or tax credit, the law must once again be altered.

Given constant revisions, governments then publish up-to-date versions of legislation. If someone requests an "official" copy of the *Act*, they would in fact be requesting the last consolidated version, along with any changes that have occurred since then.

Thus, when de-taxers request an "official" *Income Tax Act*, they are in fact requesting the last consolidated version, which currently runs to over 1,400 pages, plus any additions and deletions to that *Act* passed by Parliament since the last consolidation. And then of course, there are the *interpretations* to the *Act*.

Naturally, no one carries around the "official" version of the *Act*. Moreover, it does not matter if someone from the Canadian Customs and Revenue Service can show a taxpayer the actual legislation; it is still in force. For example, police always write out tickets to speeding motorists without also handing over a copy of the provincial traffic Act. If police carried a copy of every law they are empowered to enforce, they would have to attach U-Hauls to the back of their patrol cars.

"If you paid income tax once, you have voluntarily consented to become a 'taxpayer' and changed your status from a 'Natural Person' to the fictitious and artificial entity known as a 'taxpayer.'"

This is one of the more outlandish claims on the already bizarre evolutionary scale of weird fringe legends about income tax.

This particular claim was tested in court in 2000 when a retired Ottawa schoolteacher, Thomas Kennedy, argued that income tax was voluntary, and only applied to a business (an "artificial person") and not "natural persons," or as some de-taxers called themselves, "corporation sole" persons.

Confused? Bafflegab is the hallmark of a badly thought out argument. And the judge didn't buy it. Justice Gordon Sedgwick of the Superior Court in Ottawa found that "a 'person'... includes both a natural person and an artificial person. It follows that the applicant is a 'person' and a 'taxpayer.' His obligations include the filing of annual income tax returns and the payment of any income tax owing under his returns." The judge also ruled that there is no support in the common law for the idea taxes are merely voluntary.[13]

Summary: Want a 30-percent GST?

Lastly, if some court somewhere in Canada magically declared federal income tax illegal in Canada tomorrow, the federal government would simply raise the goods and services tax to 30 percent to obtain the same amount of revenue.

If taxpayers in Canada want lower taxes, then they must constantly pressure governments to lower their spending or keep spending increases below the rate of economic growth. For those scenarios to come about means that taxpayers themselves must lower their expectations about what they want government to provide, how often, and at what price. It also necessitates private involvement and market-based reforms to widely desired income-support programs for example. An incantation in front of a judge about how federal income tax is illegal will not do it.

8

Business pork
Corporate welfare

If we say to this chip manufacturer, 'you get $100 million or you get a special loan or a loan guarantee,' what do we say to other, smaller companies who received absolutely nothing, who established businesses on their own hook without any government assistance?

Alberta premier Ralph Klein, in 1999, declining to reverse the Alberta government's opposition to corporate welfare banned in legislation since 1996.[1]

Trough Seeking Inc.

If there is any group in the country more confused about what it wants from government than corporate Canada, they have yet to show up on the public radar screen. Many corporate CEOs preach the virtues of low taxes, free trade and open competition. They correctly argue that high taxation, whether personal or business, serves as a drag on economic growth and its benefits: more jobs, better opportunities and improved living standards. And when it comes to government intervention in the economy, the country's best-known business lobby groups such as Canadian Council of Chief Executives (CCCE), the Canadian Chamber of Commerce and the Canadian Manufacturers and Exporters[a] decry "inflated spending levels."[2]

But such groups and their public advocacy are undercut by their very members who, in the past and now, continue to receive direct taxpayer cash from government, a policy known politely as "business assistance" and more frankly as "corporate welfare." The examples are not difficult to find. Prominent among the membership of the Council of Chief Executives are businesses legendary for their

---

[a] Previously known as the Business Council on National Issues and the Alliance of Canadian Manufacturers and Exporters, respectively.

attendance at the public trough. They include aerospace giants Pratt & Whitney—Canada's worst offender, more so than even Bombardier (also a CCCE member) who is often incorrectly thought of as the top corporate welfare recipient.

Corporate welfare harms competitors who must fight against government- (taxpayer-) financed companies. It slows the economy at large through the transfer of tax dollars from productive companies and individuals to less productive sectors. And taxpayers and consumers must make do with higher prices, higher taxes, less competition, and a lower standard of living than otherwise would be the case.

Business associations and corporations who wink at corporate welfare undercut any moral credibility they might otherwise have on the issue of government spending and taxation. The public sees some business at the public trough and then wrongly concludes that a healthy dose of state favouritism for some corporations may actually help the economy. If business wants to know why it has the Rodney Dangerfield problem of so little respect, the addiction to corporate welfare is one key reason.

The excuse of history

One excuse for taxpayer assistance to business is that it has always existed. The federal government financed the Canadian Pacific Railway, some companies received hefty subsidies to build it, and lucky as well as unscrupulous land speculators made a killing. By one estimate, the CPR's cost was $150 million (about $4.5 billion today) and 59 percent of that was paid by taxpayers.[3] But that was the late 19th century; it would indeed have been fanciful to expect a private company to build a railway line across 3,000 miles just to reach 25,000 people in British Columbia.

To assume what *might* be necessary for the development of an agrarian colony in the late 19th century is still useful for urban Canada 140 years later, is to live—apologies to Aristotle—the unexamined policy life.

So how do Canada's companies and the politicians we elect justify the rip-off? On grounds that such subsidies are, naturally, good for us. Call it the nanny approach to economic policy. In some cases, as with small business or start-ups, capital access *is* a problem. But much corporate welfare in Canada goes to the country's top firms with market capitalizations and revenue in the billions of dollars.

Pratt & Whitney is not 'tiny Tim'

For example, Canada's largest corporate welfare recipient, Pratt & Whitney, was authorized to receive over $176 million in contributions from the federal department of Industry over a 15 year period and another $773 million in conditionally "repayable" contributions over the same time frame. Pratt & Whitney, a division of United Technologies Corporation, with a market capitalization of US$27.9 billion, hardly qualifies as the "tiny Tim" of the business world.[b]

And if tax dollars for some of Canada's largest companies was not enough to dispel the myth that such subsidies are about start-up capital or small business, the same programs that write cheques to the big aerospace companies also hand over money to the favourite corporate sport: golf.

Exhibit A on this is Newfoundland's Gander Golf Club that received almost $1 million in 1998 from Atlantic Canada Opportunities Agency (ACOA), another federal pork department. ACOA also handed out another $20 million to other golf courses, fly-fisher societies, tennis clubs, snowmobile associations, and sailing clubs.

Two ways to define corporate welfare

So what is corporate welfare? In very broad terms, it can be argued that corporate welfare should include industry-specific tax credits. For example, the film industry is the favoured recipient of generous tax credit programs federally and in some provinces. The usual justification is to attract an industry that might not otherwise come to a province.

But such rationalizations are weak, given that provincial tax credit programs often do nothing more than shift film production from one province to another. That makes sense for a local politician's re-election campaign, but it is less than compelling in a wider national or international context. Governments should concentrate on tax rates and tax credit programs that actually create wealth in the long term all over the planet. With film tax credits, they instead merely shift a highly mobile industry such as film from one province to another in search of the latest sucker government willing to help finance the newest Hollywood production.

However, not all would agree with such a definition of corporate welfare. Thus, a stronger definition is anything that helps a *specific* business or industry vis-à-vis other businesses or industries as opposed

---

[b] Under the federal *Access to Information Act*, it was possible to discover how much was authorized for disbursal to companies. But it is not usually possible to determine how much a specific company repaid. In the case of Industry Canada, grants and contributions are straight handouts. There is no repayment required. In the case of conditionally repayable contributions, full repayment may occur, or only partial repayment, or none at all. Conditional contributions are tied to projected sales.

to neutral government policy, where a government does not intervene on behalf of one business or any one sector.

For example, when a government gives $1 million to "Widget Maker
A," it automatically puts "Widget Maker B" at a competitive disadvantage; that's not a neutral position on the part of government. If the
government raises or reduces taxes on *all* businesses, that may be
desirable or undesirable as a policy, but it is a neutral action toward any
specific business. Lowering or raising taxes affects all businesses equally—
not the case when governments pick favourites in the marketplace.

Corporate welfare is never as useful as proponents claim. And
this becomes obvious when one looks at the issue of economic
activity and job creation from a national and then international perspective. For example, consider the absurdity of the "have provinces," which now number only two (Alberta and Ontario), and the
transfer of their tax dollars to "have-not provinces" and territories.
Provinces often try to lure specific businesses from each other with
straight grants or loan guarantees or through other means. When a
business is lured from Alberta and Ontario, *have-not provinces attract businesses in part with the very money transferred to them by
taxpayers in Canada's two richest provinces.*[c] Quebec alone spends
over $3.1 billion on business subsidies. Insofar as have-not prov-
inces compete with each other for companies via grants and loans,
have-not provinces again use taxpayer cash from have provinces, an
economically bizarre transfer of wealth in both cases. A more sensible approach is for provinces to compete on land costs, labour rates,
and tax levels without business-specific "bribes."

Economically questionable tax credits and straight cash handouts or
industry- or business-specific loan guarantees are thus a defensible and
proper definition of corporate welfare.

Everybody does *not* do it

As ill advised as corporate welfare is economically, so long as governments continue to offer money, companies are only partly to blame.
If a competitor receives a grant or contribution from government, most
companies argue they too must take subsidies or they will be at a
competitive disadvantage. There is a solution to such a conundrum:
politicians should not offer any money to any business.

In Canada, two provinces have recognized the case against corporate welfare and (mostly) outlawed the practice. Taxpayers in

---

[c] See chapter 12 for more on inter-provincial transfers. The $3.1-billion figure is from the
Atlantic Institute for Market Studies.

Alberta lost over $2.3 billion in grants, loans, and loan guarantees to Alberta-based businesses in the 1980s and 1990s due to policies enacted under previous Conservative governments.[4] Thus, in 1996, the Alberta government of Ralph Klein ended taxpayer assistance for companies with its *Business Financial Assistance Limitation Statutes Act*. British Columbia passed similar legislation in 2002.

The art of pork: Federal largesse

Despite the example of two provinces that refuse to subsidize most business, Ottawa has so far refused to change its policy on corporate welfare.[d] The excuse of history (i.e., the CPR) is one reason. Another is political; until recently all federal parties preferred the practice. The Department of Regional Industrial Expansion under Pierre Trudeau was broken up and simply reformulated into new corporate welfare departments (named regional development agencies) in the 1980s under the Mulroney Tories, and continued under the present Liberal government. Despite the stated purpose of these agencies to create economic growth, they more often simply redistribute wealth, that of tax dollars from one taxpaying business and productive sector to another.

Federally, four such agencies now exist: Western Economic Diversification (WED) in the four western provinces, Canada Economic Development (CED) in Quebec, Atlantic Canada Opportunities Agency (ACOA) for the Atlantic provinces, and one for northern Ontario— FedNor. In addition to those Crown corporations, the federal department of Industry gives out grants, contributions (grants by another name), loans, and loan guarantees.

Over the last decade in Alberta, British Columbia, and federally, and to a lesser extent in the eight other provinces, the Canadian Taxpayers Federation has obtained a large amount of data on corporate welfare. Here is a summary of some federal results, all based on *Access to Information* requests.[e]

---

[d] There are exceptions. Alberta did provide a loan to Canadian Airlines in the mid-1990s before it legislated its then-informal policy against business assistance, and it still makes loans of less than $1 million to small business. B.C.'s recent legislation does not cover business loans to Aboriginal businesses.

[e] Credit here should be given to Walter Robinson and Bruce Winchester in the federal office of the Canadian Taxpayers Federation for the information obtained through their *Access to Information* requests. Portions of the federal CTF reports on corporate welfare can be found on the Federation website at www.taxpayer.com. All of these agencies are summarized in this chapter except for FedNor.

Atlantic Canada Opportunities Agency

$1.8 billion in free money over a decade

Time frame:

- 1989 to 1999.

Amount disbursed or authorized:

- $2.577 billion, in the four Atlantic provinces.

Number of disbursements:

- 22,867.

Amount authorized in <u>grants or contributions</u> (i.e., non-repayable):

- Over 72 percent, or <u>$1.85 billion, in the form of non-repayable grants and contributions.</u>

Loan write-offs during the 1989-1999 time period

- ACOA loaned out $591 million during this period and <u>wrote off an amount equivalent to 34 percent</u> of the amount lent during this time period, <u>or $205 million.</u>

Repayment records:

- The government has not yet made such information available.

Other noteworthy facts:

- In the case of ACOA, 4.2 percent of all funding recipients accounted for $1.498 billion or 58 percent of all funds received. In straight figures, 475 (out of 11,297) recipients received $1.498 billion.
- Over $5 million was given to fund business groups such as chambers of commerce while $20 million was spent on golf courses, snowmobile clubs and other recreational activities.
- ACOA admits that it approved $20.2 million in loans even though the agency, according to its own records, has no idea what the funds were to be used for.

Famed corporate recipients of authorized grants/contributions/interest buydowns: A sample list.		
Recipient	**Grant/ contribution in $**	**"Repayable" contribution in $**
Air Atlantic, St. John's	122,719	
Air Nova Inc., Bedford	79,970	
Andre's Wines Atlantic Ltd.	52,352	
Bombardier	531,228	
Canada Steamship Lines	67,275	
Canadian Pacific Hotels	296,845	
Can-West Maritimes Television Inc.		782,415
Cavendish Farms (Irving Pulp & Paper)	5,772,287	714,000
Decima Research	29,086	
DEW Engineering and Development		850,000
DMR Group Inc.	123,435	
General Dynamics Corp.	10,248	
Global Television		640,000
Hershey Canada Inc, Moirs Division	150,000	
High Liner Foods Inc.		150,000
Iron Ore Company of Canada	340,725	4,356,000
McCain Foods	2,380,000	
Pollara Inc.	305,354	
Pratt & Whitney Incorporated	8,663	
Royal Oak Mines		6,825,000
Salter Street Films Limited	212,049	71,500
Sears Canada	559,033	
Standard Life Assurance Co.	122,850	
Sunday Herald Limited	488,161	
Trenton Works Inc.	621,695	97,406
Trenton Works Limited	280,171	212,000
Valleyfield Tobacco	43,763	
Westinghouse Canada	23,000	92,500

Canada Economic Development (in Quebec)

$1.4 billion in free money over 12 years

Time frame:

- 1989 to 2001.

Amount disbursed or authorized:

- $1.778 billion in Quebec.

Number of disbursements:

- 8,964.

Amount given in <u>straight grants or contributions</u> (i.e., non-repayable):

- Over 78 percent, or <u>$1.4 billion, in the form of non-repayable grants and contributions.</u>

Loan write-offs for the 1991-2001 time period

- Since 1991, CED-Q has written off 378 loans worth over <u>$118 million</u>. This is <u>over 33 percent</u> of the value of CED-Q's total loan portfolio between 1989 and 2001.

Loan repayment records:

- $118 million repaid as of 2001.

Other noteworthy facts:

- In the case of CED-Q, $817 million was doled out to small, medium and large Quebec businesses either in the form of contributions, subsidies, or "repayable contributions." They include a who's-who of corporate Canada including SR Telecom, Johnson & Johnson, Intranets, the Royal Bank, Banque National, Ingersol-Rand Canada, and Siemens.
- Over $119 million was given to tourism initiatives, golf courses, bicycle manufacturers, festivals, and hotels.

- Associations, unions, and chambers of commerce and other organizations received over $154 million in funds.
- The fashion industry received over $10 million.

Corporate recipients of authorized grants/contributions/interest buydowns: A sample list.		
Recipient	Grant/ contribution in $	"Repayable" contribution in $
Abrafab Inc.	110,578	97,500
Adorable Lingerie Inc.	355,000	
Asten Johnson		1,140,000
Avalon Hosiery Inc.	859,950	337,200
Banque du Montreal		1,250,000
BioAgral Inc.	410,000	
Canadian Yarns		2,000,000
DBM Reflex Enterprises Inc	498,750	740,000
Enterprises David Lauzon Ltee.	1,143,750	
Enviro-Acces Inc.	327,000	328,500
Johnson & Johnson	2,000,000	
Marche International	1,355,000	
Parc Biomedical du Chus Inc.	320,000	
Pillsbury/Green Giant of Canada	729,750	
Produits Forestiers Canbo Inc.	113,000	
Royal Bank of Canada		6,250,000
Technoparc Saint-Laurent	2,090,140	
Usinatech Inc.	306,050	
Zenon Laboratories	601,750	

Western Economic Diversification (WED)

$1.25 billion in free money over 13 years

Time frame:

- 1987 to 2000.

Amount disbursed or authorized:

- $2.003 billion to the four western provinces.

Number of disbursements:

- 13,776.

Amount given in <u>straight grants or contributions</u> (i.e., non-repayable):

- <u>Over 62.7 percent</u>, or <u>$1.25 billion, in the form of non-repayable grants</u> and contributions, though $34 million was for flood relief—a justifiable expenditure.

Loan write-offs for the 1987-2000 time period

- <u>$65.9 million—or 8.8 percent</u> of a loan portfolio value of over $746 million—was written off by 2000.

Loan repayments 1988-2000

- WED loaned out over $132 million in <u>conditionally</u> repayable contributions but has only received $4.5 million in repayments or a 3.4-percent rate of return on these royalty or level-of-sale agreements.
- WED loaned $4.5 billion in repayable contributions and has received back $351 million or 57 percent.
- The <u>average repayment total</u> then for <u>both</u> types of contributions was thus <u>49.5 percent</u>.

Other noteworthy facts:

- In the case of WED, the "who's-who" of western corporate Canada (either operating there or with a head office located in the region) received $96 million in grants, contributions, or loans. Money went to companies such as Canadian Pacific Hotels, Domtar, Harris Canada, Ballard Power Systems, Bristol Aerospace, Canadian Airlines, Inex Pharmaceuticals, Sherrit Inc., Western Star Trucks, and Canadian National Railways. Pratt & Whitney and Bombardier, though Quebec-based, also received money from Western Economic Diversification.

- Over $3.3 million was given to golf courses, fairs, resorts, yacht clubs, and wine and food festivals.
- Associations, unions, and chambers of commerce and other organizations received over $77 million in funds.

Corporate recipients of authorized grants/contributions/interest buydowns: A sample list.

Recipient	Grants in $	"Repayable" contribution in $	Conditionally repayable contributions in $
Agrium Inc.	697,854		
Alta Genetics Inc.	157,047		
At Plastics		3,961,263	
Avcorp Industries	6,836	885,200	
Ballard Power Systems	7,000		6,472,520
Bristol Aerospace	5,999	4,612,220	
Canfor Corporation		3,500,000	
Cangene Corporation	19,975	4,824,456	14,624
Coincard International	112,500		
Cott Corporation	233,291		
Creo Products	20,000	5,450,000	
Domtar Inc.	20,000	5,101	
Foremost Industries	75,000		
Harris Canada Inc.	188,082		
Inex Pharmaceuticals	150,000		
Maple Leaf Foods	568,625		
MDC Corporation		970,018	
Monarch Industries	44,042	627,672	
NQL Drilling Tools	20,000	1,319,957	
Pratt & Whitney Canada		2,350,000	
Royal Bank of Canada		15,750,000	
Saskatchewan Wheat Pool	59,834		533,721
Toronto Dominion Bank		11,600,000	
TransAlta Utilities Corporation	127,848		
United Grain Growers		263,800	
Western Star Trucks	21,993	5,365,515	

Industry Canada

$5.8 billion in free money since 1982

Time frame:

- 1982 to 1997.

Amount disbursed or authorized:

- $11.279 billion across Canada.

Number of disbursements:

- 32,969.

Amount given in <u>straight grants</u>, <u>contributions and interest contributions (i.e., non-repayable)</u>:

- $5.796 billion.

Loan repayment records:

- As of 2001, <u>21 percent of the money</u> ($904 million) for 1,773 different projects between 1982 and 2001 <u>was repaid</u>.

Loan write-offs for the 1987-2000 time period / repayments:

- Information withheld by government.

Other noteworthy facts:

- Over 18 percent ($2.1 billion) of the $11.279 billion was authorized through various forms of assistance to *five* companies: Pratt & Whitney ($949 million), De Havilland ($425 million), Bombardier/ Candour ($245 million), El Groupie MIL Inc., ($244 million) and Air Ontario ($241 million).
- Over 49 percent ($5.6 billion) of the $11.279 billion was authorized to 75 of some of Canada's largest companies.
- Over $25 million was disbursed to various companies involved in the recreation/tourism sector: West Edmonton Mall's playland ($5 million), water parks in Moncton, NB ($957,600), Colio Wines of Harrow ON ($296,400), a Howard Johnson hotel in Edmundston, NB (143,500), and the Holiday Inn Crowne Plaza in Edmonton ($251,780).

Top Corporate Authorizations
Industry Canada Financial Assistance April 1, 1982 - October 14, 1997

	Corporate Entity	Grants	Cont	Repayable Cont's	Conditionally Repayable Cont	Loan Guarantees	Interest Cont's	Direct Loans	Other Assistance	Total
1	Pratt & Whitney Canada		176,554,351		773,161,660					949,716,011
2	De Havilland		7,439,676	8,941,506	389,004,652	19,743,127				425,128,961
3	Bombardier/Canadair		22,503,160	17,761,044	204,751,890					245,016,094
4	Le Groupe MIL Inc.		196,650,000	28,499,998	18,850,600					244,000,598
5	Air Ontario					241,855,370				241,855,370
6	Bell Helicopter Textron (Textron Canada)		5,166,140		219,264,100					224,430,240
7	Spar Aerospace Ltd.		93,189,522	14,118,378	62,462,634				72,000	169,842,534
8	Air BC					133,983,308				133,983,308
9	Trentonworks Limited		103,900,000	23,853,226						127,753,226
10	Time Air Inc.					115,033,619				115,033,619
11	Canadian Marconi Company		7,326,789		102,793,513					110,120,302
12	Canarie Inc.		26,000,000		78,500,000					104,500,000
13	Allied Signal Aerospace Canada		6,391,269	979,204	96,601,571					103,972,044

#	Company						Total
14	Bombardier Inc.	6,185,147	2,000,000	93,339,250			101,524,397
15	Petromont Inc.	55,800,000		40,000,000			95,800,000
16	Litton Systems Canada Limited	433,418		93,347,775			93,781,193
17	Curragh Resources Inc.				85,000,000	8,750,000	93,750,000
18	CAE Electronics Ltd.	28,682,468	9,701,006	53,368,808			91,752,282
19	Air Nova				91,664,854		91,664,854
20	AllCell Technologies Inc.			12,600,000	75,000,000		87,600,000
21	Repap Enterprises Inc.	39,082,000		47,910,000			86,992,000
22	Air Atlantic				86,771,780		86,771,780
23	Messier-Dowty Inc.	7,204,710	4,607,500	63,497,745			75,309,955
24	American Motors (CDA) Inc.		67,800,000				67,800,000
25	Piedmont Airlines Inc.				67,000,000		67,000,000
26	Connaught Laboratories Ltd.			60,000,000			60,000,000
27	Hyundai Auto Canada Ltd.	55,000,000					55,000,000
28	DOMTAR Inc.	52,714,296					52,714,296
29	General Motors of Canada Ltd.	5,858,000	31,771,000	13,200,000			50,829,000

#	Company						
30	CAMI Automotive Inc.	47,000,000					47,000,000
31	Metro Express Inc.	46,600,000		46,600,000			
32	KPMG Management Consulting	45,000,000	45,000,000				
33	Air Canada	45,000,000		45,000,000			
34	Stateswest Airlines Inc.	43,966,700		43,966,700			
35	CC Air Inc.	42,505,000		42,505,000			
36	Noranda Inc.	41,668,750	41,668,750				
37	Boeing of Canada/Boeing Canada Tech.	40,497,811			39,058,493	1,439,318	
38	McDonnell Douglas Canada Ltd.	39,558,612			31,500,000	7,500,000	558,612
39	Wingco Leasing Inc.	38,266,932		38,266,932			
40	Cornerbrook Pulp & Paper Ltd.	38,089,234					38,089,234
41	MacDonald Dettwiler & Associates	36,041,475			36,013,725		27,750
42	Precarn Associates	35,404,550					35,404,550
43	COM DEV Limited	32,345,820			26,547,243	2,313,750	3,484,827
44	Menasco Aerospace Coltec Industries	31,377,644			27,661,294	3,400,000	316,350
45	Computing Devices Canada Ltd.	29,491,617			23,658,836		5,832,781

No.	Company					
46	Eastern Gypsum Inc.	29,120,650	5,952,800	6,286,000		
47	Eurocopter Canada Limited	26,660,659		16,881,850	26,660,659	
48	Dominion Textile Inc.	26,300,000	2,300,000			24,000,000
49	Indal Technologies Inc.	25,690,015	1,407,000		23,869,982	413,033
50	Hudson Bay Mining & Smelting Co. Ltd.	25,000,000	25,000,000			
51	Bristol Aerospace Limited	23,785,485	1,325,582		9,567,347	12,892,556
52	Canadian Airlines Corporation	20,000,000	20,000,000			
53	GEC Alsthom Energies Inc.	19,500,000				19,500,000
54	Yarrows Limited	19,000,000				19,000,000
55	Magna International Inc.	18,019,576	11,964,048		4,555,528	1,500,000
56	Dale Corporation	17,892,00		17,892,000		
57	Canadian Shipbuilding & Engineering Ltd.	17,400,000			9,100,000	8,300,000
58	Leigh Instruments Ltd.	17,308,430			13,809,145	3,499,285
59	Precision Fineblank Components	17,026,000				17,026,000
60	Control Data Systems Canada Ltd.	17,000,000			17,000,000	
61	Newbridge Networks Corp.	16,681,447	870,000		15,618,297	193,150

									Total
62	Cape Breton Precison Components Ltd.	15,903,200							15,903,200
63	Linamar Corporation		2,094,941	12,507,430	1,280,847				15,883,218
64	Ericsson Communications Inc.			15,500,000					15,500,000
65	Firestone Canada Inc.		15,000,000						15,000,000
66	Heroux Inc.		930,987	3,063,375	10,800,529				14,794,891
67	DY4 Systems Inc.		353,988		14,168,537				14,522,525
68	Hope Brook Gold Inc.				14,000,000				14,000,000
69	Louisiana-Pacific Canada Ltd.					13,600,000			13,600,000
70	Sterling Pulp Chemicals Ltd.		12,092,500		459,600				12,552,100
71	Grant Forest Products Corp.		10,262,500		2,200,000				12,462,50
72	Mitel Corporation		1,490,000	2,100,000	8,868,398				12,458,398
73	Rolls-Royce (Canada) Ltd.		17,000	11,635,250	750,000				12,402,250
74	Fag Bearings Limited		109,900		11,391,390				11,501,290
75	Montupet Ltee.			11,300,000					11,300,000
	Top 75 Totals:	0	1,191,374,090	329,611,415	2,791,194,048	1,167,164,540	28,636,000	20,000,000	86,740,750	5,614,720,843
	16 Year Industry Canada Totals:	836,302,506	4,927,592,081	895,628,269	3,210,770,262	1,247,802,370	32,578,000	20,000,000	108,963,104	11,279,636,592
	Top 75 Companies' Percentage:	0.00%	24.18%	36.80%	86.93%	93.54%	87.90%	100.00%	79.61%	49.78%

Grants and Contributions represent sunk costs and a straight handout from government. Repayable contributions and Direct Loans represent fixed financing agreements with set repayment schedules for the assistance provided. Loan guarantees represent the government's willingness to be held liable for loan defaults. Interest Contributions represent government forgiveness of interest owed. They are grants by another name. Conditionally Repayable Contributions represent loans with repayment schedules based on royalty and/or sales agreements. There is absolutely no guarantee that conditionally repayable contributions will be repaid to the government.

Technology Partnerships Canada

Technology Partnerships Canada was Industry Canada's successor to several other programs, most notably the Defence Industry Productivity Program. As of 2001, Technology Partnerships Canada authorized $1.6 billion and spent $947 million. Repayment thus far is 2.58 percent (and is part of the 21-percent repayment record documented by Industry Canada and noted previously). Various federal ministers have defended Technology Partnerships Canada as "long-term" and assert that royalty agreements will take years to show results.

There is reason for scepticism. The repayment record for the similar previous program, the Defence Industry Productivity Program (DIPP), was and is poor. By 2001, five years after DIPP was ended repayments amounted to only <u>18 percent ($393 million out of $2.159 billion in expenditures) for 654 loans, loan guarantees, and conditionally repayable loans that date back to 1982</u>.

Time frame:

- April 1996 to December 2001.

Amount authorized / spent:

- $1.661 billion authorized / $947 million spent.

Number of disbursements:

- 148.

Loan repayments:

- Repayments as of December 2001 amounted to just under $24.5 million, or 2.58 percent of the $947 million disbursed between April 1996 and December 2001.

Loan write-offs for the 1996-2001 time period:

- Information withheld by government.

Other noteworthy facts:

- 26 projects worth $378 million in approved funding were not announced publicly by 2001 even though some approvals dated back as far as 1997.

- Five of those unannounced projects amounted to over $20 million each, which means they required federal cabinet approval. As of 2001, they were also not publicly announced even though approvals took place in 1997.
- Three projects were announced publicly *before* ministerial and potential cabinet approvals were received. Those three projects were worth $149 million.

Funding recipient	Date announced	Date authorized	Authorized amount
Bombardier	October 21, 1996	March 26, 1997	87,000,000
Ballard Power Systems	November 20, 1996	March 26, 1997	30,000,000
CAE Electronics Ltd.	March 7, 1997	March 27, 1997	32,000,000

The evidence against corporate welfare

In 2000, the Canadian Taxpayers Federation found that actual loan losses and projected loan losses on business assistance programs in British Columbia ranged from seven to 30 times that of loss provisions planned for by Canada's major chartered banks.[5]

As of 2001, the Canadian Chartered Bankers Association reported that the average business loan loss provision was 0.3 percent. In other words, Canada's major lenders expect 99.7 percent of their business loans to be repaid.[6] Compare that to any government loan program. Compare it specifically to Canada Economic Development Quebec, which has written off 33 percent of its 1989-2001 loan portfolio: a write-off ratio 110 times that of Canada's chartered banks and, in the case of CED-Q, all done with our tax dollars.

Governments are not adept at picking winners, but losers are excellent at picking governments.

Lower personal and business taxation levels facilitated by an aggressive anti-subsidy stance at the World Trade Organization and other multilateral organizations are key elements to promote economic growth and raise the real incomes of citizens. This two-track approach should be adopted instead of direct government intervention in the marketplace.

The core problem with corporate welfare is that it does not deliver the promised goods. Despite the widespread practice of corporate welfare around the world, there is no solid evidence that such programs actually promote economic development.[7]

This should not come as much of a surprise. In his 1995 *Report*, the Auditor General of Canada examined the issue of regional economic development programs. While the government spent nearly $4.5 billion on these programs between 1988 and 1995, the Auditor found no "appropriate accountability information about the results achieved."[8]

Even proponents recognize that the lack of supporting evidence imperils the future of these programs.[9] As such, an area of scholarly research exists on how to evaluate the benefits of "economic development" programs. But such efforts fail to counter the growing body of evidence that direct government incentives to retain, attract or expand business do not significantly influence the location or growth of economic activity.

Professor Terry Buss of Suffolk University reviewed over 100 targeted industry studies and concluded that corporate welfare programs in the United States are based on poor data, unsound evaluative methods, and faulty economic reasoning.[10] While such studies are routinely used to justify the annual expenditure of tens of billions of taxpayer dollars, their effectiveness has never been empirically proven.

Did government intervention contribute to growth and development? Or were other factors responsible for change? What were the positive and negative effects, unintended consequences, and long-term impacts? Did the costs exceed benefits? What public investments were foregone in favour of the interventions? Buss could find no studies that answered these important questions; nor could his critics.[11]

Even when proponents point to apparent successes, the underlying economic premises in the evaluations are so deeply and seriously flawed that the benefits are illusory. And for every illusory success, there are mountains of costly failures.

So, why do so many governments throw tax dollars at private business? While there are no certain economic benefits, there are clear political reasons.[12] Corporate welfare programs allow politicians to take credit for addressing important public concerns and protect themselves from blame for not acting to prevent relocation of firms to other jurisdictions.

Professor Kenneth Thomas of the University of Missouri at St. Louis, recognized as North America's leading academic on corporate welfare, reaches a similar conclusion in his landmark book on North American and European subsidies.[13]

Elected officials need economic development programs to deliver quick, visible projects in their attempt to solve their jurisdiction's economic problems, manage business climate problems, and achieve other aims. Ribbon-cutting photo opportunities, sod-turning events, and upbeat press releases are clearly worth the millions in debt, taxes, and lost opportunities, at least for the elected officials.

Regrettably, such pork is never worth it for taxpayers and represents a tremendous opportunity cost where public dollars could have been left in taxpayers' pockets or directed toward useful projects.

Reasons why corporate welfare does not work

A summary

1) Market decisions should be made by the market, not by politicians and bureaucrats.

The function of private capital markets is to direct investment to projects, industries or firms that offer the best and most secure rate of return. Different pools of capital from institutional and non-institutional sources are available depending on the technology involved and levels of risk inherent in each project. To attempt to replace or mimic this judgment through government intervention is fundamentally flawed and unnecessary. The difference between a good investment and a bad investment for a private investor can be the difference between a life of luxury and permanent unemployment; no comparable discipline exists for government bureaucrats or politicians.

2) Selecting winners and losers is not a task to which government officials are well suited.

The best investment decisions are made in an environment characterized by experience and a "vacuum" of politics. In contrast, corporate welfare decisions are often made by people with no experience in private investment and where goals are set by politicians. For example, to ensure that taxpayer-financed projects meet geographic and political criteria is often an end in itself. Politically driven investments are motivated by political imperatives and the number one factor in these decisions is a preoccupation with "how many jobs are created" (an inexact science in its own right) regardless of profitability or sustainability.

It is precisely the reason why Alberta's taxpayers lost $2.3 billion over a decade in loans and loan guarantees and why the federal government subsidized mines in Nova Scotia for eight decades at a cost, by at least one estimate, of at least $5 billion over that period.[f]

3) Corporate welfare is inherently unfair.

Business subsidies create an uneven playing field. Credit and capital can be diverted from successful firms to less successful, politically connected firms. Worse, firms that do not receive government assistance subsidize their government-supported competitors through their corporate taxes.

4) Corporate welfare undermines confidence in our democratic institutions.

While portrayed as helpful to Canada's economic growth, there is a growing perception that government assistance to industry is little more than reciprocal payola for financial support at election time. A series of funding analysed by the Federation (noted in this chapter) and data from Elections Canada only serve to reinforce this perception. For example, Pratt & Whitney, Canada's number-one corporate welfare recipient, donated $83,283 to the ruling Liberals between 1998 and 2000. Another corporate welfare recipient, Bombardier, gave the Liberals $240,567 in donations between 1998 and 2000—including $100,502 in election-year 2000.[g]

5) Corporate welfare runs contrary to free markets.

Business owners and entrepreneurs can become so adept at securing government money that they lose sight of their core function: the creation of wealth and maximization of product/service value. In essence, some become better lobbyists than businesspeople.

6) Corporate welfare is unfriendly to the environment.

In the late 1990s, the B.C. government spent over $400 million to keep an old, inefficient and polluting pulp mill running; the subsidy forced two other newer and cleaner pulp mills to close. Business

---

[f] For more on this, see Chapter 13.

subsidies are often given to sunset plants and declining industries and the perverse result is that they are often the most harmful to the environment compared to newer facilities and sectors.

7) Corporate welfare creates a culture of dependency.

Business owners become so reliant on government assistance that they build expectations of such into financial plans for various ventures, which has the perverse of effect of slowing the growth of other non-institutional sources of financing, including venture capital funds and a critical mass of angel investors.

8) Corporate welfare leads to higher taxes.

Someone must pay the bill for years of corporate welfare— inevitably, both individual and business taxpayers.

9) Corporate welfare is not a public good.

Tax dollars should be directed to purposes that offer the largest societal benefit or to those areas where voters have decided (through their politicians) that government should spend money for other reasons, sometimes extraordinary ones, i.e., the late 1940s Marshall Plan, which rebuilt Western Europe.

Examples of a public good include infrastructure such as roads and sewers and services such as national defence, policing, customs, border control and immigration, hospitals and assistance for the disabled. Placed against these priorities, subsidies for business should not even rank.

Trade subsidies for tax reductions

It is due time that corporate Canada gave up its addiction to taxpayer welfare. Instead, a trade-off of business subsidy money for lower business tax rates, and an end to economically damaging taxes such as the capital gains tax and the capital tax would do more for Canada's employment rate, productivity, and standard of living.

---

[g] As I argue in Chapter 5, donations to political parties is not corruption, and many companies give money to more than one political party. But such money is certainly "insurance" so the ruling party designs programs and contracts with an eye to who has helped finance their re-election.

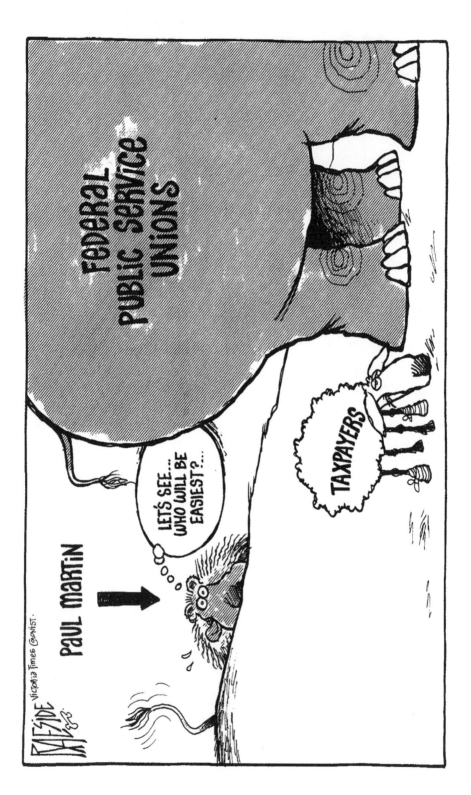

9

Pay equity pork and public sector unions

Some will pay off some of the outstanding debts they have; perhaps some might even buy a house with a decent down payment.

Daryl Bean, president of the Public Service Alliance of Canada after the government union won their $3 billion pay equity case. 200,000 PSAC members received cheques of between $5,000 and $60,000 each.[1]

Taxpayer casualties

Whenever governments and unions battle with each other, taxpayers are the first casualties. Governments with negotiators and lawyers square off against public sector unions with lawyers and negotiators and the public pays the bill for both sides.[a]

In such battles, governments rarely win and sometimes it is not clear that they intend to. Too often, Canadians are squeezed between politicians unwilling to stand up to public sector labour and government union leaders more than happy to keep the taxpayer spigot open and flowing for their members, no matter the tax burden on other Canadians.

1970s love-children: Disco and state interventionism in salaries

A textbook case of this was demonstrated in the multi-billion-dollar pay equity dispute, triggered by a badly written and vague 1978 human rights law when state planning as to wages and prices was all the rage. Federal unions then exploited the disco-era legislation for two decades

---

[a] Government unions sometimes argue that it is not fair to characterize the money spent by unions as taxpayer dollars. The characterization is entirely appropriate. The money spent by public sector unions, which comes from dues, would not exist if private sector taxpayers did not first place money in the public treasury, from which salaries are paid to government workers.

until they won a 1999 court victory in federal court at a significant and ongoing cost to taxpayers.

Pay equity sounds like a fine concept. After all, who could oppose something with the word "equity" in it? But pay equity was (and is) about the spurious concept of equal pay for work of equal *value*, not the relatively straightforward method of calculating equal pay for equal *work*—an important distinction much of the Canadian public grasped only after the pay equity bill came due.

The 1978 pay equity law committed the federal government to the nebulous concept of equal pay for work of equal value and public sector unions took it from there. On the agenda was higher wages for some female-dominated professions in government, though "female-dominated" was often defined rather widely. If 55 percent of workers in a particular government sector were women, pay equity adjustments were activated.

By 1990 the government paid out $317 million in back pay to comply with its own legislation and adjusted salaries by $76 million annually. (By 2002, the original cost and annual adjustments totalled $1.3 billion.[2])

That was not nearly rich enough for the country's largest government union, the Public Service Alliance of Canada (PSAC) which already began lawsuits against the government in 1983, first before the Canadian Human Rights Tribunal and later in the courts, a dispute they finally won in the Federal Court of Canada in 1999, at no small expense to taxpayers.

Why pay equity is appealing

To understand why taxpayers paid out billions in the 1990s (and will shell out money for years because of reclassified positions) it helps to understand the allure of the pay equity argument.

That women have the right to the same salary as the man in the next cubicle performing the same tasks—equal pay for equal work— was never at issue. Since the 1950s, the federal government and a number of provinces had "equal pay for equal work" legislation on the books. By the 1970s, every jurisdiction forbade employers from paying different wages to employees on the grounds of gender. Instead, the pay equity argument in government was always about the transfer of more tax dollars from a female private sector secretary to a female public sector secretary.[b]

But pay equity, the idea of equal pay for work of equal value, is a public policy thicket. It is virtually impossible to calculate in most cases, yet the concept was and is attractive to some politicians and policy wonks for at least two reasons. (The attraction for the government unions is obvious.)

First, it appeals to a basic sense of fairness. The concept sounds egalitarian. Second, since historically there were (are, in many cases) fewer women in high-income fields, gender-gap arguments are trotted out as proof that pay equity is needed to right what seems to be an obvious wrong.

Problem is, the wage-gap most often cited—"women earn two-thirds that of men"—does not take into account that fewer women than men are working full-time. In addition, those in the workforce work fewer hours than men on average—women work 38.7 per week and men work 43.8 hours a week, according to Statistics Canada. The statistical agency notes: "First, women work much fewer hours than men. Second, they have less labour market experience than men have. Third, other factors such as education level and major field contribute to the pay difference between men and women."[3]

Once those differences are accounted for, or the attempt to account for them is made, Statistics Canada notes that women's hourly average wage is 89.4 percent of men, which leaves about a ten-percent gap unaccounted for. As for the remaining gap, some researchers surveyed by the federal statistics agency assume discrimination; others do not. Some argue that out of that ten-percent gap, a further four percent can be explained away as due to something other than discrimination (leaving six percent for the "discrimination gap"); others argue almost the entire gap can be explained by factors other than discrimination.[4]

Even a study prepared for the former New Democrat government of British Columbia concluded the wage gap due to alleged discrimination was at most 13 percent. The difference between that and the oft-repeated "one-third" gap was due to factors described above according to the B.C. government study.[5]

It is noteworthy though that the Statistics Canada analysis, as with the British Columbia government study, is about work performed in both the government and private sectors, not just work done by government employees. And as noted elsewhere, very few employees paid by government are underpaid (on average) compared to their private sector counterparts. The private sector is paid less on average.[c]

---

[b] I was Alberta director for the Canadian Taxpayers Federation when the pay equity dispute showed up on the public radar screen in the summer of 1998. Increased public awareness resulted from a ruling from the Canadian Human Rights Tribunal (the first in a series from the Tribunal and then courts) that ordered the government to pay billions to the federal civil service. About half a dozen people phoned the Edmonton office and all said the ruling was absurd and they opposed it. None of the callers were men; all were women in the private sector who understood that the judgment was about transferring money from taxpaying secretaries in the private sector to secretaries in the public sector.

Discrimination or choices?

To put the pay equity dispute in perspective, and to use an example from the private sector, if one compared the per capita earnings of female lawyers with their male counterparts, the wage gap would likely be even more pronounced than the two-thirds gap often cited by pay equity advocates.

Because women have only recently flocked into law school at the same rate as men, a majority of the most senior lawyers, judges, and law professors—those with the money—are male. Because it takes several decades to reach the top rung of any profession, it will take that long for the wages of women in the legal profession—and thus the per capita comparison, to equal that of their male counterparts. And *that* assumes that one day both sexes will work the same number of hours over the course of their careers, have identical qualifications, and perform work similar enough that each will bill per hour at exactly the same rate. If even one female lawyer did more *pro bono* work than the average male lawyer did, the first statistical "wage gap" would then appear between the sexes.

And the same example could be true in reverse. If 50 years from now, law is a female-dominated profession where the majority of the most senior and longest-serving lawyers and judges are women (and even if both sexes worked the same number of hours at that point), the wage gap due to seniority reasons alone would then favour women.

Point being, any decision to stall one's career climb, whether to raise children or to backpack around Europe, will affect one's future earnings in relation to those who opt *not* to make similar choices. Granted, the person who takes time off to raise children or goes to Europe may be a more balanced person; they may have a fuller life than the workaholic lawyer. But none of that is relevant to wages. The wage gap that would exist between male and female lawyers in this example is there because of different choices, not discrimination.

That is why the more important statistic is the one that compares never-married men with never-married women. Just after the federal government boosted public sector salaries in 1990 in a vain attempt to appease federal unions, Statistics Canada data from 1993 showed that single women who worked full-time earned 96 percent of what men did. In 1992, the figure was 99 percent. The difference in both cases is statistically within the usual margin of error, which means that single men and single women earned virtually the same salaries, all other factors being equal. And when one compares another apples-to-

---

[c] For more on the wage disparity between the private sector and the public sector (to the advantage of the latter) see Chapter 2.

apples statistic—single female university graduates with single male university graduates—Statistics Canada data showed that women earned more: $40,024, compared with men at $39,342.

Statistics aside, the attempt to calculate the relative "sweat equity" of a job is a public policy thicket, since almost any job could be argued to be "worth" more. Are the lowest-paid officers in the Canadian Armed Forces worth more than professional hockey players?

But choices, talent, even blind luck and a thousand other variables lead people to choose different lifestyles including careers and how devoted or not they will be to work. Secretaries earn less than plumbers because the latter are in greater demand. Why women are in the lower-paid occupation and not the latter higher-paid category is an interesting sociological query, but the result is not itself proof of the supposed cause: hidden discrimination.

Besides, if most public sector secretaries are underpaid, what should we make of Canada's pathetically underpaid soldiers? Are members of Canada's Armed Forces—largely a male ghetto—victims of gender discrimination?

The cost of pay equity to taxpayers

During the tribunal and court battles over pay equity, union heads from PSAC often claimed the government inflated what the possible pay equity bill would cost taxpayers. Some estimates ranged as high as $5 billion,[6] including a Treasury Board analysis that the union's demands would cost $5.3 billion.[7]

The union balked and PSAC representative Elizabeth Millar argued that the government had "been escalating the numbers wildly in order to give a political justification for their refusal to agree to a settlement." The union pegged it at $3 billion. (Both estimates did not take into account the already-paid 1990 settlement and the annual costs of the wage adjustment.) When the Federal Court finally ruled in 1999, the public accounts in just 2001 showed that complying with the court decision did cost $3,020,925,593,[8] about what the union forecast. More of the settlement may show up in subsequent years however.

But the $3 billion did not include the 1990 payment or the annual wage adjustments. Thus, the bill for taxpayers to PSAC members never mind any other government union once the 1990 adjustments and the annual payout was included was an additional $1.3 billion, for a very conservative total of over $4.3 billion by 2002.

There was more

That number does not include any settlements and back pay given to *other* federal unions. For example, in 1995, it was estimated that 1,700 members of the Professional Institute of Canada, another government union, would receive retroactive cheques of $11,000 to $58,000 each. The cost to taxpayers was $62 million in back pay and another $12.7 million in annual salary increases.[9] And then another $34 million was paid out in 2000 to employees at the food inspection agency and the RCMP who argued they were entitled to PSAC-style compensation.[10] That came after a $45.7-million deal with Aboriginal health care workers.[11]

At the time, Treasury Board argued the additional settlements would not open the floodgates. Open? The "gate" was open long before. Thus, three other pay equity settlements alone amounted to another $141 million, not including the annual cost of boosted pay packets.

Attempts to reclassify salaries throughout the 1990s meant departments spent $500 million just to comply and recategorize various positions. The estimate for the new classification *after* the 1999 judgment was also to cost an additional half-billion dollars. So taxpayers, in addition to retroactive and annual pay equity costs, would also pay $1 billion just to adjust pay scales and attempt to make them "fair" and "of equal value."[12]

So there was the $4.3-billion bill for pay equity settlements to PSAC over the course of the 1990s, incalculable annual costs of the wage adjustments to other non-PSAC salaries to make them permanently higher, and a $1-billion bill to push it all through. That did not cover all government unions,[d] many who were under the public radar screen, nor costs to taxpayers for pay equity settlements in the provinces. Given the expense, taxpayers might have thought that public sector union members who had received $5,000 or even up to $60,000 in a pay equity settlement might moderate present wage demands.[13]

No such luck. By September 2001, the federal government offered PSAC clerical workers wage increases of 3.2 percent, 2.8 percent, and 2.5 percent. Not exactly CEO-type salary increases to be sure, and looked at in isolation as a mere percentage, not dramatic. But given the 1990s pay equity settlements, and the fact that some clerical jobs in the federal government already paid $41,025 plus generous benefits,[14] the government's offer would boost such salaries to $44,610, or about what

---

[d] To use just one provincial example, is was estimated that one settlement with one Quebec union representing 45,000 people would cost that province's taxpayers $151.5 million according to a 1994 *Globe and Mail* article.

someone with a Master's degree would make in Canada three years after leaving university. The union held out for a while and then, after it gained two extra vacation days and other benefits, agreed to the increase.

But even that was not the end of it. By May 2002, the federal government promised still *more* pay equity and additional reclassifications.[15]

When PSAC won the federal court battle in 1999 after the court ruled the 1978 human rights legislation must be interpreted close to PSAC's interpretation, union president Daryl Bean broke out the champagne, literally. He also tried to soothe the feelings of injured taxpayers and said that at least some of the money would return to the public treasury in the form of taxes paid by the lucky PSAC "lottery" winners.[16] It would be small compensation for taxpayers that were taken to the cleaners by a flawed and nebulous 1978 law, but it was Bean's public olive branch.

Alas, by 2002, the union was arguing with Canada Customs and Revenue to make sure that a good chunk of the settlement—the interest paid on the original awards—would be given to workers tax-free.[17]

The high ground of equal pay for equal work

Governments in Canada will continue to battle with public sector labour over the issue of pay equity unless they retreat to a more sensible and defensible terrain. Current pay equity legislation across the country is philosophically incoherent and, as the last decade has shown, impractical to implement without the creation of additional grievances which are continually spurred by the reclassification of various jobs.

The only sensible ground for politicians (and taxpayers that foot the bill for such wrangling) is to re-enact laws that ban discrimination in clearly similar jobs. To pay men and women different salaries for the exact same duties has long been illegal, as it should be. And while the buzzwords connected with pay equity—"discrimination" and "fairness" and "equity" itself—appeal to Canadians' generous side, Ottawa and the provinces who engage in pay equity games should change their laws to require exact job-to-job comparisons only, not nebulous equal-value comparisons.

To go beyond that is to assume governments can determine the "appropriate" salary for each and any profession. That assumes an all-knowing wisdom that has thus far proved elusive for government. In the end, the marketplace—combined with what taxpayers can afford—should determine public sector salaries, not bureaucrats, lawyers, human rights tribunals and courts.

10

Major League Pork
Why 22-year-old millionaires on skates want your tax dollars

If we begin to subsidize baseball teams, all sorts of business enterprises would demand the same thing.

Robert F. Wagner, then-mayor of New York City in 1957.[1]

There should be some payment from our government that makes money from our games. I believe we simply have tolerated for many years the use of our assets—the teams—to generate revenue for the coffers of provincial governments.

Rod Bryden, owner of the Ottawa Senators, on why lottery money should be diverted to his professional hockey club.[2]

It's *your* fault, Canada

If there was ever a taxpayer issue that has crystal-clear moral clarity and a simple solution, it is the self-created, self-absorbed "dilemma" of National Hockey League teams in Canada and the issue of taxpayer bailouts.

Moreover, every time this issue pops up in Canada, it is *always* thanks to made-to-order economic "studies" commissioned by a National Hockey League team and dutifully cooked up by accounting firms that could make Enron look like a model of unblemished accuracy. The demand for NHL-specific property tax reductions and outright subsidies has never originated with ordinary Canadians or even diehard hockey fans; instead, publicity firms on contract to NHL teams crank it up.

NHL teams and their apologists never let the facts get in the way of a decent subsidy. In 1999, the head of the NHL Player Association, Bob Goodenow, argued, "I think the real issue here is not so much player salaries. The real issue is what's going on in the United States and Canada. It's a cross-border economic issue; that's really where the problems lie."[3] The League's commissioner, Gary Bettman, said the problem was the Canadian tax burden: "In fact, we think it's the tax burden. The Canadian clubs by and large have lower payrolls."[4]

Did they have a point? Only one that almost any Canadian business could make, to say nothing of the average overtaxed hockey fan. Sure, Canadian taxes were and are higher than American levies. And the Canadian dollar is pathetically low compared to the American buck and to historical standards.

But every business in Canada faces the same high taxes. And the low dollar, while theoretically good for some export companies, hurts every Canadian as it reduces their buying power. Moreover, any Canadian or company that bought U.S. goods—say a restaurant that imports kitchen equipment—is nailed just as bad and probably worse by the low dollar. And restaurants, unlike NHL teams, did not quadruple the salaries of their staff in the 1990s.

And NHL commissioner Gary Bettman, despite his comments above, admitted elsewhere that escalating salaries *are* the main problem:

> It is no secret to anybody that we have teams losing money...
> we have too many clubs losing money, and we are paying
> out too much on the expense side, and that is something we
> are going to have to do something about.[5]

The 1990s ramp-up in player salaries

In 1990, the average NHL player made US$271,000 or about $305,000 Canadian.[a] That was a respectable sum that, after taxes, might allow an NHL player to buy a house in most Canadian cities, although, if they wanted to pay in cash, they might need to save up for two whole years if that city was Vancouver or Toronto.

By 1999, the average salary skyrocketed to US$1.3 million or about $2-million Canadian—almost *five times* the 1990 average if measured in U.S. dollars, and thanks to the plunging loonie, *over* five times the 1990 salary if measured in the northern peso.[6]

But did Canadian teams have lower payrolls on average than American teams? Sure, just as most Canadians have lower incomes on average than their U.S. counterparts. But it wasn't as if Canadian teams starved their players while their U.S. counterparts jacked up American pay packets. In 1992, Canadian payrolls ranged from US$8.5 million in Edmonton to

---

[a] Assuming an exchange rate of 89 percent at the time.

US$10.3 million in Montreal. By 2000, payrolls ranged from US$21.6 million in Calgary to US$34 million in Toronto.[7]

Canadian NHL team payrolls—in US dollars			
Team	1992-1993	1999-2000	Percentage increase over 1992
Calgary	8,822,306	21,613,750	+ 145%
Edmonton	8,522,121	23,980,500	+ 181%
Montreal	10,285,023	33,770,000	+ 228%
Toronto	9,177,069	34,000,000	+ 270%
Vancouver	8,793,457	33,990,000	+ 287%

Source: HockeyZonePlus.Com

Bettman's frank comment was the accurate one: player salaries are the biggest problem for Canadian hockey clubs. And the ramp-up of paycheques over the 1990s should have been enough to bar any NHL publicist from getting a hearing from the press or politicians. But cities and provinces (and almost the federal government) often gave in when pressed.[b]

Edmonton city council: Hook, line and sinker

You had to admire the chutzpah of NHL teams pleading poverty. But on occasion, it worked. In 1994, Edmonton city council, at the pleading of Oilers' owner Peter Pocklington, instituted a new ticket tax on all events (not just NHL games) at the city-owned Northlands Coliseum. The cash was then transferred to the Edmonton Oilers. By 1998, the

---

[b] Actually, the federal government has given out money for NHL subsidies. In 1995, it was discovered that Lloyd Axworthy helped direct $533,000 to the design of a proposed new NHL arena for the Winnipeg Jets. The money was awarded under the guise of studying the economic impact of the building on the local economy. The city and province also contributed another $1.5 million to the proposed building. "Ottawa wanted $500,000 for Jets arena," *Vancouver Sun*, 26 September 1995.

ticket tax amounted to $2.4 million annually, equal to the rent the Oilers paid to the city-owned coliseum. In essence, because of the Oilers-initiated and directed ticket tax, the team paid zero rent by 1998.

By 1998, a $2.4-million annual subsidy was not enough for the new owners, who once again lobbied council, this time to ask that the rent—for which a tax had been instituted years earlier—be scrapped entirely. There was just one catch: they still wanted their annual proceeds from the ticket tax.

While the debate raged, the Oilers and their local boosters—including the local chamber of commerce and the city's economic development arm—put out the usual bogus "economic impact" studies about how the city depended on the Oilers; economic perdition would occur if the team packed up and left. They estimated that $75 million in economic activity would be lost if the Oilers left town, a nonsense figure, but similar to ones always published by professional sports teams out to shmooze local politicians into doing a deal.

In Winnipeg, before their NHL team left, local boosters claimed that the Jets were worth $47 million annually to that city's economy. Both the Winnipeg analysis and the Edmonton study missed key economic points, including the inconvenient fact that when teams leave town, fans do not throw their disposable income into the fireplace; they spend it somewhere else and create jobs and revenues elsewhere in the local economy.

Edmonton councillors around for the 1994 Pocklington plea were unimpressed that the Oilers were back in their chambers four years later and wanted yet another break. But they were also in the minority; most voted to forego the annual $2.4-million rent.

Thus, by 1998, the local government engineered a $4.8-million turnaround in the professional for-profit hockey team's bottom line. (The $2.4-million annual ticket tax given to the Oilers to pay the rent, plus the annual $2.4-million forgiveness of rent.)

Given the Edmonton experience, it was only natural that other teams across the country would pressure their local councils for property tax breaks. And taxpayers across the country should expect as much in the future. But taxpayers and politicians should be aware of the games that professional sports teams play, including the blatant massaging of numbers in economic impact studies, the assumptions of which would never pass muster in a first-year economics course.

Bogus arguments from pro sports teams

Of course, as with any agile athlete, as soon as critics slammed the teams and pointed out that salary escalation, free stadiums south of the border, and obscene breaks on property taxes by American cities was the NHL's real problem, the millionaire-on-skates apologists slid over to other strategies.[c]

Brian Burke, general manager for the Vancouver Canucks, whose own salary was $984,845 at the end of the 1990s,[8] thought the subsidies given to U.S. teams by politicians was just fine. He wondered about the judgment of Canadian politicians who seemed more reluctant to allow NHL teams to slurp at the taxpayer trough. Speaking of lottery money, he offered this thought:

> I'm curious why politicians faced with these same issues south of the border have concluded that it is a valid and useful way to spend tax dollars. Are we that much smarter than they are? Do we have a better grip on what's best for the use of public money? I don't think so.[9]

Burke's musing that American politicians were somehow just as careful with American tax dollars and thus could justify giving pork to for-profit sports franchises was wrong. Voters in many U.S. cities and states often rejected taxpayer aid in any form for sports teams; the problem was that politicians often just ignored the results of such plebiscites.[d]

In Canada, as with south of the border, politicians often feel obliged to show that they are "doing something" as opposed to slamming the door on subsidy-seekers. Thus, John Manley, then federal Industry minister, looked warmly upon professional sports that knocked on his door. In 1999, he told the *National Post* that he "would be prepared to consider options for directing any federal portion of new sports lottery revenue."[10]

Ontario premier Mike Harris was publicly critical but sent out contradictory signals. According to one newspaper report, Harris said that offers of more money to the Ottawa Senators would only fuel escalating player salaries.[11] He was right, but the Canoe news service reported the same October day that Ontario's government was offering property tax breaks to NHL arenas around the province (i.e., Toronto and Ottawa) worth $16 million a year of which $7 million was the Senators' share.[12]

---

[c] There is nothing wrong with property tax breaks, even large ones to NHL team arenas, provided such large property tax reductions are also given to other businesses at the same percentage of their property taxes.

[d] For example, local voters turned down a replacement for Seattle's Kingdome baseball field in 1995. But major league baseball pushed on anyway. Seattle Mariners owners did an end-run on voters and persuaded politicians to provide $375 million in public funding for a project then budgeted for $417 million. The project eventually cost $517 million. At last note, the Mariners were demanding that taxpayers cover 60 percent of the cost overrun. ("The greed of professional sports team owners won't stop as long as there is money to be had," Michael Parks, *Business in Vancouver*, 10-16 August 1999.)

Later figures estimated the actual property tax break for the Senators at $3.9 million, with another $3.5 million in concession tax avoided after Senators' owner Rod Bryden restructured his operation to avoid having to pay it, a not entirely objectionable move. After all, if someone can legally avoid paying more tax, most people would cheer him or her on.[13] But on the issue of any government opposition on principle to a business-specific property tax change, the Ontario Conservatives dropped the puck.

Out west, the Vancouver Canucks also lobbied for property tax breaks. Their property taxes on General Motors Place had already dropped from $3.3 million in 1996 to $2.8 million by 1999,[14] but the Canucks wanted more "help" even though a slice in their salaries of 10 percent could easily take care of the property tax bill. Moreover, as Vancouver mayor Philip Owen noted, even that $2.8-million bill was not an accurate reflection of what the city already provided to the Canucks. The City, after accounting for city-related costs for GM Place, figured at best the Canucks property tax payment netted Vancouver only $500,000.[15] By 2002, media reports pegged GM Place property taxes at $2 million.[16]

Who wants to be a millionaire? The NHL and lotteries

When hockey teams are not busy pressing for a reduction in property taxes, thus leaving other taxpayers to foot the bill for infrastructure such as roads, sewers, and lighting the streets at night, Canada's NHL teams have gone after lottery money.

Ironically, Canada used to be a much more puritan country on this one. Lotteries and gambling were once considered to be harmful to the work ethic. They promoted a onetime win of free cash as opposed to a lifetime's constant and disciplined accumulation of wealth. But as Canadians relaxed their view of gambling as a slothful way to the top, there was an informal moral deal struck between governments and citizens: Lotteries were permitted so long as proceeds went to worthy causes—to hospitals, the Boys and Girls Club, amateur sports and other worthwhile community activities that might need money.

And then came the National Hockey League. The NHL, not satisfied with its property tax changes in Ontario and Alberta, did and does vigorously pursue lottery cash that traditionally goes to charities. Not that they admit it: "I think the most equitable way to deal with a problem is through a lottery because we generate that money and because it's not a direct tax," argued Canucks general manager Brian Burke, whose team was the most vocal on this issue. "It's not taking tax dollars away from a schoolteacher in Richmond or a firefighter in North Vancouver."[17]

And the NHL's New York head office argued the same line in a 1999 position paper: "We believe that the NHL is clearly entitled to some material portion or percentage of the total sales of sports-related lottery tickets attributable to NHL hockey."[18] And the league just happened to have a tidy figure in mind: Cdn$34 million is what the hockey teams figured they were owed, annually.[19]

Manley drops the puck for the face-off

While professional sports teams busily pursued property tax breaks at the civic level and lottery revenues with provincial governments, the federal government came out with a $20-million bailout package for Canadian NHL teams in January 2000. Ottawa's contribution was meant to cover 25 percent of the money; the provinces and cities would pony up the other 75 percent, or $60 million, annually.

The $80-million proposal was a publicity disaster and doomed from the start. By 1999, Canadians had not received any serious tax relief after three decades of ever-rising taxes. And the proposal to send some of their hard-earned cash to NHL players, with questionable loyalties to Canada at the best of times (many never bothered to live here in the off-season) set off a powder keg of discontent.

Open-line talk shows, newspapers, and television reports blared public opposition to the proposal, and members of Parliament heard from the public with a voice that was overwhelmingly opposed to the idea. It was unusual for Canadians to be so visceral and vocal; the last time they were this angry was over the imposition of the goods and services tax. Seeing the public reaction, the government dropped the idea after three days. "We now have clear negative views from the public, the provinces and many of the municipalities… this proposal is dead, and we will not be pursuing the issue any further," announced Manley.[20]

After that debacle the NHL teams once again retreated to their earlier talking points: it was all just a big misunderstanding. Hockey teams didn't really want subsidies; they just wanted "fairness," and a "level playing field."

Canucks GM Brian Burke argued that the public was just mistaken about what the NHL wanted: "The average fan thought it was handouts for millionaire players and millionaire owners. I think the Canadian public understands the issue now."[21] Burke also claimed that "we don't want a tax break, we want a level playing field."[22]

Contradicting Burke was his own vice-president of communications, Kevin Gass, who one month earlier (in December 1999) told the *Vancouver Province* that the Canucks were asking the government for tax breaks amounting to $15 million.[23] Given that the tax break was to be directed to one business—not all businesses in general—such tax-break proposals are subsidies by any other name.

Dave Cobb, chief operating officer for the Canucks, made constant comparisons between GM Place, a private facility, and government-owned BC Place and Pacific Coliseum. Cobb argued that government-owned facilities pay no tax at all. So why should private sporting facilities?[24]

The point is fair, insofar as businesses must compete for the same market, i.e., conventions and WWF events. But then the argument should be about why governments build and own major league sports facilities to begin with. The sensible solution—get the government out of major league sporting facilities and let all stadiums pay taxes—has never been seriously considered as an option in the debate over taxpayer funding and special tax treatment for NHL clubs. It should be.

OK, we'll take lottery money instead

Thus, it was back to the lottery revenue issue, where the teams used the "we're-owed-money-because-provinces-use-our-names-in-lotteries" shtick. Again, Burke: "We think it's grossly unfair that the governments of the various provinces think it acceptable to take our schedule, take our results, and generate fantastic sums of money and tell us we're not entitled to it."[25]

It never occurred to teams that radio and TV stations all "took" the NHL schedule, their game results, and then handed out free publicity to the same teams in every sportscast almost every hour of every day. Nor did they notice that every newspaper in the country took NHL statistics and results and wrote about the teams almost daily, thus attracting readers and advertisers to their publications. They too made a buck from professional hockey.

Of course, the reason the National Hockey League never complained was that coverage meant free publicity for the game. So NHL teams could hardly argue for a cut of ad revenues from TV, radio and newspapers, for what was essentially free advertising and threaten to sue if media owners didn't fork over cash. But when it came to government lotteries and *their* free publicity for hockey teams, well, that was different. Presumably, the difference was that media owners would tell the NHL to get lost if they didn't care for the bountiful free publicity that was bestowed upon them every day.

But politicians can be a soft touch on this issue, something the owners of NHL teams undoubtedly figured out quickly. And the provincial government seen as one of the most economically conservative government in the country gave in to oppressed 22-year-old millionaires on skates and arranged annual transfers from the public purse. Ralph Klein's Conservative government capitulated and set up a new lottery, which by 2001 gave $3 million a year each to the Edmonton Oilers and the Calgary Flames.[26] Klein defended the new lottery, for a for-profit business, by arguing that "teams serve to bind communities."[27] It was an unfortunate exception to his otherwise admirable record against most business subsidies.

The teams were thrilled: "It's no secret that Flames and Oilers have been seeking some creative solutions to the U.S. dollar problem we have," said Allan Watt, vice-president of marketing for the Oilers. "Instead of going door to door and selling lightbulbs and chocolate bars, we've got a [lottery] network in place thanks to the Alberta government."[28]

The imagery was touching. Of course, other businesses with U.S. dollar problems and high taxes would never resort to selling chocolates door to door either, but neither could they enlist a government to set up their own personal lottery.

A guide to bogus sports subsidy arguments

Canadians have heard and will hear again many arguments about why NHL teams (and other professional sports teams who make similar arguments) deserve a subsidy, though they rarely label it as such. They will hear claims that it is all really about an attempt to "level the playing field," or treat professional sports teams equal to other Canadian businesses which also receive preferential treatment.

Here's a guide to the more common claims and why they are incorrect.

Claim:

"It is better to have NHL teams here creating jobs, economic revenues, and paying taxes. If the team leaves, governments will lose that tax revenue. Isn't it better to have some of the tax revenue—even if we have to cut a deal—than to lose all of it if the team leaves town? And we also preserve jobs that way."

Fact:

Without exception, the studies produced by sports teams are designed to give the answer the sports teams want to hear:

that they are invaluable to the local economy. As well, the studies conveniently omit the substitution effect of what would happen if the team left town.

For example, if a hockey fan spends $500 per year on the Ottawa Senators for tickets, souvenirs, and hot dogs and beer, economists call that money "disposable income." That $500 goes into the team's coffers, and the team pays salaries for players and parking attendants, and those who make the souvenirs and sell the hot dogs. The government gets a share through taxes applied on all those goods and services provided.

But, tragically, if the team leaves town, Joe is not going to throw his 500 bucks into the fireplace. He is going to spend it someplace else. He may spend it on junior hockey, or he may watch professional hockey at a distance on the TV screen at his local pub. He may decide to go skiing or watch more movies the next year when the team is not around. Or he may buy a 36-inch Sony. Wherever he spends that money, jobs will be created, economic activity will occur, and taxes will be paid.

Even if Joe puts an extra $500 into the bank or a mutual fund, economic activity will still occur as banks and companies use that money to build plants, employ people, cut down trees, and so on. The argument that local economies will suffer when teams leave town is not taken seriously by economists who analyze the issue of subsidies to for-profit teams. Only the studies produced by the major league sports make the absurd claim that their presence has a major economic impact, conveniently, because they omit the substitution effect.

Claim:

"Other industries receive help from government. The film industry receives special tax credits and the aerospace industry receives direct taxpayer subsidies. So too should professional sports."

Fact:

It is true that the aerospace industry and others have received taxpayer subsidies over the years. But some provinces (B.C. in 2002 and Alberta in 1996) have banned business subsidies in legislation. Corporate welfare is poor economic policy (see

Chapter 8), and there is no reason to extend it to yet another sector, especially one with average salaries in the millions of dollars.

As for tax credits, there are useful tax credits—like the basic personal exemption and RRSP deductions—but they apply to everyone, regardless of where they work. Business expense deductions (for items such as a company's payroll or capital investment) also apply equally; any business can use such deductions.

But industry-specific tax credits are in most cases unwise economic policy. Governments give them to the film industry because the film industry is "sexy." It's a dumb reason, and the lobbyists for the film industry have been persistent; but both reasons are poor justifications for industry-specific credits. There is no reason to extend corporate welfare or industry-specific tax credits to enterprises whose main problem is escalating player salaries. Besides, in 2001, over 10,400 businesses went bankrupt in Canada. Should government have helped out each one of them?[29] To ask the question is to answer it.

Claim:

"The U.S. states and cities subsidize their professional sports teams much more than do Canadian governments."

Fact:

True. But as most people's mothers used to ask, "If your friend jumps off a bridge, will you as well?"

American state and local governments do subsidize their teams and build free stadiums. But many local voters when offered a chance to vote on the issue also reject such taxpayer-financed assistance. And in Canada, a 1999 poll showed that 71 percent of Canadians thought a salary cap was the most effective way of dealing with the NHL's woes.[30]

Solutions

There are things taxpayers and governments can do to make Canada more competitive, not only for NHL teams, which ultimately, every Canadian would like to keep, but to make Canada richer. There is no reason, save poor economic policy, why Canada cannot be a wealthier country vis-à-vis the U.S. And then one day Americans can complain about those wealthy Canadians who use their more valuable dollar to buy U.S. sports teams on the cheap. In brief, here are some suggestions:

Resolution #1:
Negotiate an end to subsidies for professional sports teams.

Where pro sports subsidies are concerned, negotiate an end to subsidies in Canada and the United States. American taxpayers have spent a minimum of US$14.7 billion on major league ballparks, stadiums and arenas in the 20th century and may end up on the hook for another US$9 billion.[31]

The elimination of obscene subsidies that Americans give their teams would kill one of two major problems Canadian teams face; it would also help eliminate the other. (The other is skyrocketing salaries, which would stop skyrocketing if taxpayers in both countries were not so generous to sports teams to begin with.) Canadian taxpayers have allies in American taxpayers who are also tired of subsidizing pro sports.

The inevitable political claim is that such an agreement could not happen. Nonsense. Countries that negotiated two free trade agreements for the three North American countries can certainly end taxpayer subsidies to 22-year-old millionaires on skates.

Resolution #2:
Cut taxes (and the most economically inefficient ones).

Cut taxes across the board, not just for specific individuals, businesses, or industries. Our political class should resist caving in as Ontario did in 1999 on specific property tax deals and as Alberta did on sports lotteries. It is not for politicians to pick winners and losers through either direct subsidies or through manipulating the tax system. More than 10,000 businesses went bankrupt in Canada in 2001 and undoubtedly would have liked subsidies, but they didn't have lobbyists in Ottawa and provincial capitals to argue their case.

Provincial and federal governments should also look carefully at what taxes ought to be cut. Economist Jack Mintz and many others have correctly argued that the top taxes to be cut are high personal taxes and business taxes, as they are both the most economically damaging to a country.[32] Canada began to cut both of those briefly, but not enough, and not before reversing course and raising other taxes as of late.

Resolution #3:
Cut out the anti-wealth creation political rhetoric of the last three decades.

Hockey teams do not deserve taxpayer subsidies, not because they receive large salaries but because they are for-profit businesses that should be forced to sink or swim without special help from governments.

Resolution #4:
Cap player salaries.

It is long overdue for the National Hockey League to cap player salaries—at whatever the revenues for each team amount to—without counting existing taxpayer assistance.

The moral argument

There is no compelling economic argument for governments anywhere to help a for-profit entertainment industry that in one decade quadrupled its already-high salaries.

Ironically, the higher the team payrolls have become, the more necessary it is for teams to raise ticket prices to try and prove to governments (that would bail them out) that teams will do "their part" and maximize gate receipts. The irony is that the inflated salaries and the increased ticket prices long ago barred average taxpayers from attending such games—the very Canadians whose tax dollars support millionaires on skates where subsidies exist, or pay higher property taxes because NHL teams have their property taxes wiped away or substantially reduced.

Thus, there is a compelling moral argument in all of this: Transfers to the poor make sense; transfers to the rich do not. Governments should deny for-profit sports teams any public money, at any time.

How private enterprise built sports stadiums without government

Taxpayers have mostly forgotten this but Raymond J. Keating of the Cato Institute notes that major league sports stadiums were once built privately:

> All the pre-Depression baseball stadiums in use today were originally built with private funds: Wrigley Field, Tiger Stadium, Yankee Stadium, and Fenway Park.
>
> In 1912, Tiger Stadium (originally known as Navin Field) opened in Detroit at a cost of $500,000. That same year, Fenway Park, built at a cost of $364,500, opened in Boston. Chicago's Wrigley Field was erected in 1914 at a cost of $250,000. "The House That Ruth Built," a $2.5-million structure built on land purchased for $600,000, opened in New York in 1923.[33]

Of particular interest to Canadians, Keating notes how Maple Leaf Gardens was built privately by the Eaton family:

> Hockey's Toronto Maple Leafs put down roots in Maple Leaf Gardens in 1931 (they had previously played in the Mutual Street Arena). The story of the Maple Leaf Gardens shows how, even in the direst of economic times, the private sector can build sports facilities without government assistance. David Mills explains:
>
> Although money was tight because of the Great Depression, [Conn] Smythe bought land in downtown Toronto for $350,000 from the T. Eaton Company (which took a second mortgage of $300,000 and $25,000 worth of stock). In order to build an arena, Smythe borrowed $900,000 from the Sun Life Assurance Company, which held the first mortgage, and another $900,000 from the Bank of Commerce; both institutions had their own men on the board of directors of Smythe's company. They not only provided the capital for the creation of Maple Leaf Gardens, Ltd., they participated in the financial decision-making of the company. Maple Leaf Gardens opened on November 12, 1931, with a standing-room-only crowd of 13,542. Moreover, Smythe's company had

been able to overcome a financial crisis that left it short of funds; the construction unions in Toronto had finally agreed to take 20 percent of their wages in common stock. C. Smythe Ltd., also provided the sand for the construction of the Gardens.[34]

11

MoreGovernmentFunding.org
How taxpayers subsidize special interest groups that love big government

Toronto feminist Beth Symes received a [government] grant to challenge the limit on tax-deductible childcare expenses. At the time her case was heard by the Supreme Court, Syme's annual family income was $200,000.

Ted Morton and Rainer Knopff
The Charter Revolution and the Court Party[1]

Say 'oink' and fill in the grant application

Most Canadians might think that government policy is at least partially determined by interest groups and lobbyists that fight it out in the public square *mano a mano*. A tax-and-spend group saddles up against a limited government lobby and they dual it out in front of politicians in scenes reminiscent of *Gladiator*. In other policy areas, a pro-choice group may cross swords with prolifers, business groups hash it out with labour, gay liberation groups with traditional Presbyterian types. In this view of politics, such groups pick up their rhetorical weapons, studies, soundbites and whatever else is within reach, and after they fight it out for a season, politicians and bureaucrats decide on the policies and legislation for the next year, or 20.

Truth is, Canada's governments long ago stopped being neutral in public policy fights. To extend the Gladiator example, many politicians and the multi-billion-dollar departments they control are more likely to load up their favourite "non-governmental" organization with taxpayer cash and other weapons of choice such as access to themselves, influential bureaucrats, and political staff who write the regulations and laws. Meanwhile, groups not in political favour might as well have a ball-and-chain wrapped around their ankles.

That this is a terrible distortion of the democratic process is obvious to any honest observer. Sure, politicians and bureaucrats will always and obviously have their biases, and some often make up their mind long before cross-country hearings are held on an issue. But when governments use tax dollars to fund advocacy groups, government is no longer on the receiving end of various pleas and demands from the public. Instead, it becomes a major voice in the naked public square— one that carries with it all the resources, funding, and power that a state possesses, which is substantial. With such power, most other voices— the ones *not* favoured by government—are shunted to the side.

Any attempt to provide a complete breakdown of government funding for special interests is destined for an exercise in frustration. When it comes to interest groups at the public trough, a comprehensive list of subsidy-seeking (and receiving) groups would fill several telephone books. Every level of government—federal, provincial, municipal, and government-owned businesses—dish out cash to non-profits, registered charities, labour unions, and chambers of commerce. Social, political, and legal advocacy groups are all funded to wage public campaigns on behalf of their favourite cause. John Bryden, a Liberal member of Parliament from Ontario who has looked extensively at government funding of charities and non-profit organizations estimates the total amount of money that flows from all governments in Canada to those groups is $49 billion.[2] (If the number seems large it is because he includes all charities and hospitals, for example, in that number.) [a]

Often, many groups have a vested interest in government intervention because they themselves are so dependent on government (taxpayer) money for their budgets. And the fact that such groups rely so heavily on government funds reveals that their public base of support is indeed narrow. If it were not so thin, they would raise money directly from the public. From environmental groups to teachers' unions to lobby groups that want government to be more involved in various aspects of Canadians' lives, many special interests have a vested interest in high taxes precisely because such taxes flow to their bottom line.

---

[a] "Charities" are non-profit organizations that are given a tax-deductible number by government that allows them to give tax-deductible receipts to donors. Those without such tax-deductible status are simply non-profits. The difference between the two as far as government is concerned has to do with the purpose of the organization. Generally, charities are supposed to be philanthropic or educational in nature and are to be limited in their direct political activities and their lobbying of government. Non-profits face no such restrictions but also do not have the advantage of attracting donors with tax-deductible receipts.

The battle in Seattle and the granola gang in Genoa

One illustration of how taxpayers fund advocacy against their own best interest and against the interests of the poorest citizens on the planet, is when governments fund anti-globalization groups, their protests, and others associated with such events.

The anti-globalization protesters who travel around the world from Seattle to Genoa to Quebec City are no doubt sincere. But they are also misinformed, would cut Third World countries off at the knees, and limit the ability of the poor to improve their lot. The anti-free-trade movement in Canada and around the world is merely hard-left socialism dressed in drag. With apologies to Churchill, never have so many protested so often for so wrong a method to relieve poverty around the world. Access to rich countries' markets will lift the poor into better conditions; in contrast, an expansion of protectionist policy under any guise will only guarantee more misery.

But if many Canadians assume as much about the protesters vis-à-vis free markets, they are likely unaware that much of the anti-globalization fervour is taxpayer-funded. When professional protesters show up at every G-8 gathering, much of the ensuing circus is financed by tax dollars, either indirectly or directly.

Remember the 1999 "Battle in Seattle?" The British Columbia Teachers Federation sent 100 union activists to that melee. That union's take from taxpayers was $4.6 million in grants and contributions from the British Columbia government between 1992 and 2001 and another $700,000 in contracts the then-New Democrat government arranged with the teachers' union.[3]

And then there was Quebec City in 2001. The Canadian Teachers Federation helped along anti-free-trade festivities there and that union has received $579,000 from the federal department of Multiculturalism since 1996.[4] Besides such indirect taxpayer funding for the anti-globalization crowd, politicians also feed them direct cash. Quebec City anti-free-trade activists were given $300,000 by the federal government and $200,000 from Quebec to hold their own so-called "Peoples' Summit."

But if education unions are at the taxpayer trough and feed anti-free-trade sentiment, they are not alone, as sponsors of a 2002 anti-G8 gathering in Calgary illustrated. Participants at that anti-G8 fiesta included the Canadian Labour Congress, itself a recipient of $304,480 based on an analysis of just *two* federal departments, Canadian Heritage and Environment.[5]

Also in Calgary was Matthew Coon Come, chief of the Assembly of First Nations (AFN). His group so annoyed the federal government when it bashed reforms to the *Indian Act* that AFN funding was cut in half, but Mr. Coon Come's lobby still receives $10 million annually.

On the environment side, tracking taxpayer funding for every anti-globalization group is near impossible; there are multiple agencies from all governments that disburse grants to environmental lobbyists. But here are several examples from those present at the 2002 Calgary protests: The Canadian Environmental Network, whose website offered to help protesters deliver their message to the "corporate media," took $481,250 in 2001 from the federal government, which takes taxes from, among others, corporations.[6]

Environment Canada gave the Sierra Club over $175,000 in grants and contributions to that lobby's British Columbia and Alberta branches in 2000 and 2001. According to ministry lists, much of the money Sierra received was "to support activities which contribute to the objectives of the Climate Change Action Fund." (The Sierra Club also received over $213,000 from the BC government when New Democrats were in charge.)

But the money that flowed to groups that protested in Seattle, Quebec City and Calgary is just the tip of the proverbial funding iceberg. To examine just one federal department in one year, consider the example of Environment Canada. That ministry has a funding category for those who wish to lobby in favour of the Kyoto Protocol on Climate Change, which disbursed $6.7 million in 2001. A complete reckoning of how much environmentalists receive from taxpayers is impossible to calculate, as other federal ministries and every level of government in Canada also give subsidies to greens. But Environment Canada alone handed out $51 million in grants and contributions for environmental causes in fiscal 2001.[7]

Of course, the unions, environmentalists, and social activists will argue that no indirect taxpayer cash goes to their anti-globalization fiestas. At other times, chambers of commerce and business lobbies argue that some of the money they receive goes to conferences. Both are weak defences.

Business groups ought to hold their conferences without government sponsorship on principle; and on a practical level, many of those same groups call for lower taxes and then undercut their call by taking government cash. Not very smart, PR-wise.

And regardless of which favourite cause a lobby group spends money on—an anti-free-trade rally or a Kyoto newspaper ad—the tax dollars that flow from governments allow such groups to engage in more advocacy than they otherwise could if forced to rely only on fundraising from the public or from union dues. When governments give money to such organizations, taxpayers finance the agenda of groups whose protest abilities would be restricted to what they could raise from donations or dues.

If teachers' unions or others want to mistakenly protest free trade, an activity which, unlike the protests, has been of immense help to the world's poor, they should pay their own way, not snatch cash from taxpayers unaware that their pockets have been picked.

How governments fund their very own lobby groups

Undoubtedly, some money goes to worthy environmental projects worth doing by someone, but much taxpayer cash also goes to groups busy promoting one view of the issues of the day, such as the Kyoto Protocol. For example, the Alberta-based Pembina Institute, critical of Alberta Premier Ralph Klein for his Kyoto stance, received at least $291,371 in 2000 and 2001 from Ottawa to push the federal government's view of Kyoto.[8] How it received the money is no surprise; it is on friendly terms with Environment Minister David Anderson with whom it once held a very public black-tie dinner.[9]

Naturally, while such lobby groups receive government funds, it is of course easy for them to oppose and kill off development and the accompanying jobs in the country's mines, forests, and at the rigs. But if forced to live in the real world and raise support there, many groups would wither up and die and lose their jobs instead of being able to put others out of work. When governments fund lobby groups, it gives the public the mistaken sense that more Canadians support the views of such groups than might actually be the case. That is helpful to governments who may hold unpopular views or are themselves unpopular.

A provincial example of this occurred in British Columbia. Throughout the 1990s, the New Democratic government funded the Canadian Centre for Policy Alternatives (CCPA), an organization with offices across the country who, not coincidentally, constantly press for higher taxes and more spending.

To say that a fair majority of Canadians would disagree with the Centre's heavily redistributionist policies is an understatement. The CCPA, which has tax-deductible status, is solidly in favour of higher taxes and more government intervention in the economy including, oddly, corporate welfare. (Curiously, its call for higher taxes, if implemented, would negatively affect high-income workers on the auto assembly line who are probably unaware their labour bosses at the Canadian Autoworkers Union *also* fund the group.)

In British Columbia, the New Democrat government in power between 1991 and 2001 funded the Canadian Centre for Policy Alternatives over the last decade to the tune of at least $410,231.[10] And $200,000 of that was doled out in the last three months of the NDP's mandate in 2001. *Freedom of Information* requests to government reveal that in some cases the CCPA gave 25 copies of each study they produced to government ministries or Crowns in exchange for funding.

This enabled the Centre to argue that it performed contract work or sold goods and services to the government. What it did do, in fact, was charge several hundred dollars per report for 20-page opinion pieces produced by the Centre that were available free on its website.

In essence, the Centre charged for reports that other organizations from every end of the political spectrum regularly give to governments for free; i.e., their advice in the form of studies and pre-budget submissions. It was a covert way for the then-NDP government to subsidize a lobby group that would routinely call for higher taxes and more spending, something that government thought useful to have an ally on.

And by granting $200,000 to the CCPA in the last three months of office in 2001 when it knew it faced certain defeat at the polls, New Democrats supported—at taxpayer expense—an ideologically similar lobby group guaranteed to be critical of the expected (and eventual) new B.C. Liberal government. One "contract" given to the group by the NDP government was for studies to be conducted through to 2005 which, not coincidentally, is the time frame up to the next election. It was political advocacy paid for by taxpayers, many of whom were no doubt unaware that their tax dollars were used to fund views and positions with which they might disagree.

Ottawa and SOW

In a federal example of how state funding is used generously to promote one view of contentious issues, it is hard to find a better example than the Status of Women (SOW) Secretariat under the federal department of Canadian Heritage directed by Sheila Copps. The Status of Women currently receives over $23 million every year[11] and over $10.8 million of that is given out in the form of grants and contributions.[b]

Included in the recent department grants list is the Canadian Feminist Alliance Action for $194,988, the National Association of Women and

---

[b] Readers should not confuse the National Action Committee on the Status of Women— an advocacy group—with the Status of Women Secretariat, a branch of the department of Canadian Heritage. Though, over the years, there is indeed little difference between the lobby group and the Secretariat itself in terms of positions.

the Law at $262,250, Feminists for Just and Equitable Public Policy ($110,712), the "52% Coalition" which noted that it wanted to make "women's issues" a priority in the British Columbia election ($18,000), and the Ad Hoc Group Raising Awareness of Lesbian Lives ($20,000).

Those are but a few examples and as with environmental lobbies and Environment Canada, Canadian Heritage and its Status of Women Secretariat, has a symbiotic relationship with so-called women's groups: the ones that share the department's bias receive the vast amount of funds. For example, the conservative group REAL Women has received $89,346 in its two-decade history while in the 1980s alone, the National Action Committee on the Status of Women received over $3.7 million.[12] Moreover, since 1999, REAL Women lost all government funding. And while the National Action Committee on the Status of Women had its funding reduced slightly, most feminist groups have not, as a scan of the almost $11 million in annual grants from Canadian Heritage makes clear.

Not all of the Status of Women's grant funding goes solely to lobby groups; money also flows to a few agencies that run women's shelters, grants that every Canadian could agree with. But that sort of funding has become, unfortunately, the minority of disbursements in a much larger sea of activist funding for groups that promote one view of abortion, gender and racial quotas, and other issues on which Canadians are genuinely and sincerely divided.

When such groups claim to speak for women, it is safe to assume that they speak for women who think as *they* do on their favourite issues. On the tendency of radical feminists to be anti-free trade and anti-free market, it is unlikely that such groups speak for the average business-woman, *National Post* columnists Elizabeth Nickson or Diane Francis, *Toronto Sun* money editor Linda Leatherdale, or *Maclean's* columnist Barbara Amiel. On social issues, such groups are also not likely to speak for REAL Women founder Gwen Landolt, a Catholic pro-life woman with seven children, or a stay-at-home culturally conservative Baptist mom opposed to state-funded daycare who wants a better tax exemp-tion for *her* choices.

Some groups on the conservative side of the ledger refuse to apply or take government money; others such as REAL Women were opposed on principle to government funding for their organization but have applied and received some funding on the justification that the government refused to stop funding their opponents. Regardless of the positions of the various groups and their stand on government funding, Canadian Heritage ought to do taxpayers and honest public debate a favour—and cut off *all* the groups.

The Court Challenges Program

The politicization of government funding has extended far beyond the grants given by one corner of Canadian Heritage. There is the example of the Court Challenges Program (CCP), originally set up in 1977 by Pierre Trudeau's government in response to the election of the Parti Quebecois. It was set up to provide funding for English speakers in Quebec and francophones outside of that province to challenge laws they thought discriminated against them despite Canada's official two-language policy. Quebec's Bill 101, which banned English on some signs in that province, was the most obvious example. Rather than challenge the PQ government directly, the Trudeau government opted to wait for citizens to challenge laws (with help from the CCP) and then intervene; it was thought this would be a smarter political strategy vis-à-vis the Quebec government.[c]

Over the years, those who want to advance their agenda in the courts on issues that might receive a cold shoulder in democratically elected legislatures have often used the Court Challenges Program. Using arguments from Section 15 of the Constitution (the equality clause) and money from the Court Challenges Program, many groups bring cases to court or seek intervener status in cases they believe will advance their agenda. The budget of the Court Challenges Program has also expanded dramatically, from several hundred thousand dollars per year in the mid-1980s to $4.4 million at present.[13]

Thus, arguments over what constitutes discrimination against gays and lesbians are conducted in court and funded largely through the taxpayer-funded Court Challenges Program. The feminist organization Women's Legal Education and Action Fund (LEAF) and Equality for Gays and Lesbians Everywhere (EGALE) have been in the forefront of such legal and constitutional challenges and many of their court fights have been funded in part by the Court Challenges Program. Calgary political science professors Ted Morton and Rainer Knopff explain:

> The Court Challenges Program has been a funding bonanza for LEAF and other equality seeking groups on the left. In addition to funding almost every other language rights case that has made it to the Supreme Court, the CCP has directly funded the litigants in a number of leading equality rights cases, including *Canadian Council of Churches* (challenging limits on third-party interventions), *Schachter* (authorizing

---

[c] More extensive details of the Court Challenges Program can be found in *Friends of the Court: The privileging of interest group litigants in Canada* by Ian Brodie and *The charter revolution & the court party* by F.L. Morton and Rainer Knopff.

judges to impose affirmative remedies), and *Sauve* and *Belczowski* (affirming prisoners' voting rights).... Janine Brodie, one of Canada's leading feminist scholars, has bluntly referred to the CCP as providing the "financial underpinning for LEAF."[14]

After its founding in the mid-1980s, LEAF received a $1-million grant from the Ontario government, and professor Ian Brodie from the University of Western Ontario estimates that about half of its current annual budget is from government with most of the rest coming from large tax-deductible foundations.

As with many activist organizations that favour government intervention by default in one manner or another, and also claim to speak for the "public interest," such organizations are invariably dependent on government for a large portion of their revenues and not the very public they claim they represent. And then there is the inevitable conflict of interest when government agencies (or those created with public funds) pick partisans to determine who should receive taxpayer assistance. One of the founders of LEAF, Shelagh Day, now sits on the Canadian Court Challenges Program, the same program that has given money to LEAF in the past and presumably still does.

As Morton and Knopff note, CCP grants often have little to do with financial need and everything to do with connections and ideology:

> Toronto feminist Beth Symes received a CCP grant to challenge the limit on tax-deductible childcare expenses. At the time her case was heard by the Supreme Court, Syme's annual family income was $200,000.[15]

Of course, Canadians of all views can and should challenge laws they believe to be unconstitutional. The question is whether taxpayers should fund one view, often the most strident one, on a particular issue. The Court Challenges Program is biased heavily to one side, and neither the conservative REAL Women nor EGALE or the feminist LEAF should receive any money from taxpayers for any reason.

Does the taxpayer-funded Court Challenges Program fund challenges to child pornography laws?

One final note about the Court Challenges Program: despite the $4.4 million in taxpayer money it disburses to sympathetic allies every year, the public is no longer allowed to know who receives the money. Ted Morton explains why:

> On 24 October 1995, the Liberals made good on the [election] promise, announcing the formation of a new CCP as an independent, limited corporation with an annual federal grant

of $2.75 million. This independent corporate status means that Ottawa cannot shut down the CCP in the future.... The reorganization of the CCP was guided by the premise that "The program must belong to those groups likely to use it."[16]

As a result of its new independent status, taxpayers fund it but they will never know where their money goes. The CCP will not publish the names of organizations or challenges that it funds, nor is such information available through *Access to Information* requests. In 2001, Beyond Borders, a Winnipeg group that fights child prostitution and pornography was denied funding by the Court Challenges Program to intervene in the child pornography case involving Vancouver's John Sharpe and his challenge to Canada's child pornography laws. The CCP refused to disclose whether it was funding Sharpe's constitutional challenge.[17]

This lobby group brought to you courtesy of Ottawa

Many groups active politically and in the courts would likely disappear or be severely restricted in the activities they pursue were it not for their tax deductible charitable numbers or their government funding. Canadians have wide and divergent views on a number of issues, especially those most controversial. On abortion, polls over the years revealed that most Canadians want neither unrestricted access to abortion for nine months, nor do they want a complete ban; they come down somewhere between those two stark choices and between the two sides most firmly committed to their own positions. On gay marriage, Canadians are evenly split. On racial quotas, there is likewise some support for affirmative action, opposition to it, and a wide berth of Canadians who give it little thought.

But it would not matter if Canadians were 100 percent in favour or opposed on any question. A healthy democracy needs dissent and must preserve room for the same. When governments fund one side of an issue in advocacy work or in the courts, they in effect stifle dissent by virtue of the "megaphone effect." Groups with a funding pipeline from government hire a plethora of lobbyists, researchers, and spokespeople to influence the public debate in a manner they could not if they were actually dependent on a membership base reflective of the public at large.

How bad has the situation become? Morton and Knopff note two academic studies that reveal the depth of dependency that many activist lobby groups have on government funding:

> Pal's seminal study found that Canadian feminist, multicultural, and official language minority groups typically depend on

government grants for 50 to 80 percent of their budgets....
Pal's findings are replicated in McCartney's study. McCartney
found that federal and provincial funding accounted for three-
quarters of the budgets of Native organizations, approximately
half for women's groups, and one-third for multicultural and
environmental groups.[18]

Why taxpayer funding is wrong and undemocratic

First, subsidies to special interest lobbies take scarce tax dollars.

Every time governments write a cheque, they make a choice on
behalf of those who pay the bill. Whether the citizen is an English
language teacher helping immigrant children or a blue-collar worker on
the assembly line in southern Ontario, most taxes are paid by middle-
income Canadians because that's where most Canadians are: in the
middle income tax brackets. Yes, the poor and rich pay taxes as well,
but the poor are largely (and properly) exempt from most taxes and the
rich are few in Canada, so the tax burden falls on the middle-income
earners.

Thus, when governments cut a cheque they do so largely at the
expense of middle Canada. When governments give money to a
lobby group, the pool of cash available for more worthy causes
shrinks. And whether the tax rates in a country are low, high, or
whether a country is rich or poor, there will always and should
always be a limit to the amount of money a government can spend.
In addition, the impact of special interest group funding on taxpayers is not just limited to the grants and contributions such organizations receive. Taxpayers are also affected by what those groups ad-
vocate for: in many cases, special interest groups put pressure on
government for ever-higher per capita spending and its corollary:
higher taxes.

Second, subsidies for political or legal advocacy distort the democratic process.

One core assumption of the Canadian Constitution and of our
democratic tradition is the limitation of the power of the state to
compel citizens to act in ways they do not wish to. We assume
people are free to do whatever they wish unless actions are ex-
pressly and explicitly forbidden in law—not the other way around;
i.e., it is not that everything is forbidden unless explicitly approved
by the state.

Moreover, this assumption also limits the possibility for collective action. Some people may want to restrict freedom of speech for example, or the right to vote, but Parliament cannot simply and collectively remove such rights. There is the historical assumption, tradition, and—since 1982—the Constitution, which limits the collective action of parliamentarians, or anyone else, to remove anyone's rights or force one to do that which they do not wish to do. (There are exceptions to this of course; few rights are absolute. But the exception is not the rule.)

Within the context of taxpayer funding for special interest groups, governments ought not only to respect the rights of individuals, but when it comes to collective action (which is what legislatures and parliaments are about), governments ought to at the very least, listen first. None of this prevents politicians or parties from expressing their views or even leading public opinion on occasion in those roles; but government itself, as an institution, ought to be neutral and not fund one side in a debate.

For example, it is assumed that politicians and political parties will have views and will be elected in part based on those views. When elected, that they will transform at least some of their views into policy and legislation is also assumed.

But when governments fund advocacy, then they cannot know if the views that lobby groups trumpet are legitimately held by a wide swath of Canadians, or are simply a parroting back of what some politicians and mandarins wish to hear. Liberal Member of Parliament John Bryden sums it up clearly: "Lobbyists shouldn't be funded because it distorts the political agenda."[19]

The democratic process can be distorted in another way. Some special interests that receive funding from governments also donate money to political parties. Bryden noted in his 1994 study on government funding of special interests that the Canadian Labour Congress received a whopping $41,370,247 in one decade from the federal government.[20] The CLC is a regular contributor to the federal New Democratic Party in elections, and most recently gave $734,899 to the federal New Democrats in 1999 and 2000.[21]

Unions should not receive money from government for the same reason that corporations such as Bombardier and Pratt & Whitney should not be given grants and contributions. No matter what the recipients claim, government handouts are added to the budgets of such organizations and thus those groups have extra cash with which to lobby, donate to a political party, or both. Taxpayers ought not to be forced to subsidize unions, corporations and then, possibly by extension, political parties.

Third, government subsidies compel people to support groups and political positions they might disagree with.

Funds given by politicians to lobby groups do not originate magically within the public treasury; they are compelled by government and delivered to government coffers by taxation.

Citizens might be tempted to overlook their forced donation of funds to organizations because on occasion they may agree with some of the organizations that receive such funds; but that is shortsighted.

Government unions may like it when they receive taxpayer cash, but are they thrilled to know that chambers of commerce also receive money? Between 1989 and 1999, the federal Crown corporation Atlantic Canada Opportunities Agency (ACOA) gave $5,032,728 to chambers of commerce, boards of trade, and business associations in Atlantic Canada. Included on the list were the St. John's Board of Trade ($435,212), the Nova Scotia Chamber of Commerce, ($161,546), and the Atlantic Chamber of Commerce ($1,247,473), to name but a few.[22] Environmentalists may love their time at the ministry of Environment trough, but do they also appreciate it when the Canadian Association of Petroleum Producers receives $427,837 in non-repayable contributions from a federal Crown corporation, Western Economic Diversification?[23]

Because government is an institution separate from politicians and political parties, politicians and bureaucrats should not use government and taxpayer dollars as their own personal fiefdom and slush fund and give tax dollars to groups they favour. To do so is a distortion of the political process; for those who do not agree with the agendas of the groups that receive their tax dollars, it is tantamount to theft; and the entire process is simply immoral.

How to dry up government funding for special interests

It is one thing to know that governments fund all manner of advocacy groups that then are involved in the public, political, and legal debates of our country. But how do ordinary citizens cut off such illegitimate funding flows? Here are a few steps to follow:

One:

Refuse to donate to organizations that take government money.

Canadians have many different views on many controversial issues. Some are pro-choice or pro-life. Some favour gun control and others are against gun registration. Some Canadians may favour unlimited development; others desire a human-free Eden. Some groups do legitimate contract work for government but even then it can be used as a way to covertly fund advocacy work. If you suspect that the latter is happening, tell groups you favour that you will write them a cheque when and if they refuse to accept any government money.

Help government-funded groups kick the subsidy habit and strike a blow for a more robust democracy at the same time.

Two:

If you suspect a group has abused its charitable number by lobbying too often or it openly supports a political party, report them to the Canada Customs and Revenue Agency.

Over the past several years, Canada Customs and Revenue Agency has stripped the charitable tax number of a number of organizations that engaged in political action and lobbying above the allowed limits (defined as no more than 10 percent of its budget to be spent on political activities). Greenpeace and the Friends of Clayoquot Sound both had their charitable tax-deductible status revoked after they engaged in too much political as opposed to charitable and educational activity. Both groups can still function as non-profits but cannot give tax receipts. That is fair; groups must choose whether they want to have the luxury of a tax-deductible number, and stick to education, research and charitable work—or whether they want to lobby.[d]

Contact the Charities Directorate at CCRA at:

Charities Directorate
Canada Customs and Revenue Agency
Ottawa ON K1A 0L5

Toll-free in Canada:
1-800-267-2384 (English) or 1-888-892-5667 (bilingual)

Fax:
(613) 954-2586 (Director General's office)
(613) 946-2423 (Policy & Communications Division)
(613) 952-6020 (Determinations)
www.ccra-adrc.gc.ca/agency/directions/charities-e.html

Three:

Contact the media and your member of Parliament or member of your provincial Legislature.

Tell them you want your tax dollars to go to programs and services, not to political lobbyists. Tell them you want fair debates in the public square.

---

[d] The Canadian Taxpayers Federation is a federally registered non-profit association and has never sought tax-deductible status, precisely so political action and positions can be taken. For the record, the CTF does not apply for nor accept government funding.

RAESIDE
VICTORIA TIMES COLONIST-DIST. BY KOKO PRESS INC. www.raesidecartoon.com
MARTIN
NOW, DON'T GO WILD WITH IT.
TAXPAYER DOLLARS

12

Hooked on subsidies
How Alberta and Ontario
support everyone else

Incentives to create wealth through good policies and institutions may wane because of the relatively effortless ability to extract wealth from the soil or the sea. Manna from heaven can be a mixed blessing.

Economist Thorvaldur Gylfason, on why some resource-scarce nations succeed economically while some resource-rich countries do not.[1]

Reversing the Industrial Revolution

Never let it be said that Canadian politicians lack ambition. Who else would attempt to reverse 200 years of worldwide migration from the countryside to cities? Ever since technological progress began to shift people from farmyards to urban courtyards, the flow of people to cities has been unparalleled in human history. Worldwide, only three percent of the population lived in cities in 1800, whereas today 47 percent find their home in an urban area. In Canada, the flight from the rural countryside is even more pronounced; city dwellers now make up 77 percent of the country's population compared to just under 20 percent in 1871. Canadians may love the great outdoors and cottage country for their vacations, but most do not live or work there.

So what has been the response of Canadian federal and provincial governments to this mass migration into the cities? Naturally, they spend a large number of tax dollars in a Sisyphus-like attempt to defy a worldwide two-century trend, and instead bribe individuals and businesses to move to more remote locations.

Think of transfer payments to have-not provinces and transfers to remote Indian reserves. Remember the awful story of young Native peoples sniffing glue on a remote Newfoundland reserve? The government solution was to move the reserve to *another* remote area, barely less isolated than the first, as opposed to a suburb of a major city where the young people might have a chance to connect with the larger world and solid educational and employment opportunities. This is progress?

Whether funding for Native reserves far away from urban Canada, or funding for have-not provinces that encourages them *not* to develop their resources or their human capital, the economic illogic of large transfer payments continues unabated in Canada. Far from retreating from an ill-advised policy, in 1982 Canada's governments instead entrenched such absurdities in the Constitution.

Canada's first transfer payments and the deal: 80 cents per person and no provincial trade barriers

Federal transfers to the provinces are as old as Confederation but not because the founding fathers wanted it that way. Canada's founders wished to avoid subsidies to the provinces entirely. The conundrum was that the Dominion government did not want to risk the prospect of provincial tariffs on each other's goods (tariffs then being the main source of revenues for governments) and in so doing create trade barriers within the new country.

Another option was to give the provinces greater revenue powers. They were given the right to collect direct taxes (i.e., on income) in order to raise revenues, but the provinces were not expected to actually use that option, given the rank unpopularity of that tax. As tax historians Milton Moore and J. Harvey Perry write, with the exception of Ontario, where property taxes and some local income taxes already existed, "it is evident from the speeches of the day that the founding fathers counted on the very unpopularity of direct taxation to prevent its extensive use."[2] Thus, while the provinces were given direct taxing power, they were unlikely to use it, or so went the theory, which proved mostly correct for Canada's first few decades.[a]

At the time of Confederation, the provinces were given responsibility for welfare and education and not much else, and those two items were not particularly burdensome in 1867. Moreover, given the sentiment of the times, they were never expected to be overly costly. In fact, provinces were expected to decline in terms of per capita expenditures as municipal governments grew.[3] The federal government, then known as

---

[a] As noted in Chapter 1, British Columbia was the first to introduce a provincial income tax in 1876.

the Dominion government, was responsible for developing the country's railway system, bridges, roads, harbours and other infrastructure, and thus was given much of the needed revenue base.

The expected change in position and dominance is in fact what did occur. Examining expenditures from the year before Confederation (1866), total government revenues across Canada amounted to $20 million, with 70 percent ($14 million) accruing to the provinces (then colonies) while the remaining portion, 30 percent ($6 million), went to municipalities. Upper and Lower Canada, as well as the Atlantic colonies, were the biggest kids on the government block.[4]

Seven years after Confederation, the role of the provinces decreased dramatically. In 1874, out of revenues of $33 million, two-thirds flowed to the Dominion government while the next largest jurisdiction was that of cities and towns, which garnered $8 million, or about 24 percent of all revenues. The provinces were then a distant third with $3 million, or nine percent.[5] Thus, their revenues had dropped to one-fifth their pre-Confederation collections.[b]

Given that the provincial responsibilities were forecast to decline, the possibility that they would use income tax to raise revenue was remote, and as tariffs would create trade barriers, the default option was a federal subsidy to the provinces. Thus, Ottawa chose what is best described as the first transfer payment. Subsidies were agreed upon and amounted to 80 cents for each person in each province, though there was a cap for any province over 400,000.[c] But there were exceptions to the general rule; New Brunswick was given an extra ten-year grant, for example.[6] After that, and because of the reluctance of the Dominion government to dole out subsidies to begin with, the agreed-upon settlement at the time was stated to be the "full and final" settlement of all claims by the provinces upon the new Dominion government.[7]

It did not last. As other provinces joined Confederation, additional special annual grants were made, and soon "special" disbursements (annually) were made from the central government to Nova Scotia, Prince Edward Island and British Columbia. With those major changes accommodated within the first decade of Confederation, the subsidy

---

[b] Their third-place role (in terms of revenues) continued until 1947 when revenue flows to the provinces once again overtook that of municipalities for the first time since 1867.

[c] Only Quebec and Ontario exceeded that number. In 1871, Quebec's population was almost 1.2 million while Ontario's was over 1.6 million. Prince Edward Island possessed 94,000 inhabitants, Nova Scotia 388,000, New Brunswick 286,000, while 25,000 inhabited Manitoba and 36,000 lived in British Columbia. The Northwest Territories, which then also encompassed the now separate Nunavut and Yukon territories, had 48,000 people.

program remained mostly unchanged for the next forty years. At that point, the introduction of new provinces (Alberta and Saskatchewan joined Canada in 1905) prompted Prime Minister Wilfred Laurier to convene a general conference in 1906 to reconsider the subsidy question. One result was the removal of the subsidy cap that limited the 80-cents-per-capita subsidy to only a province's first 400,000 people; the effect was that average subsidies increased by one-third.

This too was to be the "final" settlement but, as federal Finance ministers and prime ministers would discover throughout the 20th century, finality was an elusive goal. Experimentation with conditional grants (for agricultural instruction) began in 1913. In the 1920s, additional federal grants were given for vocational education, highway construction, employment offices, venereal disease prevention and old age pensions. The provinces were to be responsible for half the money spent on such programs.

The Depression, World War Two and Postwar arrangements

The onslaught of the Depression knocked Canadians and their governments into a tailspin. The country's gross national product, which reached a high of $6.2 billion in 1929, plunged to $3.6 billion by 1933, a descent of 57 percent in four years.[8] The provinces and the federal government taxed as never before but even that was not enough to meet the multiple needs that arose out of the Depression.[d] The Dominion government gave special assistance to the provinces to prevent defaults in debts and to continue the financing of essential services.[9]

Over the next 40 years, transfer payments and tax agreements between the provincial and federal governments changed several times. For example, during World War Two, the provinces agreed to forego income and corporate tax revenues in exchange for compensation from the federal government. The federal government levied much of the increased tax burden (as the government also raised taxes in general to prosecute the war effort and to take over the provincial tax room). While tax increases and other sacrifices were the price of war, there was at least one side benefit: the confusion and overlapping jurisdictional authority on some taxes was removed between 1941 and 1946.

By 1947, a new tax rental agreement was in place where the provinces agreed to continue not to tax personal incomes in exchange for

---

[d] For example, in unadjusted dollars, total government revenues dropped from a pre-Depression high of $932 million in 1929 to a low of $701 million in 1932. Thus, in the early 1930s deficits reached record proportions, as high as 42 percent of all government expenditures in 1931.

guaranteed federal payments; provinces were also restricted to a maximum five-percent corporation tax under the terms of the deal. (Ontario and Quebec opted out of that particular arrangement.)

Between the 1950s and 1980s, federal-provincial arrangements shifted from the immediate postwar arrangement where the federal government levied all income and business taxes and transferred an agreed-upon portion to the provinces (who stayed in the postwar arrangements) to a system where the provinces once again levied their own specific taxes. With the exception of Quebec, they did allow Ottawa to collect and process income tax.

The changing nature of federal and provincial tax agreements and policy as regards transfer payments over the past half-century would test the intellect and alertness of all but the most dedicated tax historian. For the lay reader, the simplest way to understand the shift over the past several decades in federal subsidies to the provinces is to examine the current arrangements to gain a sense of how the system functions.

The big three: Equalization, Canada health & social transfers, and tax transfers

Besides redistribution through its own programs, the federal government uses three main instruments to transfer money between taxpayers across the country via the federal government in Ottawa.

The first, **equalization** payments, consists of money transferred to eight have-not provinces and three have-not territories. As the name suggests, the money is intended to "equalize" (to some degree) per capita revenues among the provinces.

The second, **health and social transfers,** also consists of cash transfers but is given to every province and territory.

The last part of Canada's current federal-provincial transfer system is in the form of **tax transfers**. A few have occurred throughout Canada's history, and the most recent was in 1977. In essence, the federal government gave up tax "room" and let the provinces tax citizens for the same amount instead.

Equalization for dummies: a refresher course for the rest of us!

Equalization is by far the most difficult of the three federal transfer programs to understand. The complexity of determining which province is a "have-not" versus which one is a "have," and then how much each "have-not" province will receive from federal coffers, is complex.

The federal department of Finance describes equalization this way:

> The Equalization program enables less prosperous provincial governments to provide their residents with reasonably comparable levels of public services with reasonably comparable levels of taxation. Equalization payments are unconditional in that receiving provinces are free to spend them on public services according to their own priorities.[10]

OK, a Canadian might ask, that's the *justification*, but how is equalization calculated? Here is the simple version:

- The federal Finance department examines 33 sources of revenue in each province.
- It then calculates how much each province raises from those 33 taxes.
- Five provinces considered "middle income" (Quebec, Ontario, Manitoba, Saskatchewan and British Columbia) are examined to arrive at a "standard" average.
- Provinces below that standard then receive equalization payments to bring them up to the five-province average.

As of 1999, British Columbia joined the list of have-not provinces, which meant eight out of ten provinces were officially have-not provinces.[e] Add in the three territories (Northwest, Yukon and Nunavut) which also receive generous transfers under a separate but similar program, and 11 out of 13 sub-national jurisdictions in Canada receive some sort of equalization payment from the federal government.

The most recent figures available show that the federal government will pay out just over $10.2 billion in equalization payments. Territories receive $1.5 billion under a similar formula.[11]

The Canada Health and Social Transfer

As large as equalization payments are, the Canada Health and Social Transfer (CHST), is an even larger expense for the federal government. It is also easier to explain.

In 1966, the Canada Assistance Plan (CAP) was introduced, which was a cost-sharing arrangement for the growing Canadian welfare state.

---

[e] British Columbia joined the rank of have-nots in 1999 in large measure, I would argue, due to economically damaging policies enacted by that province's 1990s government. For more, see *Barbarians in the Garden City—The BC NDP in Power*, published in 2001.

Four decades later, and after several mutations, CAP has now become the CHST, which will transfer $19.1 billion in 2003 for health care, post-secondary education, welfare and other social services.

In straight cash, how much does Ottawa hand out every year? Equalization and CHST payments amount to $29.4 billion. But there is a massive *per person* difference between what Ottawa transfers to the provinces and what is doled out to the territories.

On average, the provinces receive $893 per person from the federal government while the territories receive $15,610. Note to readers in the south: the federal government would like *more* people to live and work there. Want to save taxpayers some money? Encourage more northerners to move south. Twenty thousand more people south of the territorial lines would save taxpayers over $300 million every year.

$29.4 billion in cash transfers from the federal government to provinces/territories (Canada Health & Social Transfer plus equalization payments 2002-2003 estimate)	Cash transfers (in $ billions)	Per person average federal transfer (in $)
10 provinces	27.85	893
3 territories	1.56	15,610
Total	29.4	940

Sources: Statistics Canada. Information on federal transfers from department of Finance. The value of tax transfers from 1977 are not included in this chart. Calculations by the author.

Tax transfers

And then there is the issue of tax transfers. If Canadians are confused about equalization and the Canada Health and Social Transfer, it is also because when federal politicians speak, they want to emphasize their past generosity to the provinces as it concerns the "tax transfer." Provincial politicians have amnesia on this as it helps their public case when they demand more money from Ottawa.

The tax transfer is just as it sounds. In 1977, the federal government literally "transferred" taxing room to the provinces. In 1977-78, the federal government agreed to give up 13.5 personal income tax (PIT) points (under the previous method of calculating income tax) and one corporate income tax (CIT) point. In return, the provinces raised their taxes by the same amount; that meant it was revenue neutral for taxpayers.

But it was not revenue neutral for provincial revenues. The federal Finance department still reminds Canadians on its website and in departmental releases that the tax transfer given up in 1977 is now worth almost $16.6 billion annually, up from $2.7 billion when it was first sacrificed by Ottawa.[12]

Alberta and Ontario write the cheques

Are the various transfer payments good public policy? Some argue yes. The justification is that equalization helps provinces provide roughly comparable levels of services to citizens.

Others would say no. When the vast majority of sub-national governments, as opposed to the very few and poorest jurisdictions, receive equalization payments, the tax burden must necessarily be higher on the residents of the have provinces (now only Alberta and Ontario) than would otherwise be the case. And it is perverse as it punishes the regions that have the most to offer in terms of economic potential, job creation and wages.

The federal government's position is that tax dollars come from taxpayers in *all* parts of the country, have provinces and have-nots. Thus, as taxpayers in every province pay federal tax, it is technically incorrect to say that the rich provinces (the haves) finance the have-nots. The claim is technically true. But while taxpayers in have-not provinces do contribute to federal coffers, have-not provincial governments receive much more back in transfers than residents pay in federal taxes.

Examine the issue from a different angle: assume there was no federal government but that transfer payments yet occurred. In that scenario, two provinces would cut cheques and every other provincial Finance minister, from Victoria to St. John's, would be a recipient of provincial taxes from the Alberta and Ontario treasuries.

This is why it is financially perverse for anyone in the remaining have provinces of Alberta and Ontario (and British Columbia once it recovers its have status) to call for more transfer payments. When such demands originate in Alberta and Ontario governments, they in effect demand that their own taxpayers hand over even more federal cash to Ottawa only to receive back *less* to their own provincial government later in the form of transfer payments.

NET TRANSFERS BETWEEN CANADIAN FAMILIES
Census Family Total Income, Post-Tax and Post-Transfer

	$20,000	$20,001-$30,000	$30,001-$40,000	$40,001-$50,000	$50,001-$60,000	$60,001-$75,000	$75,001-$100,000	>$100,001	ALL	Per Family Average
	In percentages according to income category									In $
Newfoundland	70.8	48.5	28.0	15.7	8.4	1.1	0.1	1.2	25.4	$6,690
PEI	61.2	36.8	19.8	7.1	-2.3	-8.9	-13.0	-12.8	10.2	$2,976
Nova Scotia	52.8	28.6	10.8	-1.1	-6.5	-10.4	-13.6	-18.0	6.6	$1,807
New Brunswick	54.4	29.6	11.6	-1.9	-6.8	-11.3	-16.0	-14.8	6.2	$1,738
Quebec	48.4	23.0	3.2	-7.5	-13.5	-17.7	-21.8	-27.0	-2.2	-$652
Ontario	36.2	18.8	-2.8	-12.3	-21.2	-24.9	-29.7	-36.9	-16.1	-$5,742
Manitoba	43.8	22.4	2.1	-8.0	-12.1	-16.3	-20.8	-25.4	-4.9	-$1,551
Saskatchewan	44.9	16.0	-1.5	-14.1	-18.2	-22.1	-25.6	-34.8	-9.0	-$2,659
Alberta	28.8	11.3	-9.0	-18.1	-21.9	-27.3	-31.4	-35.8	-17.6	-$6,007
British Columbia	44.1	8.4	-5.2	-16.4	-21.4	-23.5	-29.9	-35.6	-15.9	$5,156
All Canada	42.8	19.1	-0.5	-10.9	-17.9	-21.9	-27.0	-33.7	-10.7	-$3,480

Average dollars per family

	$20,000	$20,001-$30,000	$30,001-$40,000	$40,001-$50,000	$50,001-$60,000	$60,001-$75,000	$75,001-$100,000	>$100,001	ALL
Per family average	$5,191	$3,959	($133)	($3,469)	($6,731)	($9,828)	($15,243)	($32,849)	($3,480)

Notes: FEDERAL NET BALANCE AS A PERCENTAGE OF FAMILY INCOME. Net balance is federal direct and indirect transfers less federal taxes. Transfer amounts used in the calculations are for fiscal year 1996/97.
Source: Poschmann, Finn. Where the Money Goes: The Distribution of Taxes and Benefits in Canada, CD Howe Institute, Toronto, 1998.

Taxpayers in the have provinces would be better off if the federal government transferred tax room once again to the provinces; that way, have provinces would at least recoup the full tax dollars as opposed to the half-loaf they now receive. Finance ministers in Toronto and Edmonton (and soon Victoria) who call for ever-increasing federal transfers are not helping taxpayers in their own provinces when they make such demands of the federal government.

How a $30,000 Albertan helps out a $75,000 Newfoundlander

Worse than the economic inefficiencies created by the system of transfer payments, where Canadians are encouraged to live in regions with few opportunities, the chronic subsidies have led to a bizarre situation where middle-income Albertans subsidize families in Newfoundland with *higher* incomes.

The best demonstration of this came from economist Finn Poschmann, who showed that when all government-to-government transfer pro-

How much does Ottawa transfer to the provinces?
Equalization, Canada Health & Social Transfer, Territorial Funding and Tax Transfer

Major federal transfers ($ millions)	2000	2001	2002	2003
Canada Health and Social Transfer	14,500	15,500	18,300	19,100
Equalization	10,717	10,828	10,318	10,233
Territorial funding	1,415	1,471	1,467	1,507
Value of 1977 federal tax transfer to the provinces/territories	15,568	16,413	16,100	16,564
Total value of cash & tax transfers	40,840	42,911	44,825	45,978

Source: Major federal transfers to provinces and territories, department of Finance, Ottawa, 4 April 2002. Totals may not add due to rounding. 2003 figures are estimates. Equalization associated with CHST tax transfer is included in both CHST and Equalization. Totals have been adjusted to avoid double counting

grams (equalization and the Canada Health and Social Transfer) and government-to-individual transfers are analyzed together, families in Saskatchewan, Ontario, British Columbia and Alberta that earn between $30,000 and $40,000 every year are net contributors to federal transfers, contributing (depending on the province) between one percent and nine percent of their incomes to families in other provinces.

Anything wrong with that?

There *is* when families in Newfoundland (the most stark example) that earn as much as $100,000 in income are net *recipients* of such transfers from families in Alberta who earn less than $40,000. Thus, lower-income earners in at least four provinces (including a have-not province like Saskatchewan) send their tax dollars to Ottawa only to have their money redistributed to families, who in some cases, earn much more than they do.

Expressed simply, a $30,000- (and higher) income family in Calgary pays taxes to support not only Newfoundland families that earn less than they do, but also families that earn up to $100,000. Meanwhile, the lower-income Calgary family faces a higher cost of living.

Even in Atlantic Canada, where a middle-income taxpayer makes a net contribution to transfers, there is an imbalance vis-à-vis the same income earner somewhere else. For example, as Poschmann points out, families in New Brunswick with $50,000 to $60,000 contribute seven percent of their income to federal transfers. If that same family moved to Alberta and remained at the same income level, their net contributions would equal almost 22 percent of income. Thus, the Alberta family (*at the same income level* as the New Brunswick family) pays three times as much to support federal transfer programs.

Please, mug me again

One other way to understand how much select areas of the country subsidize others is to examine the Canada Health and Social Transfer payments once more. When provincial governments signed a new CHST deal in 1999, they reinforced the perverse incentive where politicians from the have-not provinces could promise their voters the sky and have it paid for by taxpayers in the have provinces.

On average, when the provinces signed a new CHST deal in 1999, the taxpayers in the have-not provinces would pay 67 cents in federal income tax for every dollar their governments would receive from Ottawa in CHST payments. In contrast, for taxpayers in Ontario and Alberta, for every $1.30 they pay to Ottawa in federal income tax, the federal government in essence writes back a cheque for only one dollar.

This creates obvious political tensions and economic disincentives. Politicians in have-not provinces (now the vast majority of the country) can feel free to promise their voters any manner of election-time goodies at the expense of taxpayers elsewhere, i.e., Alberta and Ontario, who will finance a large portion of such election promises anyway.

Many taxpayers in Canada are already not sure what level of government is responsible for what tax and for which particular spending program; transfer payments only further cloud this already weak understanding for many Canadians. Accountability for taxes raised and money spent is served best by clear and direct links between the taxes a government collects and the money it spends. Large transfer payments do not help clear up that fog.

Moreover, it also creates a perverse incentive as it concerns the control of government spending. For example, ferry workers in Newfoundland recently demanded wage parity with ferry workers in British Columbia (both ferry systems are government-run). However, St. John's has a much lower cost of living than Vancouver or Victoria. Marine Atlantic, owned by the federal government and thus subsidized by taxpayers, should pay local wage rates to reflect local conditions and the local cost of living. But when governments are not directly responsible for the cost of their programs or some of their local services are run by another level of government, the accountability link is weak. Instead, because of transfers, governments feel free to pay inflated rates, in part because large portions of the wage bill will be paid by taxpayers in other provinces.

Nunavut Inc.

Thus far, no argument against the continual subsidies which Canada's founders were so wary of, have yet convinced most politicians it is time for a policy change; quite the opposite.

The most recent example of this rather perverse fiscal policy is the creation of Nunavut out of what used to be the Northwest Territories. Consider that while a chronic have-not province such as Newfoundland receives 38 percent of its provincial revenues from the federal government, Ottawa's support of Nunavut is 88 percent of that territory's budget. Thus, as much as Newfoundland's government is criticized on occasion as chronically dependent on taxpayers elsewhere in the country, the "rock" is a deal compared to Nunavut.

Even the two other northern territories are less dependent on Ottawa. The Yukon Territory budget is reliant on Ottawa for 78 percent of its revenues; the now-shrunken Northwest Territories budget needs federal taxpayers for almost 40 percent of its budget. In comparison, Alberta is least reliant on federal transfers, which account for just 9.8 percent of its provincial revenues; Ontario and British Columbia click in at 9.9 percent and 11.6 percent respectively.[13]

And it doesn't work anyway: The tragedy of Atlantic Canada

Some bright spots on the horizon have appeared to challenge the status quo including from Atlantic Canada itself. One of the better analyses of the folly of such redistribution comes from the Halifax-based Atlantic Institute for Market Studies (AIMS). Their 1999 study noted how well Ireland and the New England American states performed in comparison to Canada's Atlantic provinces.

Two decades ago, Ireland's per-capita economy was 40 percent less than that of Canada; now it has a per-capita economy 10 percent *higher*, and regional subsidies from the European Union are minuscule in comparison to what the Atlantic provinces receive from Canada's federal government. Moreover, such EU subsidies are never touted as the reason for Ireland's astonishing catch-up over the past two decades.

Rather, the success is credited to lower tax rates (10 percent for businesses) and labour agreements where workers agreed to modest wage increases in return for increased investment by business. The net effect over time is that increased investment led to a booming economy and wages rose as demand for workers increased.

Not that provincial Finance ministers from Atlantic Canada are ready to consider the Irish evidence. In 2001, Patricia Mella, the provincial treasurer for Prince Edward Island, told the Senate Committee that reviewed equalization that Atlantic Institute analyses and others do not take into account the "fiscal capacity" of the have-not provinces.[14]

The "fiscal capacity" argument is one often given by Finance ministers for the have-not provinces; this writer heard the same from provincial finance officials in British Columbia in pre-budget discussions. Essentially, the "fiscal capacity" argument is that some provinces are richer than others, i.e., Alberta has oil and Ontario has manufacturing, so of course such provinces have a much better economy and consequent tax revenues.

But the argument ignores the choices that governments have and their long-term effect on the economy. When the British Columbia government almost shut down the mining industry in the 1990s through a variety of measures—some intentional, some not—the fiscal capacity of that province was indeed restricted. When Newfoundland for years refused to allow the development of Voisey's Bay for political reasons (the mining company did not promise enough Newfoundland jobs), the fiscal capacity of that province was likewise kept small.

There are, worldwide, numerous countries with little in the way of natural resources that have prospered. Japan, Hong Kong, Singapore, Taiwan, and South Korea are now prosperous to a degree unimaginable 50 years ago.[15] Some countries rich in natural resources such as Venezuela and Congo are not.[f]

Some academic evidence even suggests that natural resources are not naturally a help to countries, as those nations tend to rely on such natural wealth instead of concentrating on economic fundamentals such as trade and investment and post-secondary education opportunities, for example. Economist Thorvaldur Gylfason explains it this way:

> Abundant natural resources may imbue people with a false sense of security and lead governments to lose sight of the need for good and growth-friendly economic management, including free trade, bureaucratic efficiency, and institutional quality. Put differently, abundant natural capital may crowd out social capital, by which is meant the infrastructure and institutions of a society in a broad sense: its culture, cohesion, law, system of justice, rules and customs and so on, including trust. Incentives to create wealth through good policies and institutions may wane because of the relatively effortless ability to extract wealth from the soil or the sea. Manna from heaven can be a mixed blessing.[16]

Far from helping Prince Edward Island, Nova Scotia, Newfoundland, and New Brunswick, transfer payments have created a perverse situation, where economic development is discouraged both corporately and individually.

On a provincial level, every new dollar in economic revenue mostly reduces the take from Ottawa by a similar amount. Thus, the incentive for a have-not provincial government to promote economic development through sensible regulation and appropriate tax rates is reduced.

Positive signs

There is a changing attitude in Atlantic Canada. It was first signalled by the Atlantic Institute for Market Studies and their analyses of the Irish and northeastern U.S. states' prosperity in relation to Canada's Atlantic

---

[f] For an excellent analysis of how and why nations prosper, see *The World Economy: A Millennial Perspective* by Angus Maddison. The OECD economist traces economic history since AD 1000 and analyses the reasons why some countries prosper and notes the remarkable progress of many formerly poor countries since just the 1950s.

provinces. Recently, Scott Brison, the federal member of Parliament for Kings-Hants, Nova Scotia, and the federal Finance critic for the Progressive Conservatives, has called on the federal government to scrap the regional subsidy programs in exchange for the elimination of business tax in Atlantic Canada.

Brison has noted that federal corporate income taxes take in only $380 million, while the budget for the Atlantic Canada Opportunities Agency is $447 million annually.[17] While the cancellation of business taxes may not be feasible for one region in isolation, the cancellation of the federal subsidy agency would itself be a positive move.

Scott Brison did not extend his call to the elimination of all federal transfers—equalization is, tragically, constitutionally entrenched.[g] But the very possibility that an Atlantic politician called for the elimination of business subsidies is a positive political development in that region. The founders of Confederation, wary of subsidies as they were, would likely applaud.[h]

---

[g] That some form of equalization is entrenched in the Constitution does not mean it cannot be substantially changed and lessened in its perverse effects. And, unlikely as this is any time soon, if enough provinces became have provinces or the have-nots recognize some of the long-term disincentives in equalization for Canada's prosperity as a whole, it could be dispensed with at some future point. But short-term political horizons combined with immediate provincial interests make that unlikely in the short term.

[h] To its credit, the Alliance party and its predecessor, the Reform party also called for the elimination of business subsidies. If Scott Brison's comments are reflective of his caucus, there now is little difference between the two parties on this issue.

Percentage of provincial revenues from Ottawa
Provincial and territorial government revenues and expenditures (Millions)

Year	NF	PEI	NS	NB	PQ	ON	MB	SK	AB	BC	YK	NWT	NT	All Prov.
Total Federal transfers	1,775	421	2,210	2,044	9,358	7,731	2,398	1,540	2,365	3,355	446	442	695	34,780
Total revenues	4,672	1,129	6,841	5,945	59,859	78,342	9,333	7,704	24,195	28,984	572	1,111	792	229,479
Federal transfers as a % of revenues	38.0%	37.3%	32.3%	34.4%	15.6%	9.9%	25.7%	20.0%	9.8%	11.6%	78.0%	39.8%	87.8%	15%

Source: Statistics Canada, Financial Management System Basis, 2001/02. Total transfers may differ from other estimates as Statistics Canada includes general purpose transfers and specific purpose transfers.

The Canadian Senate:
Hooked on the equalization drug

The Canadian Senate once again reinforced the impression that it is a 19th-century body with its release of a report in 2002 that would make Canada's equalization programs even more expensive for taxpayers.[18]

The Senate panel listened to economists such as Ken Boesenkool, professor Paul Boothe (a former deputy minister of Finance from Saskatchewan) and professor Dan Usher who urged reform of equalization to make it less costly. Others such as Atlantic Finance ministers and the Canadian Union of Public Employees (who have a vested interest in having large, inefficient governments) also presented. The first presenters recommended wholesale changes to reduce the perverse economic incentives associated with equalization; the second group wanted more money. No prizes for guessing which presenters the Senate listened to.

The Senate panel recommended the federal government lift the ceiling on equalization payments and restore the ten-province standard in determining the same. *Translation*: more money for have-not provinces from the two remaining have provinces—think of it as an unlimited VISA from Ontario and Alberta.

The Senate also recommended that the "floor" provision in equalization—that ensures population change and other factors cannot reduce payments to the have-not provinces—be kept in place. So the Senate committee *favoured* subjecting federal finances to the risk of ever-increasing transfer payments (e.g., lift the "ceiling") but would not accept that if a province becomes richer that it should accept less federal tax dollars (e.g., keep the "floor").

The summary of the Senate Committee's position is this: open up the cash register and let the provinces take whatever they want, forget about substantial reform to equalization and heaven forbid it ever be abolished. In short, the Senate committee sided once again with the spenders. The Senate and provincial subsidies from Ottawa are 19th-century relics. Perhaps the fact that one endorsed the equalization drug of the other should not be a surprise.

13

Boondoggles:
The pan-Canadian list

Only the best projects are funded.

> A spokesperson for the federal Social Sciences and Humanities
> Research Council on a $50,000 grant to study strippers.[1]

Triumph of the absurd

George Orwell once remarked that some ideas are so absurd only intellectuals could believe them. A twist on that observation is that there are some studies and projects so absurd that only government could fund them.

Canadian governments have funded a list of projects and loaned or given money to so many questionable recipients over the years that to catalogue them all would require a separate book. From a $50,000 grant to a Vancouver professor to study erotic strippers to $500 million spent over seven years to keep a polluting, inefficient coalmine in Nova Scotia running, governments in Canada have elevated boondoggles to high art.

Both the occasional grant from governments to fund legitimate research and the transitional payments to the unemployed (e.g., unemployment cheques) are justifiable in most cases given their straightforward connection to real needs, though even then there are exceptions; dependency can be problematic as governments discovered in the 1980s and 1990s. But then there are the cheques cut by our governments that *cannot* be defended.

To expand on the example of the subsidized coalmine in Nova Scotia, that $500-million subsidy between 1990 and 1997 to the Cape Breton Development Corporation (Devco) amounted to over $260,000 per employee.[2] And that half-billion dollars was neither the beginning nor the end of it. The mine was subsidized since the late 1920s and again after the federal government took it over from its British owner in 1967 and right up to and after 1999 when another $328 million was spent to close Devco.[3] Between 1967, when the federal government took over the mine, and its closure, the federal government estimated the cost was at least $1.7 billion.[4] Adjusted for inflation and including subsidies from the 1920s to 2002, Fred McMahon, an economist who has written extensively on subsidies in Atlantic Canada, pegs the seven-decade subsidy at $5 billion in current dollars.[5]

Subsidies to sunset companies are not restricted to the East Coast however; the British Columbia government spent over $400 million between 1997 and 2002 to keep open an inefficient and polluting pulp and paper mill (Skeena Cellulose) in Prince Rupert.[6]

As with most subsidies, once governments get suckered into owning the "commanding heights of the economy," taxpayers would almost always have been better off if a onetime cheque were cut years ago to Devco miners or to Skeena Cellulose workers in exchange for an earlier shutdown of the inefficient mine and out-of-date pulp mill. But when businesses are owned, loaned to, or guaranteed by governments, sensible decisions (albeit tough ones on occasion) are derailed by politics. Thus, cash that could have been left with other businesses and individuals (by not taxing it away) or spending tax dollars on more worthy government projects, like upgrading the Trans-Canada Highway or a replacement of aging military helicopters, are lost.

But boondoggles and questionable expenditures big or small are, tragically, not rare for federal or provincial governments. The selection of boondoggles here is entirely arbitrary; there are too many to list in any complete sense. Some are the result of straight grants by governments; others the result of well-intentioned but fatally flawed loan guarantees. Others on this list are merely interesting grants given out on taxpayers' behalf, at which most people might raise an eyebrow. In some cases, the money is gone forever. In others (such as outstanding loans), taxpayers can always hope the money does return to the public treasury one day.

Dead rabbit exhibits to porn funding: Selected examples of government boondoggles

- In June 1999, the taxpayer-funded Canada Council for the Arts gave Winnipeg resident and artist Disney Thorneycroft a $15,000 grant for her art exhibit entitled Monstrance. "We must give credit to God for the body's return to the earth," said the artist. The exhibit featured 12 dead bunny rabbits hung from trees. Canada Council also gave $60,000 to a film company for "Bubbles Galore," a 1996 lesbian pornography fantasy film.[7]

- In 1995 the Federal Business Development Bank loaned $105,000 to the Montreal Rockers Bike Club for its clubhouse. One biker at the club noted that the clubhouse with bullet-proof glass, double steel doors, and perimeter security cameras was a "place to get away from the wives and kids." The bank thought it had lent money to a vending machine business.[8]

- In 2002, the Federal Business Development Bank was again snookered. It lent $750,000 for the creation of a business training centre, or so it thought. It turned out that the loan helped build a $2-million, 12,000-square-foot riverfront mansion in Ottawa.[9]

- In 2002, the family of suspects in the Air India bombing court case were being paid by the British Columbia government to perform duties for the defence team. Defence team costs were estimated at perhaps $1 million per month; it was unclear how much made its way to the families of the accused Air India bombers.[10]

- A federal government lawyer sued the federal government for "wrongful hiring," after "enduring utter boredom" for three years at his $70,000-a-year job. The government initially refused to award him compensation but later settled out of court with an undisclosed payment in 1995.[11]

- The Saskatchewan government lost an estimated $30 million when a Crown corporation, SaskWater and its subsidiary "Spudco" built massive concrete potato storage facilities in that province in a bid to attract farmers to potato growing. Once potato prices plummeted, farmers could not afford the expensive rents and it was downhill from there. A later auditor general's report noted that "SaskWater's rules and procedures for managing its investment in the potato industry were not adequate" and "objectives for the investment in the potato industry were not clear or measurable." In addition, the Auditor pointed out that major decisions were made without a comprehensive assessment of the risks of investing in the potato industry or a proper cost-benefit analysis being done.[12]

- In 1997, the National Film Board of Canada spent $288,336.52 on a profile of anti-free-trade activist Maude Barlow.[13]

- The federal government gave $1,000 to a Montreal filmmaker to present a film on civil disobedience to protesters gathering to object to the World Trade Organization (WTO) in Seattle in 1999.[14] Another artist, Roshell Bisset, was given $500 to travel to Paris to present her film, Cotton Candy, a film about a Japanese girl who works at a sex trade shop. Ms. Bisset defended the grant this way:

"We're always talking about creating Canadian culture and creating an identity separate from that of the United States. How are we supposed to do that without some kind of freedom of expression to do that as well?" As with some other artists who receive such grant money, freedom of expression was equated with taxpayer *funding* of freedom of expression.[15]

- The federal government spent $612,500 in 1999 for a contract with Groupaction of Montreal to study whether the government was getting fair value for its sponsorship of events related to fishing, hunting, and recreation. Such sponsorship deals were mostly handled by Groupaction, meaning the company was essentially paid over $600,000 to tell government whether it did a good job with its existing contracts.[16]

- $1.7 million to double the number of "Canada" signs across the country. In defending the project, Alan Way, a federal civil servant said "it's to establish a federal presence across the country. It's similar to IBM and others who say 'Here we are, this is our building and you can get programs and services here.'" In addition, the federal government via Crown corporations also placed such signs at a cost of $2.4 million in NHL hockey arenas and Canadian Football League stadiums (as one way to unofficially subsidize such professional sports). Apparently, Canadians might forget that the federal government exists if it does not advertise.[17]

- In 1981, the BC government bought five locomotives for $2.5 million, never used them for a planned Vancouver-Mission commuter route, paid $20,000 annually for insurance and storage for the trains and, despite being urged to sell them by government staff for at least $500,000 in 1986, neglected to do so. They were sold in 1994 for $65,000.[18]

- In 1997, Pierre Thibault received $600,000 in grants from the Transitional Jobs Fund and $1,325,000 in loans from the federal government after meeting with his member of Parliament, Jean Chretien. The prime minister announced the grant three weeks before it was actually and officially approved.[19]

- In 2002, the prime minister noted that "perhaps a few million dollars was stolen in the process," referring to the federal government's attempt to boost its "image" in the 1995 Quebec referendum on secession. The RCMP were investigating the possibility that Groupaction of Montreal was given $1.6 million in contracts by the federal government at the time but did not actually perform any work in exchange.[20]

Every spring the Canadian Taxpayers Federation awards a "Teddy" to the politician or bureaucrat who has been most proficient at wasting tax dollars or for suggesting new and higher taxes. Past recipients include former BC Premier Glen Clark and Heritage Minister Sheila Copps. Former Conservative Finance Minister Michael Wilson was given a "Lifetime Achievement Award" for the introduction of "bracket creep" into the political lexicon, a subtle tax that cost taxpayers $90 billion over its 14-year existence. The award is named after a former federal bureaucrat, Ted Weatherill, who was fired in 1998 for running up his expense accounts, including a $733.43 lunch for two in Paris at the RPG Arpege. Federal director Walter Robinson is seen here with a local model at an Ottawa press conference announcing the annual awards.

- Remember the 1993 promise by the then-Opposition Liberals to tear up contracts signed by the Conservatives to replace aging Sea King helicopters? In 1996, the government paid out $478 million to various contractors in compensation only to talk about tendering for the same helicopters nearly one decade later. As of 2002, a contract for the replacements had not yet been signed. In contrast, and very hastily at the end of the budget year, the prime minister ordered two Bombardier jets for himself at a cost of $100 million to replace his current planes—a purchase his own government said was not necessary.[21]

- Between 1980 and 1994, the Alberta Conservative government wrote off over $2.3 billion in loans and loan guarantees to various Alberta companies. Costs included $646 million (Novatel) and $209 million to Gainers, a Peter Pocklington-owned meatpacking plant that the government took over and ran for several years after the company defaulted on a $55-million government loan guarantee. As a result of the cost to taxpayers, the Alberta government banned (most) subsidies, loans, and loan guarantees in 1996.[22]

- $50,000 from the federal government to a Vancouver professor to study strippers, in 2001.

- $1.7 billion to Cape Breton Development Corporation for subsidies regarding the coalmine, between 1967 and 1997. It is estimated that between the 1920s and 2002, total subsidies might equal $5 billion in today's dollars.[23]

- In the mid- to late-1990s, three "fast ferries" were constructed by the British Columbia government and originally forecast to cost $210 million by then-minister responsible and later premier, Glen Clark, who in 1994 guaranteed that cost "right down to the toilet paper." The cost of the ships escalated to $463 million by the time of completion. By 2002, their book value had been written down several times and it was estimated that all three together would fetch no more than $75 million.[24]

- MuchMusic, owned by millionaire Moses Znaimer, received $250,000 from Multiculturalism Canada in 1999.

Two boondoggle lists:

Alberta & Atlantic Canada

Are there concrete reasons why governments should steer clear of business loans and subsidies—besides the overwhelming academic case against such intervention in the marketplace? In chapter eight, I noted the academic arguments against corporate welfare. When governments become involved in corporate welfare they regularly produce boondoggle lists. Here are two examples:

The first is from just *one* federal economic development agency, the Atlantic Canada Opportunities Agency (ACOA), where $97 million was lost between 1987 and 1994. The second is from the Alberta government's disastrous experiment in business subsidies, loans and loan guarantees over a 14-year period, a costly venture of $2.3 billion to taxpayers in that province.

The misadventures of ACOA

In 1995, the Canadian Press received a confidential inside audit of the Atlantic Canada Opportunities Agency (ACOA), the federal Crown corporation that hands out loans, loan guarantees and grants in the four Maritime provinces. The internal audit examined 17 large projects that collapsed after receiving federal grants and loan guarantees. Details of the ventures by province are followed by the date of agency approval and then the receivership year and the cost to taxpayers.

Newfoundland

St. Christopher's Resort Inc., Terra Nova Provincial Park - 1989-92, $4 million

Governor's Park Inc., Kelligrews - 1986-91, $3.6 million

Prince Edward Island

Marine Harvesting Ltd., Georgetown - 1987-88, $2.4 million

Charlottetown Metal Products Ltd., Charlottetown - 1989-91, $370,000

Nova Scotia

Avstar Aerospace Corp., Sydney - 1988-90, $22.7 million

N.S.C. Diesel Power Inc., Sheet Harbour - 1988-90, $10.5 million

Gasco Manufacturing Ltd., Mulgrave - 1985-91, $5.7 million

Arrow LM Ltd., Port Hawkesbury - 1987-89, $4.5 million

WCN Communications (Canada) Inc., Sydney - 1987-91, $4.5 million

High Tech Woodworkers Ltd., Hammond Plains - 1989-91, $4.3 million

Technitread Tire Manufacturing, Glace Bay - 1988-1990, $3 million

New Brunswick

Presswood Pallet Partnership, Grand Falls - 1988-91, $17.5 million

Ampal Pallets Ltd., Saint John - $10.1 million

La ferme pisicole Theriault Ltee., Drummond - 1987-89, $1.4 million

Negoot Gook Salmon Farms, Perth-Andover - 1989-92, $1.4 million

Softwood Fencing Supply Ltd., Woodstock - 1988-89, $850,000

Valley Land and Water Ltd., Woodstock - 1986-90, $510,000

Total: $97.3 million, of which $56.5 million was already paid out.

Source: *Access to Information* request by the Canadian Press, reported 5 September 1995, *Vancouver Sun*

Alberta government business boondoggles 1980-1994

Novatel	$646 million
Swan Hills Waste Treatment Plant	$410 million
Lloydminister Bi-provincial Upgrader	$392 million
Gainers	$209 million
Millar Western	$199 million
Magnesium Company of Canada	$164 million
Syncrude	$81 million
Chembiomed	$58 million
Northern Lite Canola	$51 million
General Systems Research	$31 million
Fletcher's Foods	$15 million
Northern Steel	$12 million
North West Trust	$11 million
Alberta Pacific Teminals	$11 million
Myrias Research	$8 million
Peace River Fertilizer	$8 million
Alberta Terminals	$6 million
General Composites Canada	$4 million
Ski Kananaskis	$3 million
Teknica Resource Development	$2 million
Norstar Recreation Products	$2 million
Others Under $2 million	$7 million
TOTAL	**$2,330 MILLION**

Source: Alberta Public Accounts,1980-1995. Compiled by the Canadian Taxpayers Federation

14

Rethinking Canada's third world

To believe that the power which is conferred on the state is merely transferred to it from others is erroneous. It is a power which is newly created and which in a competitive society nobody possesses. So long as property is divided among many owners, none of them acting independently has exclusive power to determine the income and position of particular people.

Friederich Hayek, The Road to Serfdom[1]

1867 and the question of modern racism

One of this country's best political thinkers, Gordon Gibson, has bluntly noted that Canada in 1867 was a far different country than the one we know today, and one not positive for many people:

> When our constitution was written, in 1867, the world of that day was racist, sexist and bigoted. Indians were thought inferior, and so were Chinese, women and Jews, even Catholics. One hundred and thirty-some years later, women, Chinese, Jews and so on are part of ordinary society. Indians aren't, and I suggest to you that that is because they have the defect of being mentioned in the constitution.[2]

But, as Gibson also argues, 21st-century Canada is not the Dominion of the 1860s. Most Canadians' present-day attitudes are fairly liberal towards what some refer to as "minorities."[a] That most Canadians now have good intentions towards Native Canadians is undeniable though exceptions unfortunately do exist.

---

[a] While the term "minority" is widespread, the term itself is philosophically and politically problematic and carries with it a number of rarely examined assumptions. For more on this discussion, see the excerpt at the end of this chapter.

Racism or regressive economic policy?

Not everyone agrees that discrimination is a diminishing problem and some assume that racism, either stark or what some label as "systemic," is still the main cause for what ails Native Canadians. The Chief of the Assembly of First Nations argued from this view in his speech in Durban, South Africa, in 2001:

> However, at home in Canada, the oppression, marginalization and dispossession of indigenous peoples continue.... The lesson for me is that colonial and discriminatory policies and practices are not restricted to less-developed parts of the world. They are also to be found in Australia, Canada, New Zealand, the United States and Scandinavia, to name a few examples. Indigenous peoples everywhere are being "pushed to the edge of extinction"—even in Canada, where the plentiful land, resources and capacity exist to correct these ongoing injustices.[3]

Mr. Coon Come's assertion can be challenged on a number of grounds, not least of which is the multi-billion-dollar funding provided to Native Canadians annually. One could also point to set-aside government contracts and racial quotas in government and in business. But his assertion is unfortunate as it assumes that racism is mainly to blame for the poor condition in which many Native Canadians find themselves. Little thought is given to the possibility that it may be more likely due to regressive economic policy.[b]

The belief that racism (in whatever form) is the core problem is to assume a 19th-century cause as the main reason for present-day conditions in some Indian communities: rampant poverty, Third World living conditions, and social problems multiple that of the mainstream population.

But the claim of racism as the main reason for the lack of substantive economic progress is questionable. It no doubt applies in specific cases and forms *part* of the reason for the lack of economic progress. But

---

[b] The words Aboriginal, Native and Indian are often used interchangeably to describe those peoples whose ancestors lived in North America before European contact and whose descendants live here now. Much of the government funding in Canada is directed towards status Indians, Inuit and Metis (though significantly more to the first and not the third group) so defined as such under the *Indian Act*. There are Native Canadians who are not status Indians; there are status Indians who do not live on reserves. I am reluctant to use the term Indian as it carries with it its own historical baggage, but it is the official term insofar as the *Indian Act* is concerned. In this chapter, I use the term Indian to refer to reserve-specific and *Act*-specific matters. At other times, I use the words Aboriginal and Native interchangeably.

other minorities have also been heavily discriminated against in the past and have propelled themselves ahead of other Canadians in their wealth and living standards. Japanese Canadians suffered discrimination when they were stripped of their land and shunted to internment camps during World War Two. Worldwide, Jews have suffered historic discrimination as well and perhaps more than most. But over the last half-century, both groups have prospered despite that tragic legacy.

To bring up the discrimination suffered by other Canadians or groups in history would usually be pointless; the suffering of one person is hardly alleviated by the knowledge that someone, somewhere else in time, has also been victimized. But in terms of political remedies, the successful economic progress of Japanese and Jewish Canadians to overcome the effects of stark racism should serve as a clue that there may be other, more systemic reasons for the awful social and economic conditions of Native Canadians (and on reserves in particular) as opposed to racism.

The record of taxpayers is one of generosity

In the 1990s as all other programs were cut, money spent on Native Canadians by the federal government continued to rise. Presently, about $6.5 billion is spent federally every year with additional spending by the provinces. With just federal spending on Native programs, real per-capita spending in the 1990s rose to $8,479 by 2002 from $7,289 in 1991—and the 2002 figure is *after* accounting for inflation.[4] And it is money spent in addition to other services available to Aboriginal and non-Aboriginal people alike.

The money: There has been progress

Insofar as money spent, it would be incorrect to say that it has had no effect. On life expectancy, between 1991 and 1996, Native Canadians improved to 68.2 years for males and 75.9 for females (from 66.9 years and 74 years respectively). And the gap *between* native life expectancy and other Canadians has narrowed, marginally, to a gap of 7.5 years from 7.7 years (males) or to a gap of 5.6 years from 6.9 years (females) over the same census period. There are also some positive indicators regarding family income and education.[5]

Causation or correlation?

As positive as some trends are, it is not clear that increased funding has been the sole or even primary cause of it. For example, life expectancy has increased worldwide as have health indicators. And while some trend lines are up as regards those measurements for Native Canadians, is it because of money spent on reserves or is it because more Native Canadians moved to cities? (In 2000, 42 percent of Indians lived off reserve, compared to 30 percent in 1980.[6]) In urban areas, living conditions and socio-economic status have always been higher compared to rural areas.

Meanwhile, some troubling statistics remain. On reserves, unemployment was 29 percent in 2001, a figure which understates the joblessness given that Native participation in the labour market is about two-thirds of that for the general population. Moreover, welfare dependency is still high and did not drop over the 1990s compared to the noticeable decline in general for the population at large.

It is racist to ignore the problem; it is Native Canadians who suffer most

Ironically, while the charge of racism is occasionally thrown at non-Natives for the mere discussion of Native policy, the most racist approach one could take is to ignore present policies. What could be more harmful than to never question which money and which programs work and which do not?

After all, if a racist wanted to see large portions of Natives continue to live in sub-standard social conditions and to be deprived of opportunity, the status quo approach would be the method of choice. Such a person would ignore the current top-down economic "strategies" which ignore supply and demand, accountability issues, and the importance of property rights in wealth creation.

By now, based on worldwide evidence from many different cultures and countries over time, it should be recognized that incentives matter. If economic incentives are structured to reward poor governance and allow for corruption, no one should be surprised at the result. In Canada, the media in particular should treat government policy on Native issues and Native leaders with the same degree of scrutiny as they do other policies and politicians. To do otherwise is to patronize in a manner that assumes such politicians cannot handle the scrutiny given to "regular" Canadians.

The red herring charge of racism aside, it is Aboriginals themselves who suffer most because of current perverse incentives. Take crime statistics as an example. Most Aboriginal crime is directed toward other Natives. And in general, urban crime rates are 4.5 times higher than the non-Aboriginal rate in Calgary and 12 times the non-Aboriginal rate in Saskatchewan's two largest cities. Meanwhile, suicide rates are eight times higher for females and five times higher for males aged 18-24 when compared with the general population.[7]

The deficits, excessive travel budgets, and salaries

To live on a reserve in Canada is to exist in a semi-feudal political state. Money is distributed for welfare, housing and education according to the dictates of a band council; some, such as the Six Nations reserve in Ontario, have a very good record at managing band finances. Others have performed poorly. By 2002, the cumulative deficits of Native bands across Canada almost tripled to $373 million from $132 million in 1993 and that despite the constant per-capita increase in funding.[8]

Where has some of the money gone? In some cases to excessive expenses and travel. For example, the 800-member Salteaux band near North Battleford, Saskatchewan received $7.45 million from the federal government in 1998 and the band council spent $600,000 on travel that year—more than the entire travel budget for Saskatchewan's provincial cabinet ministers.[9]

Another problem is that some Native politicians have awarded themselves large salaries that are out of proportion to the communities they serve. Salaries for reserve chiefs in Canada range from an average of $29,590 in British Columbia to an average in the Atlantic provinces of $63,585. Those are tax-free, which means the taxable equivalent range is from $39,443 to $88,369 respectively.[10]

And then there are the clearly excessive salaries. The *Edmonton Journal* reported that the chief of the Alberta-based 360-member Horse Lake Indian band took home $439,425 in a tax-free salary in 2001. Two other councillors were paid $414,500 tax-free while the band's Director for Special Projects garnered $435,000 tax-free. In comparison, in 2001 the prime minister earned $144,000—all of it taxable.[11]

Too many politicians, too little accountability

One reason reserve Indians may fare so poorly is the overabundance of Native politicians. Thirty-eight hundred chiefs and council members represent Canada's approximately 368,000 Indians who live on reserves—there's one for every 97 Indians on reserve. If Canadians as a whole had such representation, we would have 321,275 politicians.

The total number of politicians in Canada is not available, but it is nowhere near that amount, which can be demonstrated by examining specific cities. If the same ratio of politicians to people existed in Regina as exists on Indian reserves, that city would have 2,082 politicians instead of 38.[12]

There are likely to be two objections to this analysis. The first will be that the sheer number of Native bands across the country means that more politicians will exist. The second is that taxable-equivalent salaries that range from $39,443 to $88,369 are similar to what mayors in many non-Native cities and towns may take home.

But such objections would not be correct. Most reserves have less than one thousand people; many are only in the hundreds. Equivalent Canadian towns and villages have, at best, part-time mayors paid very small part-time salaries. And the objection that more reserves necessitates more politicians itself points out the absurdity and the problems of numerous, lightly populated hamlets propped at a large expense to taxpayers. Elsewhere, amalgamation under a lightly staffed administrative body for a larger region would occur for reasons of cost-effectiveness. And five-figure salaries for mayors of villages of several hundred people would be out of the question. Amalgamation issues aside, there is no reason why political salaries on reserves cannot be reduced to reasonable levels and the money spent elsewhere—on proper housing

If Regina had as many politicians per person as do Native reserves

	Current population	Ratio of people to politicians	Existing number of politicians	If same number of politicians as Native reserves
Native reserves Across Canada	368,556	97 to 1	3,800	3,800
Regina*	202,000	5,316 to 1	38	2,082

*Regina numbers include city council members, MLAs, MPs and members of two schoolboards.

and repairs, for example. Native Canadians have too many politicians and some are paid far above what can be considered reasonable.

Easy money and easy water: Both are wasted

It is not surprising that there are instances of poor financial controls, deficits, corruption and nepotism on reserves. To award large amounts of money to a politically controlled entity (a reserve) from a colonial outpost (Ottawa) instead of collecting taxes by consent of the locally governed, is a recipe for such ills. It has nothing to do with skin colour or ethnic heritage.

For example, while the federal auditor general does not now have the legal authority to track money once it reaches a particular Native council, individual Natives also cannot always access band budgets and financial statements. But the accountability will not be improved merely by hiring more accountants.[c]

One primary reason for the poor accountability of reserve expenditures is the direction of the money flow. There are over 2,300 reserves in Canada. Even if the budget of the federal auditor general's agency were increased a hundred-fold to carry out the mammoth task of reviewing every band's books, the attempt would miss the point: bottom-up accountability by Native Canadians themselves is needed as an effective and permanent check, just as other Canadians have vis-à-vis their local city councils.

The current method of collection and expenditures of Native reserve money contrasts with how responsible government anywhere in the world works. That is to say, citizens are directly taxed (in most cases) within a city, province or country for (most of) the money spent by that level of government.[c] And it is that *direct* link which promotes accountability. It is not enough to be able to elect the people who spend one's money; it must be coupled with the ability to collect that money (on the part of the politicians) for it is the latter which compels voters to be vigilant.

For example, if a Montrealer did not pay taxes directly to city hall, what motivation is there for voting, other than civic duty? If all the money to run a city originates elsewhere, there is no reason to complain, pressure or even vote. Nor, assuming money for city spending came from Ottawa, would there be much reason to complain to the distant capital. One would be lost in the bureaucratic maze.

There are, admittedly, problems with even this approach. Money for "free" creates its own dependency; moreover, Native leaders themselves have argued, sometimes correctly, that the state of personal financial management by some Natives is poor. But if money is to be transferred, better that the money is given directly and that

---

[c] At the Canadian Taxpayers Federation, we often receive calls and visits from Native Canadians who are not given the documents necessary to determine how money is spent on their reserve.

people learn how to manage their own finances individually rather than allow the current state of affairs to continue. In the worst-case scenarios, Native Canadians would still have access to the social support programs now in place for all Canadians.

Ultimately, it is political pressure on politicians that compels transparency, accountability and the better use of tax dollars. And that political pressure is at its strongest when there is a direct link between the taxpayers and those who collect and spend the taxes. No additional piling on of rules, laws, regulations, or multiple auditors can have the same effect as local taxpayers who demand that their government manage honestly and lightly the public purse. Where such pressure is intense and where those in office resist it, such people are invariably turned out of office.

The effect of this would prompt more civic participation on the part of Native Canadians and inject accountability into reserve governments. If someone receives a gross monthly cheque for $2,500 but finds that $1,000 was deducted and sent to their Native councils, that person is far more likely to vote and push for reforms. Alternately, they may leave the reserve entirely if they feel the money is not handled properly and move to another area where governance is better. Or they may move to a major Canadian city. Regardless, accountability is enhanced and reserve governments that do not shape up will find that they lose inhabitants *and* their tax dollars.

It may be helpful to think of a parallel example, that of water that flows down a hill. The very availability of water in plentiful and "easy" amounts means that those who use it are not particularly judicious with its use. However, where water is scarce, when it must be pumped into an area—or uphill—the use and amount of that water is more carefully controlled, precisely because it is so expensive and difficult to obtain.

Thus, the only way to have better political accountability is not to "rain" down money from Ottawa into reserves (or have-not governments); "free" money is never as carefully used as is "costly" money. It is only when a political price exists for the extraction of money from voters that checks and balances are introduced into a political system and such funds are then handled with much more care. It is why Jean Baptiste Colbert, Controller-General to Louis the XIV, noted that the "art of taxation consists in so

[d] As noted in Chapter 12, the exception is transfer payments between different levels of government. As also noted, such payments also create a similar problem where perverse political incentives are created, i.e., prospective politicians promise "goodies" to be paid for by taxpayers in other jurisdictions.

plucking the goose as to obtain the largest amount of feathers with the least possible amount of hissing." The hissing only exists when subjects see the taxes taken and have a good idea of who carries out the deed.

Instead of the current top-down system where Ottawa sends money to reserve councils who then apportion it out, money should flow to individuals and families and then be taxed back by the local reserve government. This in fact is the intriguing suggestion from a Manitoba Metis, Jean R. Allard. The former Manitoba New Democrat MLA suggests that treaty entitlements be updated to reflect inflation, but that such treaty payments then be subtracted from the money the federal government sends to band councils across the country. This, he argues, would honour the original spirit and letter of treaties, but would remove some funding for band councils and instead direct it to those for whom the original treaties intended it: individual Natives themselves.[13] It would also help clean up the problem of corruption on reserves and make bands more accountable:

> Since there is no real separation between politics and administration on reserves, everything that is any way related to band administration is politicized. Whoever is elected is in control of just about everything on a reserve. The result is elections coloured by bitter rivalries and ugly disputes.

> Reserves are one-dimensional systems. Elsewhere in Canadian society, a variety of choices act as checks and balances on each other. The interests of unions, for instance, temper the interest of business lobby groups. Those who speak for individual rights temper those who advocate collective rights. There are no such "other voices" on reserves, leaving the single dimension of politics in which to work out solutions to social economic and political problems.[14]

Economic progress flows from property rights

Native leaders in Canada have asked for everything but what is most likely to ameliorate the rotten environment in the long term: full individual property rights and all the protections and incentives that such rights might provide.

---

[e] For more on why individual property rights matter in terms of wealth creation, see Hernando de Soto's *The Mystery of Capital* (New York: Basic Books, 2000). The Peruvian author makes a compelling case for easily registered property and transferable property as the key to unleash "dead" capital, which spurs wealth creation.

Individual property rights combined with a local tax base spurs accountability and would put Native leaders in the service of Native property-holders, the exact reverse of the current system. Every society on the planet that advances economically does so on the basis of such a model.[e]

Reserves that remain owned communally can never be used for individual collateral. Without that, there is little incentive for improvement to the land or risk-taking with the property, as there are no long-term benefits to such actions. (Few people invest much money in an apartment they rent.) As a consequence, there is no significant local tax base from which to promote responsible taxation and expenditure decisions of Indian governments.

But if that right of individual property with all its benefits and risks is not yet realized, it is due to many Native leaders themselves and to non-Native politicians who cannot conceive of individual Natives as anything but dependent on government—an assumption which is neither historical, fair, nor necessary.

For those who want economic progress, it makes eminent sense to at least parcel sections of individual reserves as private property. To go one step further, governments should recognize in law the right of Indians to treat such private property as sellable no matter the Aboriginal buyer and no matter the reserve in question.[f] Make it a fully voluntary and private transaction fully enforceable in the courts. For now, politics will dictate that reserve land is transferred only between Natives, but parcels of reserves—at least for Natives—would be a significant improvement on the current system of communally owned and controlled land that now exists.

Admittedly, there are likely two objections to this proposal. First, Indians are divided into different reserves precisely because they have different ancestral roots and it would be highly unlikely that a Cree (for example) would desire to live on a reserve that is primarily MikMaq or vice versa. While this may be true, it is also the case that such narrow affiliations are occasionally overcome over time. This is the essence and the assumption of liberal cosmopolitanism; i.e., people have the right to live with whom and where they choose without regard to public pres-

---

[f] As Tom Flanagan and Christopher Alcantara have explained elsewhere, there is a form of private property on reserves though not to the extent that exists off-reserve. Such forms include customary rights, new land codes under the recent *First Nations Land Management Act*, and leases. They point to Six Nations reserve in Ontario as a laudable example. The difference is that individual parcels on Six Nations property are privately owned in a manner similar to off-reserve property.[15]

sure or government interference. If an Italian wants to live in a predominantly Jewish neighbourhood, or a Chinese family wishes to live in a mostly Caucasian area, it is their business and not that of anyone else, especially not that of the state.

The negative word for the preference of one's own to another ethnic group is tribalism. In a world where such notions of ethnic separatism are resurgent similar to the mid-19th-century surge in nationalism, citizens who desire better relations between not only Aboriginal and other Canadians but between Natives themselves should squarely face the undesirable cultural and social assumptions that underlie such politics.

True, people always form exclusive groups, as in the choices of religion and family or friends, for example, and such exclusiveness is most often healthy. But to discriminate in the choice of one's spouse or friends is not at all similar to state-enforced segregation that promotes such ethnic segregation as an assumed policy.

A system of property rights on reserve is desirable not only for economic reasons but also for social ones. If that means that no Cree ever lives on the (reserve) private property of a Huron, so be it, if it is a voluntary choice. But surely government policy ought to allow for voluntary mingling of different peoples and not artificially prevent the same. This free movement of people of diverse races used to be a goal of most who think of themselves as progressive, liberal and cosmopolitan. Few have noticed the dramatic shift that now, by default at least, endorses ethnic separatism.

Another objection is that the limitation of private property on reserves to Natives will artificially limit its value in contrast to what it might be worth if reserve land was treated as fully private property and was tradable between all Canadians. Given that there would be relatively fewer buyers due to the fact that Aboriginals are a small percentage of Canada's population, the criticism is correct. Whenever the number of buyers for property is artificially limited, the price of it is likewise limited.

But the political reality is that many Natives and politicians are unwilling to consider this prospect at present, and some perhaps never will. But a system of fully tradable private property between Native Canadians on reserves would at least give Aboriginals the chance to own property, with all its attendant benefits and responsibilities, including leasing their property to non-Natives in greater amounts and thus plugging into the mainstream economy. It is a start, and the financial incentives for eventually opening up reserve property to all will become evident to their owners over time. Should they desire that, Native Canadians could lobby their local governments on greater freedom to do with their property as they like.

Moreover, such a system would encourage better governance. Those reserves that are better run, where the leaders are adequately but not exorbitantly paid, where the services available are consistent with those off reserve in a city, and where the schools teach lifelong skills, would attract those who wished to live under such conditions. The effect that such pressure—from the ground up—would have on Native governments could be revolutionary in the most positive sense.

The case for a new cosmopolitanism based on individual choice and not group entitlements should be made by those interested in a more liberal and cosmopolitan view of the world, Native or non-Native, especially because the trend in Canada has moved in the opposite direction. Urban liberal thought used to believe that sectarian division based on race, religion, or ethnicity was an embarrassment, a holdover from the 19th century. This view has crumbled as of late and many who now consider themselves progressive seem to have little problem with the division of peoples based on their racial or ethnic background. That some have slouched towards such thinking and policy does not also make it desirable.

Defining Minorities

The term "minority" is problematic because it presupposes a category people may not in fact care to be placed within. For example, a Japanese-Canadian may be referred to as a minority on the basis that Japanese Canadians are, visibly, a minority. But that assumes the individual in question values their ethnicity above all else. They may value their religion or their politics or their work more than their background and it may be in the former description that they choose to find their primary identity.

To assume a minority status is to make assumptions about someone that may well be unjustified. In a political context, it leads to division based on ethnicity (or in some cases, gender) and calls for representation based on the same.

For example, the argument that because women make up 52 percent of the population they should be guaranteed 52 percent of the seats in Parliament is a similar and erroneous assumption. It may well be that some women choose a political party and candidates based on political philosophy and not gender; a woman may vote for a male candidate who shares her views on the environment, for example. Similarly, British men may have voted in the 1980s, for example, for Margaret Thatcher because that particular voter preferred market economic policy to that of the British Labour party.

The gender of the person, as with other categories, may or may not be the primary way a person identifies themselves in a political context, and thus to mandate representation based on gender, ethnicity or another category is to assume—from the outside—all who fit into that category value that identification above all else. To lock people into categories, especially in any sort of preferential political sense, is to assume all Aboriginals, all Japanese, or all women see themselves in a certain way or have the same opinions and politics, or even value their ethnicity or gender above all else. They may well not.

The protection of individual rights as opposed to group rights allows people to choose which collective they will voluntarily belong to and identify with and without coercion. The attempt to cast people into predetermined categories assumes loyalties on their behalf and is the very antithesis of freedom.

15

Civilization and taxes

There is no snobbishness like that of professional egalitarians.
Malcolm Muggeridge, *Chronicles of Wasted Time*

Adam Smith and Oliver Wendell Holmes Jr.

"There is no art which one government sooner learns of another than that of draining money from the pockets of people," said Adam Smith in the *Wealth of Nations* in 1776. "Taxes are the price we pay for civilization," replied U.S. Supreme Court Justice Oliver Wendell Holmes Jr. in Compañia de Tabacos *v.* Collector in 1904.

Similar to any statement with a nugget of truth, once a saying becomes a cliché the reasonableness of the original point is lost in present justifications. What may be appropriate to live by in one age may hardly be prudent in another; the applicability of a statement depends on context. About the time Justice Holmes uttered his now-famous dictum, federal taxes in the United States amounted to 1.3 percent of the U.S. economy.[1] One century later in America, federal taxes alone amount to nearly 20 times that.

In Canada, and to go beyond just federal taxes to a more comprehensive measurement of government near to the time of Justice Holmes' remark, total government expenditures amounted to $77 million. As a percentage of the economy, that amount translated into 9.5 percent of Gross National Expenditures (GNE) in 1900 and 11.4 percent in 1910. (In contrast, in 1870 total government expenditures amounted to 6.8 percent of GNE.)[2]

Without (some) taxes and (some) government, life might well be, as the philosopher Thomas Hobbes once wrote, "nasty, brutish and short." Certainly tax-and-spend types seem to argue the result of any lower taxes would be a society where people are left to face marauding bandits akin to the characters in the 1970s film *Road Warrior*.

But Hollywood nightmare scenarios are of little help when it comes to a policy decision on actual tax rates. Follow the logic of the assumption that more taxes equals more civilization. If taxes, which presently constitute 37.5 percent of the economy in Canada (with actual government expenditures higher yet at 41.9 and total revenues at 42.7 percent), make for a superior civilization, does it follow that 38 percent or 39 percent, or 75 percent thus equals even *more* civilization?

Take the end result of such an assumption. Given the nature of the state vis-à-vis the citizen in the now-defunct Soviet Union, one can argue that almost 100 percent of that country was "taxed" as everything and everyone was in effect property of the state. Would anyone seriously argue that the Soviet Union, *gulags* and all, represented the pinnacle of civilization, and that a comparatively lesser-taxed country, say Switzerland or Canada, was *less* civilized?

Adam Smith was correct about the tendency of governments to tax as a default option. Justice Holmes was right about taxes and civilization, but only to a point. The belief that enough smart people plus more tax dollars as the solution to a problem is a perennial temptation to intellectuals and to politicians no matter their political stripe. But after 30 years of ever-higher taxes in Canada, we long ago passed the point necessary for taxes as a foundation for civilization. Instead, increased taxation has become a presumed cure-all for any public policy problem, or even private ills.

It is one thing to use tax dollars to support low-income families with relief in the dust bowl Thirties on the prairies. That makes sense and is compassionate and a more-than-justifiable use of tax dollars. It is quite another to have government departments redistribute hard-earned tax dollars to corporations, special interest groups, and even back to rich and middle-income earners through redistribution or services when in some cases, middle income and rich Canadians could purchase such services in a competitive marketplace without the middleman of government. (Think of the plethora of government-owned auto insurance companies or government-run liquor stores; in neither case does market failure exist.)

Why focused government priorities matter

If government is a given, it follows then that choices must continually be made as to what governments should spend tax dollars on. September 11, 2001, was a reminder that mortal threats to free states have not disappeared. Francis Fukuyama's much-misunderstood thesis on the end of history was prescient in that he did accurately note the absence of a coherent and attractive "idea" to compete with free markets and free political systems, competitor positions once occupied by socialism and fascism at various points during the last century.[3]

But if Fukuyama was correct about that lack of competition in the marketplace of ideas, he (and most of the rest of us) underestimated the power of belief, especially of the religious type to be taken to an extreme and to shatter assumptions about our security. In his sense of the next "great" struggle, Harvard political scientist Samuel Huntington's observation about the looming clash of civilizations was closer to the mark.[a]

After the 2001 terrorist attacks, advocates for ever-more state intervention argued that the assaults reinforced the need for government, *big* government. Anti-globalization activist Naomi Klein argued that after September 11 there was "a groundswell of appreciation for public-sector workers of all kinds. In short, 'the commons'— the public sphere, the public good, the non-corporate, what we have been defending."[4]

But it is a caricature of the case for limited government to suggest that limited government is equivalent to *no* government. And Klein, as with other anti-capitalists, mistakenly equate the commons and the public good with government spending, control, and intervention for its own sake. That much of modern education and hospitals were first preceded and set up by devoted religious adherents (nuns, for example) that responded to a higher calling often escapes those who mistakenly believe that civilization and a caring society must begin and end with government.

Most, if not all of the impulses to virtue, charity and other desirable moral characteristics are rarely inculcated by the state; they are instilled by or absorbed from parents, religion in some cases, philosophies of life in others and the society and culture in which one participates consciously and unconsciously.

But the attacks of September 11 did remind people that governments are necessary, if they ever doubted such. Properly restrained, a limited state can be a foundation for civilization if it secures its borders, enforces the rule of law, provides a basic safety net, and attends to other matters that require government power and action and, in dire situations, goes to war to defend the same.

But there is a sharp double-edge to the existence of the state and government power; unleashed, the Leviathan state itself becomes nasty and brutish. Governments in the 20th century—especially those with complete political, military *and* economic power—killed more people

---

[a] See Francis Fukuyama's *The End of History and the Last Man*, The Free Press (1992), and Samuel Huntington's *The Clash of Civilizations and the Remaking of the World Order*, Simon & Schuster (1996).

than ever before in history; Communist governments alone were responsible for 100 million deaths.[5] It is when the three areas just named are concentrated in the grasp of one entity that citizens are most in danger, which is why the division of powers and the dilution of influence, both through the structure of government and by limits to government, are critical.

The history of the last century alone should be reason enough to maintain a sceptical bias towards government as virtuous in and of itself. The onus must be on politicians and governments to prove they ought to be allowed liberty to take *our* liberties and not the reverse—where citizens must constantly prove they are capable of possessing freedom.

That noted, except for hard-core libertarians, no one who recognizes the virtue of limited government ever argued that Canada should do without a government or even a military. It was not an accident that Pierre Trudeau presided over the decline and hollowing out of Canada's once-proud defence; it was intentional. More often it was and is those who believe in government as inherently good that have argued, if not directly then often by neglect, for the decline of the armed forces.

It is those most infatuated with government for its own sake who are generally the most opposed to increases in defence and security budgets. They generally believe that most problems are structural and social and that people—even dictators who kill their own—can be negotiated with and talked out of their lust for power. It is a fatal flaw that stems from the kind-hearted assumption that ultimately all are decent; the prospect that some are consumed by their own lust for power is not understood by those who apologize for tyrants or refuse to take them seriously. Such people mistakenly think that everyone possesses the good intentions they themselves have.

And in a world where the newest threats may come from rogue states and small cabals that move in the shadows, the role of states in guarding the soft underbelly of civilization is obvious. Governments will need to spend money on the military, on the security apparatus and in other areas to build in safeguards. But that calls for focus with both their efforts and with our tax dollars, not an assumed octopus-like grasp on all areas political, economic and social.

Thus, far from a blank-cheque endorsement of government for its own sake in Canada—as opposed to its existence for its citizens—two very different starting points, the terrorist attacks should serve as an historical marker to rethink where Canadians want their tax dollars spent.

The welfare state: For better and worse

Once upon a time, there were justifiable historical reasons for the growth of government in Canada. What the *Economist* notes about pre-1950s spending in Western governments in general is also true of Canada in specific:

> Up until the 1950s, increases in public spending did seem to produce worthwhile improvements in healthcare and education. Certainly up until the 1930s, the larger part of expanding government expenditure was taken up by investment in infrastructure, the supply of essential public services, and the creation of a low-level safety net to guard against poverty. In all these respects, it could be argued, the state was attending to things that the market, left to its own devices, would neglect. In those days, a much larger share of public spending was devoted to dealing with genuine "market failures," as they would now be called.[6]

The pattern was similar in Canada. In the 1920s, the explosion of automobile ownership, for example, necessitated the building of roads that led to gasoline and registration taxes and a resulting growth in government. In the 1930s, new relief provided by taxpayers to fellow citizens was a sensible and compassionate response to the Great Depression.

But post-mid-century, government expanded far past areas where the market arguably had failed and set up programs and services for both poor *and* rich, for both the destitute and for big business. But that created inefficiencies and absurdities. For example, what ever was the point of giving family allowance cheques to millionaires? To send tax dollars back to the very people who send the money in the first place, *after* the recycling of such money through a bureaucracy, benefits no one. Targeted subsidies make sense; unfocused universal subsidies simply create a bureaucracy.

Post-World War Two, and with the exception of a dramatic expenditure rise due to the Korean War in the early 1950s, there was a substantial rise in transfers. Tax historian J. Harvey Perry:

> Social expenditures—health, education and welfare—accounted for the greater part of the rise in government expenditures between 1947 and 1977. From 1965 to 1976 the three together accounted for 68 percent of the total growth and by 1976 accounted for over 21 percent of GNE [Gross National Expenditures]—half of total government spending.[7]

Perry notes though that transfers also began to change in shape and form after the mid-1970s and dramatic increases in "non-personal" transfers occurred, which included categories such as debt interest, subsidies, and corporate welfare.[8]

Thus, from an original 1930s impulse to provide money and services to people in need and who could not provide for themselves, by the 1970s, government redistribution was at least partly transformed; now big business and provincial governments (more than before) were included in the redistributive scheme of things. And the envisioned programs were invariably always much more expensive than originally forecast.

> As the history of individual programs reveals, cost estimates presented at their time were grossly below ultimate results. But despite this recurring experience new programs and additions to existing programs continue to be introduced. One federal Minister of Finance, the Hon. Mitchell Sharp, was concerned enough to hold off implementation of Medicare for a year in the late sixties, but this had no apparent effect as an example for later programs. Despite strong inflationary pressure and growing budget deficits, in the next decade, several billions in costs were added through the expansion of Unemployment Insurance, the enrichment of Family Allowances, the introduction of the Extended Health Care in 1976 and the Child Tax Credit in 1979. As well, the most extravagant method of indexation—adjustment for the full extent of inflation—was adopted.[9]

By the last quarter of the 20th century, Canadian governments, even conservative-labelled ones in provinces such as Alberta, possessed the "commanding heights" of the economy. They owned and ran businesses that, without government ownership and intervention, would have risen and fallen as conditions and consumer preferences dictated, in other words, as happened every day for most enterprises.

Instead, government-owned businesses were subject to political control and interference. The result was that tens of billions of dollars were wasted to buy and prop up entities that were later closed or sold at a loss. (Think of government takeovers of coalmines in Nova Scotia and acquisitions of oil companies that later became Petro-Canada, as well as airlines such as Pacific Western Airlines and Air Canada, to name but a few.)[b]

In retrospect, one might argue that citizens and companies should have been responsible for the cost of such 1920s infrastructure as roads (and many environmentalists might agree but for different reasons). Perhaps, but the political reality of the time led to different results. Today, user-pay assumptions are more accepted if not always popular; for example, few argue that taxpayers should subsidize the business traveller's airline ticket or the airport itself. Increasingly, those that want such services bear the cost of its provision.

More of that can and should be done across government as a whole, including outright privatization but also competition for the provision of public services and routine duties still largely performed by government. For example, governments contract out when they lease computers or cars and would not think of setting up a bureaucracy to build such items; there is no reason that governments cannot also tender out the provision of services, be it accounting or janitorial work in hospitals. Competition is what leads private sector companies to find efficiencies and to provide better service. Canadian governments are notably behind other countries in this area, though there are exceptions. Canada's politicians should look to merely subsidize specific citizens with lower incomes for specific necessary services, not attempt to own and run such services via a ministry or Crown corporation.

Plenty of workers made generous subsidies possible

But the expansion of the Canadian welfare state beyond original, targeted (for relief of the poor and for conditions of market failure) and justifiable reasons was also helped by the demographic makeup of Canada at that time.

When the Canada Pension Plan took on its current form and government involvement in health care expanded dramatically in the 1960s, there were eight working Canadians for every one retiree. Now the ratio is five-to-one, and in several decades, there will only be three workers for every one retiree. It was thus easy to finance both health care and retirement pensions out of the public purse, out of current taxes, when the ratio of workers to retirees was plentiful.

Pre-funding for retirement (as has always been done by individuals, companies and unions and lately by the recent set-asides in the Canada Pension Plan) was unnecessary to consider at a political level until

---

[b] "Tens of billions of dollars" might be thought to be an exaggeration. It is not. The buying of the companies that became Petro-Canada alone was estimated to have cost $4.2 billion, plus $2 billion in grants when the Crown corporation went through its first privatization round in 1991. Peter Foster, author of *Self-Serve: How Petro-Canada Pumped Canadians Dry*, calculates that by 1992 and excluding grants and factoring in the borrowed money used to buy Petro-Canada, taxpayers lost $11 billion in the deal. Besides Petro-Canada, the federal government lost money on other business-related ventures described in earlier chapters. Provincial governments have also taken similar losses when they owned businesses, subsidized them, or took them over and did both, the $2.3 billion lost by the Alberta government being the most obvious provincial example.

recently. Relatively speaking, there was always plenty of tax revenues and fewer needs given the average age of the population. It was not a particularly difficult balancing act.

But as the average age of the population becomes older, pre-funding of the health care system in particular and revisions to the Canada Pension Plan (a delayed retirement age for example to ease the strain on early payouts) become necessary to not only talk about but to act on. For those interested in expanding opportunity for all, ensuring sensible safety nets based on principles of choice, sustainability, and market principles, many areas need to be considered, but here are a few of the most compelling.

The Canada Pension Plan

Canada Pension Plan taxes have doubled between 1996 and 2003 and together with Quebec Pension Plan taxes, they amount to an estimated $33.8 billion annually in revenues and $27.3 billion in expenditures. That makes the CPP/QPP the third largest federal revenue source after personal income taxes ($89.7 billion) and sales taxes ($40 billion) and the third largest expenditure for the federal government after social services ($55.8 billion) and transfers to the provinces ($28 billion).[c]

The government moved in the direction of market-based reforms when it began to invest money into equity markets, a strategy that gave the Quebec Pension fund higher historic returns than the Canada Pension Plan.

But the Canada Pension Plan serves less as a pension plan and more as a massive intergenerational shift of resources from one generation to another. Current young contributors would be better off if they invested their CPP contributions into a low-interest bank account. Early contributors to the CPP have reaped far beyond what their initial payments would have resulted in had such contributions been funnelled through a company or union plan, for example. The recent restructuring of the CPP has taken away the worst inequities. Before recent reforms, present contributors would have been awarded a net loss for their contributions due to the intergenerational transfer, but the plan is still structured primarily as a redistributive mechanism, not as a pension fund.

---

[c] Note that these figures are derived from Statistics Canada Financial Management Systems, and thus may differ slightly from other measurements of the same. The Quebec government is in charge of the Quebec Pension Plan, but to demonstrate the relative size of the state-funded programs and to be consistent with Statistics Canada measurements that combines both, they are compared here to other federal expenditures and revenues.

Canada Pension Plan
Rates of return for contributors by birth year
(annual percentages)

Birth Year	Nominal	Real
1930	15.4	9.4
1940	10.4	6.1
1950	7.3	4.0
1960	5.9	3.0
1970	5.3	2.3
1980	5.1	2.1
1990	5.0	2.0
2000	5.0	2.0

Source: 18th Actuarial report on the Canada Pension Plan, Office of the Superintendent of Financial Institutions

The result is that younger contributors who give to the current Canada Pension Plan will receive pensions that barely pay back their contributions, never mind any substantial growth. For those born in 1930, the equivalent figure is triple that at nine percent. For someone born in 1960, the real rate of return on their CPP contributions will be three percent. Those born later than 1960 see even more of a disparity, with returns of only between two and 2.3 percent. The rather rich return for early contributors was due to subsequent workers who topped up the benefits of the first recipients into the plan. Many have used another word to describe such funding, and it is wholly accurate: a pyramid scheme.

One argument for the intergenerational transfer of wealth from the younger generation to the older generation is that the older generation paid for the education of the young. While this is true, it is also unconvincing as an argument for the overly punitive effect of the CPP upon younger contributors. *Every generation* must pay for education of the young. But today's post-baby boom generation now faces a CPP bill for those whose contributions were set lower than they would be if the plan was truly a pension plan. Moreover, the post-baby boom generation must repay federal and provincial public debt and finance the growing health care costs that will occur as the baby boom generation moves to and into retirement. Those are three distinct burdens in addition to funding the education of today's young. Reforms should guarantee good pensions for existing seniors and those moving to retirement in the near future. But the inequities of the plan must also be smoothed out.

There are transitional issues to be grappled with, but even without a transition to individual accounts *a la* Chile or Singapore, reforms can be introduced to help offset the cost of the CPP on the younger generation. One key reform is to raise the retirement age from 65 to 70 over a decade or two. And such a move is entirely justifiable: Life expectancy at birth in Canada has increased to over 78 years from 71 years in the early 1960s[10]—a *seven-year* increase—but the age at which one can collect CPP benefits has remained stuck at 65 over that 40-year period. Raising the retirement age would help lower the cost of the Canada Pension Plan for the current generation, which would be fair given the current wide disparity in returns accorded to the different generations.

Employment Insurance

Employment Insurance payments amounted to $18.3 billion in 2001 while expenditures equalled $17.8 billion. Overall, the surplus,[d] though it exists only on paper as an accounting notation, now stands at $36 billion. Besides the obvious attraction for a rate reduction for employees and employers, the program should be restructured to make it at least close to an actual insurance program and not a social welfare program in disguise. That means actuarial principles should be followed and—similar to the Canada Pension Plan—the fund itself should be out of the reach of the general revenue fund and out of the reach of politicians with a short-term horizon.

Foodcare, Seniorcare and Medicare

If governments ran grocery stores, bureaucrats in Ottawa and the provincial capitals would determine how many boxes of Corn Flakes® were to be available in Halifax, Sarnia and Kamloops. Government unions would argue that because food is so vital for human survival only they should be allowed to run farms, grocery stores, and the transportation system that surrounds the provision of foodstuffs. Lobby groups

---

[d] As noted in Chapter 2, EI revenues are collected and spent out of the general revenue fund. There is no separate account with actual money.

would spring up to decry the encroachment of "two-tier foodcare" where some rich folks could buy caviar while the rest of us make do with hamburger. If Canada's governments controlled retirement in the manner that health care is regulated, retirees would not be allowed to save for their retirement outside of the Canada Pension Plan and the government would determine how many Winnebagos and trips to Florida could be bought every year.

The great accomplishment of Canada's health care system is that it is universal; the great failure is that funding decisions are forced through bureaucrats and politicians. No matter how well-intentioned such people are—and they are—the core problem that remains is one common to all top-down attempts to micromanage complex systems: misallocation of resources, and in a political context, political decisions that work against effective use of such resources.[e] The result, according to the World Health Organization, is that Canada's health care system only ranks as the 30th best in the world, not *the* best, as is often and falsely claimed by our political class.[11]

Governments that attempt to fund needed health care only through tax increases will continue to subject health care to political decisions and the predictable misallocation of resources, including a lack of planning, foresight, and pre-funding. And as they try to fund so much through government, they will again resort to tax increases for health care—a path already trod since governments became involved in this area.[f]

In so doing, they will duplicate the Canada Pension Plan increases where rates have doubled since 1996. And there will be no serious thought given to the future and to place money aside for the same.

Instead, the demand to spend money now will drive spending decisions as always happens in politically charged and politically regulated environments. The result is that if present spending trends continue, and based on 1996-2001 data, British Columbia will spend 50 percent of its money on health care by 2007 while Alberta will hit that marker by 2012. Other provinces are not far behind.

This is problematic because the remaining two have provinces of Ontario and Alberta also support the have-nots. Such a situation will pit those provinces against the have-nots and in fact already pits ministries within each province up against the health care interests who now have

---

[e] For more on Canada's health care system, including a 130-year review and comparisons around the world, see *The Patient, The Condition, The Treatment*, a CTF review of Canada's health care system, published in 2001.

[f] Governments have often introduced or raised taxes using health care as the reason. See the excerpt on health taxes at the end of this chapter.

first call on extra dollars that governments spend. Two-thirds of the
new government spending over the past five years has gone to
health care.

Universality without the straitjacket

There are a variety of misconceptions about Canadian health care,
just as there are a number of options for reform of the system that
would give the patient choices and yet preserve universality. Other
countries allow for much more private involvement than does
Canada—every European country for example—and also have universal health care coverage.

Health care as a percentage of provincial budgets: Current and future estimates				
Province	Budget on health	50% of spending	75% of spending	100% of spending
Alberta	29.06%	2012	2020	2025
British Columbia	39.93%	2007	2016	2022
Manitoba	38.30%	2014	2034	2047
Newfoundland	41.70%	2007	2020	2030
New Brunswick	35.73%	2022	2046	2063
Nova Scotia	34.76%	2197	2415	2569
Ontario	37.44%	2030	2071	2099
P.E.I.	35.50%	2025	2052	2072
Quebec	32.34%	2038	2072	2097
Saskatchewan	35.02%	2019	2038	2052

Source: Estimates by the Canadian Taxpayers Federation based on 2001 provincial
budgets. Future estimates based on revenue growth and Health ministry spending over
the 1996-2001 period, i.e., if the same revenue and health care spending trends
continue.

Physician and author Dr. David Gratzer once remarked that Canadians often mistake Medicare—the federal program—with *medical care* itself. They are not one and the same; one is a political document now enshrined in (Medicare) legislation and the other is, to be obvious, how health care is delivered. People are afraid that if you tinker with the funding mechanism (Medicare) that the actual medical care will not be there.

But there is no conflict in allowing private medical care providers to compete for government contracts even if one thinks that only government should write the cheque for medically insured services. The current legislation, the *Canada Health Act*, mandates that government must pay for medically insured services; it does not mandate in any sense who must perform those services, i.e., a government hospital, a private clinic or a non-profit hospital. In any event, the five principles of the *Canada Health Act* are not the Ten Commandments. They are legislative and can be changed.

While the nervousness of some Canadians on this is understandable, the principle of universality—that every Canadian should be covered—need not be given up in the search for more medical providers.

Save for the future

While competition for the provision of medical services is one possible reform of the Canadian health care system, pre-funding individual savings accounts as does Singapore is another option. In that case, individual accounts are kept for citizens who then use the money in their own medical account for basic medical services; past a certain point though (take the example of $1,000) government or private insurance is activated as it also is in catastrophic cases. The idea of a medical savings account, similar to RRSPs, is that individuals have control of the spending, and have an incentive to look for fine medical care but at a fair price. Now, there is no such incentive in the system; the government simply writes cheques and responds to immediate political pressure, which is not always the same as directing resources to where they are most needed. That is one option for reform.[g]

If governments attempt to pre-fund health care on a state level as opposed to an individual level through medical savings accounts, what has happened with the Canada Pension Plan will merely be

---

[g] See Dr. David Gratzer's book *Code Blue: Reviving Canada's Health Care System* for a thorough description of medical savings accounts and how they work in other jurisdictions.

duplicated. Younger contributors will pay a heavier share while they also attempt to pay down federal and provincial debts, finance other government expenditures, and pay the bills that every generation must face: for raising children and paying a mortgage. In short, younger taxpayers will be highly taxed to fund existing Medicare bills while the possibility for strategic individual-based savings accounts—those impervious to demographic shifts and to pyramid-style funding set-ups by governments—will be lost.

Moreover, pre-funding by government without individual savings accounts would negate the very discipline that Canadians themselves would exert on cost pressures within the health care system. With appropriate safeguards, medical savings accounts *de facto* prompt individuals to choose wisely and prudently regarding health care. Such ideas are not a cure-all for the health care system; there is no cure-all treatment, as any amount of money could theoretically be spent on health care or any other service: the question is whether Canada's health care system will continue to be driven by political imperatives as opposed to long-term economically sensible, sustainable, and individual priorities.

Medical savings accounts would at least replace a politically driven system with one partly influenced by individual choice and provide incentives for cost containment. Combined with other measures, such as the allowance for private insurance in the manner private retirement savings are allowed for, would also allow health care spending to increase in tandem with individual choices that make the system more effective.

Why free trade and limited government is inextricably linked

In debates over taxation, people often forget that one significant way to lower taxes is to practise free trade. And in debates over free trade, people often forget the intrinsic moral argument for free markets across countries: it gives people in poorer countries a chance to make a living by selling their goods and services to richer countries. Free trade is not only morally positive, the best reason to support it, there is also an economic benefit.

Worldwide, politicians routinely throw vast sums of money at business and justify the tax dollars because of the subsidies *other* countries provide. One classic example is the aerospace industry. Brazil has provided an interest subsidy of between $2.25 million and $3.75 million (all figures Canadian) per regional jet sold by Embraer. Six years and a thousand jets later, Brazil's taxpayers have pumped between $2.25 billion and $3.75 billion into their aerospace industry under just one subsidy program, according to their Canadian competitor, Bombardier. But Bombardier itself has of course received taxpayer dollars from Canada's government. Thus, the obvious solution is for both governments to declare a truce and spare taxpayers in both countries the bills.

As large as the dollar amounts are in international aerospace disputes, they pale in comparison to business subsidies in general. One credible estimate pegs U.S. subsidies (excluding agricultural subsidies) at between US$99.1 billion and US$131.3 billion annually,[12] while Canada's federal government allocates about Cdn$2.7 billion annually[13] at a minimum (and as much as $4 billion if indirect transfers are included) and provincial governments spend over Cdn$5.4 billion (including the Quebec government which spends $3.1 billion).[14]

To examine select figures from the European Union, that continent's governments have long subsidized various sectors at the expense of taxpayers. In 1997, the EU committed to pouring US$2.1 billion worth of subsidies into Europe's shipbuilding industry.[15] Between 1989 and 1996, Europe's automotive industry received US$6 billion in subsidies.[16]

And then there is the mother of all subsidized trade: agriculture. According to the OECD, Canada spends US$4.2 billion on agricultural subsidies, while the United States spends US$49 billion and the European Union spends almost US$90 billion.[17]

It is time that politicians around the world stopped the subsidy game, especially given that subsidies are expensive for poorer countries and outright risky for lightly populated countries such as Canada. Given our small population, Canada's ability to engage in subsidy wars is limited. While subsidy programs may be politically attractive and successful to one industry in the short term, i.e., aerospace, Canada would be buried by an all-out subsidy war on a number of fronts all at once. After all, we simply do not have enough taxpayers to finance a multi-front war, as the history of losing the agricultural subsidy battle to the Americans and the European Union demonstrates.

International free-trade agreements that eliminate subsidies, impose tough penalties on cheaters, and help give politicians a backbone to say no to corporate welfare are of immense benefit to taxpayers whose money can then be channelled to more efficient, effective, and productive uses. Morally and practically, such agreements are of substantial help to the world's poor who benefit from

being able to sell their goods to markets the world over. With grudg-
ing apologies to V.I. Lenin, taxpayers of the world unite; you have
nothing to lose but the politicians who hand out your money.

Compassion redux

Are there are other positive arguments for limited government?
There is the link between moderately taxed states and positive social indicators. It is a myth that higher government spending leads to
a better-educated and healthier population. There *is* a difference in
social indicator statistics between low-tax countries and high-tax countries, but there is no difference between medium-taxed countries
and high-taxed nations.[18]

For example, the Japanese, who spend roughly three-quarters
of what Canadians do (as a percentage of the economy) through
government, live longer, have lower infant mortality rates, almost
as many doctors per capita, and have more hospital beds per
person. Switzerland, which also spends considerably less through
government than does Canada, also ranks higher on all of the
above mentioned social indicators, including annual GDP per
person statistics; the Swiss GDP per-capita figure is US$31,000
while Canada's annual "wealth per person" stands at $28,800.
Citizens can have a limited role for government and excellent
social and economic indicators as well.

Tilling the soil: Limited government and civilization

Few would argue that universal health care, help for the disabled,
new hospitals, or pensions for seniors were the wrong road to take
in the 1920s, the 1950s or at any point. But the most successful
government policies—defined as those that actually do raise people
out of poverty and are sustainable for everyone else—are, oddly,
not those usually thought of as such. For example, Registered Retirement Savings Plans where tax deductions encourage Canadians to
save for their retirement and not rely merely on the state-funded
Canada Pension Plan. And the beauty of plans such as the RRSPs, or
company or union pension funds, is that politicians and civil servants
in Ottawa and the provincial capitals do not tell retirees where to
spend their money. And government-designed programs such as the
CPP, which avail themselves of tax dollars, are not used to restrict
private savings that also help to alleviate poverty. These actions of
government are in stark contrast to the design of the health care
system.

Similarly, the most efficient and effective government policies are not ones that attempt to capture an entire sector. Think of food. Properly, Canadians do not want fellow Canadians to starve, so tax dollars are directed to the poor. Debates over the proper level of welfare aside, no one confuses the tax dollars necessarily transferred to low-income Canadians so they can buy food with some sort of role for government in the ownership of farms or grocery stores. Governments use the marketplace as it exists and subsidize the specific person in need; they do not buy Loblaws or Safeway. (If they did, the line-ups and issues faced in health care would be replicated in food quality, selection, freshness and customer service in grocery stores.)

Government-designed programs that are modest in scope and use market incentives and targeted benefits are superior to a top-down, one-size-fits-all approach. Those that do not fall in such a category, like Employment Insurance, become political footballs where rates are raised or lowered not according to actuarial needs but to political priorities. And all manner of other uses for the fund are also present, including straight revenue transfers to the general revenue fund of which it is a part.

Most people are rightly reluctant to accept new ways of delivering a service unless they see an added benefit in comparison to the existing method. But if Canadians asked themselves which services are delivered best and which ones they are concerned about, they might—depending on their bias—be surprised. After all, no one ever reads newspaper headlines about how grocery stores are shut down again because of a budget decision by a provincial or federal government.

Limited government and civilization are not contrary in theory or in practice. Quite the opposite. Civilization is dependent on both the basic structure maintained by government—the rule of law, a sound currency, secure borders, and free markets—and from the practice of the latter. In such rich soil does civilization flourish.

Live long and prosper, even if your government is smaller than Canada's

Does the size of government need to be as large as Canada's in order for a society to be healthy, experience less crime and live as long? While many Canadians would count out the United States and argue it is less civilized than Canada, that argument is more difficult when it concerns Australia, Ireland, Japan and Switzerland, all of whom have smaller governments but enjoy similar if not better social indicators than Canada. Of course, there are many variables that influence life expectancy and other social indicators. And there are many other ways to measure a civilized country. But that is just the point: many countries prosper, their citizens live longer, they have more doctors and more beds to stay in when they are sick —with a smaller size of government.

	Current general gov't revenue % of GDP	Current general gov't expenditure % of GDP	GDP per capita (PPP) in US$	Infant mortality per 1,000 live births	Life expectancy at birth years Women	Life expectancy at birth years Men	Doctors per 1000 population	Beds per 1000 population (in patient care)	CO_2 emissions per capita
Canada	42.7	41.9	28,800	5.3	81.7	76.3	2.1	3.9	17.13
Australia	32.9	32.9	26,600	5.2	82.0	76.6	2.5	7.9	17.19
Ireland	33.9	26.4	31,400	5.9	79.1	73.9	2.3	9.7	10.88
Japan	29.4	31.9	26,500	3.2	84.6	77.6	1.9	16.4	9.10
Switzerland	34.3	33.4	31,000	4.9	82.5	76.8	3.4	18.3	5.80
US	32.8	32.7	36,500	7.1	79.4	73.9	2.8	3.6	20.57

Source: OECD in Figures. Statistics on the Member Countries, OECD Observer 2002 / Supplement 1.

Canada's past health taxes

As *Tax Me I'm Canadian* went to print, federal politicians once again hinted about new taxes to fund health care—as if taxes were not specifically introduced and raised in the past to fund health costs.

In the fall of 2002, Prime Minister Jean Chretien echoed the remark of Oliver Wendell Holmes Jr.: "It has been said before and we on this side of the House agree that, like it or not, taxes are the price one pays to live in a civilized society."[19] Thus, once again, our politicians appear ready to introduce new taxes rather than divert existing spending and at a time when Canadian taxes have rarely been so high. And it appears that substantial reform of the health care system is also not envisioned at present by Canadian governments.

It is one thing to introduce or raise new levies if government taxation and spending were low compared to historical standards—even compared to historical welfare state levels—but taxes have risen for the last several decades with only a temporary retreat in 2000.

Thus, the reflex to tax rather than to restructure health care for private medical savings accounts, or to introduce competition between the public, private and non-profit sectors for the provision of universal health care in Canada, also appears to be a low priority compared to new tax increases instead.

Increased taxes with health care as the justification is not new. Over time, some of the taxes introduced specifically for health care have gradually been diverted to other purposes. In other cases, the reason for the tax was forgotten or was made irrelevant because the money flowed into general revenues where a large portion of expenditures are already devoted to health care. But the combination of forgetfulness and a refusal to reform or divert other spending will now be used to sell new or increased health taxes to Canadians. Here are past examples of taxes or tax increases justified by the health care budget.

> **1916:** Prince Edward Island's *War and Health Tax Act* raises all taxes by one-third except for the road tax. Saskatchewan's *Union of Hospitals Act* authorizes local municipalities to set up hospitals to serve common needs and to finance the same through land tax levies.

1939: Saskatchewan passes the *Municipal and Medical Hospital Services Act*, and extends the municipal taxing right to include personal taxes though not to exceed a $50 charge per family.

1944: Ontario's *Municipal Health Services Act* permits municipalities to levy property taxes or a poll tax for health plans.

1947: Saskatchewan introduces a new tax—compulsory monthly premiums—for health insurance.

1948: Ontario enacts a 20-percent amusement tax in the *Hospital Tax Act*. British Columbia introduces a three-percent retail sales tax under the *Social Security and Municipal Aid Tax* partly to fund medical services. The same year, B.C. passes the *Hospital Insurance Services Act*, which similar to Saskatchewan mandates personal and family premiums.

1950: Saskatchewan increases and renames its two percent retail sales tax to three percent for health funding under the *Education and Hospitalization Tax Act*.

1951: British Columbia raises its health care premium rates.

1953: Newfoundland introduces an entertainment tax of five cents per theatre ticket for cancer control.

1954: Saskatchewan health care insurance premiums raised. Newfoundland broadens the entertainment tax. British Columbia increases the retail sales tax from three percent to five percent, now known as the "social services tax."

1959: Nova Scotia imposes a three percent retail sales tax known as the "hospital tax."

1965: B.C. reintroduces health care premiums.

With the introduction of Medicare in 1969, the provinces once again moved to raise or initiate new taxes over the following several years. Nova Scotia raised its retail sales tax from three percent to seven percent in 1969 and directed the money to health programs. Quebec increased the corporate tax by two percent and in 1972 introduced a payroll tax on employees, employers and the self-employed.[20]

In Manitoba, a five-percent addition to personal income taxes was labelled the Hospital Services Tax though proceeds from it were not specifically earmarked. Monthly premiums were introduced in 1969, eliminated in 1973, but a payroll tax was introduced in 1982 for health care and education costs. Saskatchewan levied a five-percent retail sales tax and earmarked half of the proceeds for health services. Alberta introduced health care premiums in 1969.

In 1984, British Columbia introduced a four-percent surtax on personal income tax as a "health care maintenance" tax and increased the surtax to eight percent in 1985.

Health care tax increases continued into the last decade when in the early 1990s, Ontario New Democrats introduced a new high-income surtax which the Ontario Conservatives later kept and re-labelled as the "fair share" health care levy. And in 2002, two governments that are supposed to be fiscally conservative—British Columbia's Liberals and Alberta's Conservatives—raised their health care premiums to pay for wage settlements in government health care.[h]

---

[h] Source: Perry, J.H. (1989). *A fiscal history of Canada: The postwar years, Canadian tax paper No. 85,* Canadian Tax Foundation, pp. 653-655.

Endnotes

Notes to Chapter 1

[1] Gillespie,W.I.(1991). *Tax, borrow and spend: Financing federal spending in Canada, 1867-1990.* Ottawa: Carleton University Press, p. 48.

[2] Adams,C.(1993). *For good and evil: The impact of taxes on the course of civilization.* Lanham,MD: Madison Books, p. 2.

[3] Duncan,A. & Hobson,D.(2001). Saturn's children: How the state devours liberty, prosperity and virtue. In N. Ferguson, *The cash nexus: Money and power in the modern world.* New York: Basic Books, p. 67.

[4] Adams,C. (1993). *For good and evil: The impact of taxes on the course of civilization.* Lanham,MD: Madison Books, p. 169.

[5] Perry,J.H.(1990). *Taxation in Canada, Canadian tax paper No. 89.* Toronto: Canadian Tax Foundation, p. 17.

[6] The various taxes in pre- and post-Confederation Canada are listed in the now out-of-print book: Perry,J.H. (1955). *Taxes, tariffs, and subsidies, Volumes 1 & 2.* Toronto: University of Toronto Press, pp. 575-616.

[7] Ibid., pp. 35-36.

[8] Ibid., pp. 33-34.

[9] Ibid., p. 75.

[10] Ibid., pp. 33-34.

[11] Urquhart,M.C., & Buckley,K.A.H. [Eds.]. (1965). *Historical statistics of Canada. Series G1-25.* Toronto: MacMillan Canada, pp. 197-200.

[12] Ibid., pp. 201-203.

[13] Perry,J.H. (1961). *Taxation in Canada.* (3rd edition). Toronto: University of Toronto Press, p. 14.

[14] Perry,J.H. (1955). *Taxes, tariffs, and subsidies, Volumes 1 & 2.* Toronto: University of Toronto Press, pp. 51-52.

[15] Ibid., p. 61.

[16] Cartwright,R.(1878). Budget speech. Cited in Gillespie,W.I. (1991). *Tax, borrow and spend: Financing federal spending in Canada, 1867-1990.* Ottawa: Carleton University Press, p. 48.

[17] Duffy,J.(2002). *Fights of our lives.* Toronto: HarperCollins, pp. 48-49.

[18] Gillespie,W.I. (1991). *Tax, borrow and spend: Financing federal spending in Canada, 1867-1990.* Ottawa: Carleton University Press, p. 51.

[19] Ibid., p. 56.

[20] Ibid., p. 59.

[21] Perry,J.H. (1961). *Taxation in Canada.* (3rd edition). Toronto: University of Toronto Press, p. 10.

[22] Perry,J.H.(1955). *Taxes, tariffs, and subsidies, Volumes 1 & 2.* Toronto: University of Toronto Press, pp. 110-111.

[23] Ibid., pp. 110-111.

[24] Perry,J.H.(1961). *Taxation in Canada.* (3rd edition). Toronto: University of Toronto Press, p. 10.

[25] Perry,J.H.(1955). *Taxes, tariffs, and subsidies, Volumes 1 & 2.* Toronto: University of Toronto Press, p. 711.

[26] Ibid., p. 228.

[27] Revenue figures from Perry,J.H. (1955). *Taxes, tariffs, and subsidies, Volumes 1 & 2.* Toronto: University of Toronto Press, pp. 640-666.

[28] While Alberta was the first province to introduce a retail sales tax, Montreal began to levy one in 1935 and was followed by Quebec City in 1940. Both city sales taxes were eventually taken over by the province.

[29] Moore,A.M. & Perry,J.H.(1953). *Financing Canadian federation, Canadian tax papers No. 6.* Toronto: Canadian Tax Foundation, p. 15.

[30] Gillespie,W.I. (1991). *Tax, borrow and spend: Financing federal spending in Canada, 1867-1990.* Ottawa: Carleton University Press, p. 154.

[31] Perry,J.H.(1955). *Taxes, tariffs, and subsidies, Volumes 1 & 2.* Toronto: University of Toronto Press, pp. 150-151.

[32] Ibid., p. 147.

[33] Ibid., p. 153.

[34] Ibid., p. 154.

[35] Ibid., p. 157.

[36] Ajzenstat, J.(1999). *Canada's founding debates.* Toronto: Stoddart, pp. 55-56.

³⁷Ibid., p. 62.
³⁸Ibid., p. 128.
³⁹Ibid., p. 130.
⁴⁰Ibid., p. 142.
⁴¹Ibid., pp. 150-151.
⁴²Ibid., p. 217.

Notes to Chapter 2

¹ Organization for Economic Development and Cooperation. (2002). *OECD in Figures.* Paris, France, p. 38.

² Ibid, p. 35.

³ Organization for Economic Development and Cooperation. (2002). *OECD in Figures.* Paris, France.

⁴ *Toronto Star.*(1994) 17 October.

⁵ *Budget plan 2001, annex 1.* (2001). Ottawa: Department of Finance, p. 165; *Budget plan 2000: Five-year tax reduction plan.* (2000). Ottawa: Finance, p. 83; *18ᵗʰ Actuarial report, Canada Pension Plan.* 31 December 2000. Ottawa: Office of the Superintendent of Financial Institutions, Office of the Chief Actuary. Calculations by author.

⁶ Statistics Canada. *The Daily.* 6 September 2002, Based on Labour Force Survey information. In contrast, the most recent information from the Public Institution Division of Statistics Canada reports 2001 data for public sector employment at just over 2.5 million people. The difference, according to conversations with Statistics Canada officials, is due to the time period measured— the Public Institution data is an average for 2001 as compared to the Labour Market Survey, which is a more current snapshot of August 2002. As well, the Public Institution Division data is based on administration records while the Labour Force Survey is based on a survey.)

⁷ Gunderson, M., Hyatt, D. & Riddell, C. (2000). *Pay differences between the government and private sectors: labour force survey and census estimates.* Ottawa: Canadian Policy Research Networks, p. 4.

⁸ Statistics Canada. (2002). EI beneficiaries data, CANSIM II, table 276-0001 11. Data includes regular maternity, fishing, training, work-sharing, job creation, adoption, parental and self-employment assistance. Canada Student Loans: full-time, not including part-time students or students with provincial loans payable. Social assistance statistics from Human Resources and Development Canada, latest data available is for 1999-2000, Table 435. To avoid double counting Canada and Quebec Pension Plan recipients *and* Old Age Security beneficiaries, only CPP/QPP recipients were counted. Survivors' pension beneficiaries were not included in this analysis, thus the numbers are conservative.

⁹ Urquhart, M.C., & Buckley, K.A.H. (Eds.). (1965). *Historical statistics of Canada. Series G26-44.* Toronto: MacMillan Canada, p. 96 of Series 219; p. 99 of Series 287.

¹⁰ Perry, J.H. (1957). *Canadian fiscal facts: principal statistics of Canadian public finance.* Toronto: Canadian Tax Foundation, pp. 102-104.

¹¹ Hum, D. & Ferguson, B. (undated). *Aspects of the Chinese head tax.* [Electronic version]. Winnipeg: Department of Economics, St. John's College, University of Manitoba. Retrieved 7 September, 2002 from http://home.cc.umanitoba.ca/~dhum/re_aspects.html. Also: Hayley, R.L. (2002). *The Chinese head tax class action: No legal basis.* Vancouver: Lawson Lundell, Barristers and Solicitors. Retrieved 7 September, 2002, from www.lawsonlundell.com. Information on provincial revenue amounts from Perry, J.H. (1955). *Taxes, tariffs, and subsidies, Volumes 1 & 2.* Toronto: University of Toronto Press.

Notes to Chapter 3

¹ Department of Finance. (2001). *Total government net debt, national accounts basis, fiscal reference tables.* Ottawa: Table 56.

² Department of Finance. (2001). *Federal and provincial net public debt, public accounts basis, fiscal reference tables.* Ottawa: Tables 14 and 30.

³ Perry, J.H. (1989). *A fiscal history of Canada—The postwar years, Canadian tax paper No. 85,* Canadian Tax Foundation, p. 466, Table 17.21.

⁴ Ibid., p. 415.

⁵ 1946-47 budget year—Perry, J.H. (2001). *A fiscal history of Canada—The postwar years,* p. 466, Table 17.21.

[6] 1976-77 budget year—Fiscal reference tables. (2001, September). Ottawa: Department of Finance.
[7] Canadian Labour Congress. (1998). *There's no shortage of ideas, it's the political will to create jobs that is in short supply, February 18* (news release).

Notes to Chapter 4

[1] Layton, J. (2002). Status quo no solution. *Victoria Times Colonist*, 1 August.
[2] Pope, K. (1995). How Eurocrats squander billions. *Globe and Mail*, 4 April.
[3] WorldCom will emerge intact, CEO promises. (2002). *Financial Post*, 23 July, p. FP1.
[4] Altman, R. (2002). The market punishes its own. *Wall Street Journal*, 23 July.
[5] Layton, J. (2002). Status quo no solution. *Victoria Times Colonist*, 1 August.
[6] Roll over, Enron. (2002). *The Economist*, 3 August, p. 42.
[7] Ibid.
[8] Associated Press. (2002). Ex-PLO treasurer says Arafat pockets millions in donations. *Victoria Times Colonist*, 19 August.
[9] Mowbray, J. (2002). Big Labor's Enron. *National Review*, 13 August.
[10] McCracken, J. (2002). Three men indicted in probe of UAW. *Detroit Free Press*, 26 September.
[11] Office of the Auditor General, Province of British Columbia. (1999). *A review of the estimates process*, February, pp. 139, 151.
[12] All details from Auditor General of Prince Edward Island. (2002). *Report of the Auditor General to the Legislative Assembly, Auditor General of Prince Edward Island*, Charlottetown.
[13] Auditor General of Prince Edward Island. (2002). *Report of the Auditor General to the Legislative Assembly, Auditor General of Prince Edward Island*, Charlottetown, p. 25.
[14] Ibid., pp. 25-26.
[15] Ibid., p. 26.
[16] Ibid., p. 27.
[17] Office of the Provincial Auditor. (2001). *Lessons learned from our audit investigations*. Winnipeg, Manitoba, March, p. 4.
[18] Office of the Provincial Auditor (2001). *2001 annual report of the Provincial Auditor of Ontario*, Toronto, p. 2.
[19] Look south, Eric. (2002). *Saskatoon Star Phoenix*, 15 July.
[20] Office of the Auditor General. (2001). *Report of the Auditor General of Canada to the House of Commons, matters of special importance—2001, foreword and main points*, Ottawa, p. 1.
[21] Ibid., p. 6.
[22] Office of the Auditor General. (2001). *Report of the Auditor General of Canada to the House of Commons, matters of special importance—2001, chapter 4, voted grants and contributions: government-wide management*, Ottawa, p. 9.
[23] Office of the Auditor General. (2001). *Report of the Auditor General of Canada to the House of Commons, matters of special importance—2001, foreword and main points*, Ottawa, p. 12.
[24] Office of the Auditor General. (2001). *Report of the Auditor General of Canada to the House of Commons, matters of special importance—2001, chapter 4, voted grants and contributions: program management*, Ottawa, p. 42.
[25] Ibid., pp. 39-42.

Notes to Chapter 5

[1] Solzhenitsyn, A. (1969). *Letter to the Writer's Union, Moscow*, originally quoted in the New York Times, 15 November. Reprinted in the *Quotable Conservative*. (1995). Holbrook, Massachusetts: Adams Publishing, pp. 215-216.
[2] Stanbury, W.T. (1995). *Reforming the regulation of the financing of federal parties and candidates*. Vancouver: Faculty of Commerce and Business Administration, University of British Columbia. Prepared for the 2nd Annual BC Taxpayers Conference, 3 June, p. 2.
[3] Notes from National Citizens' Coalition. *NCC battles gag laws*. Retrieved 7 September, 2002 from www.morefreedom.org.
[4] Stanbury, W.T. (1995). *Reforming the regulation of the financing of federal parties and candidates*. Vancouver: Faculty of Commerce and Business Administration, University of British Columbia. Prepared for the 2nd Annual BC Taxpayers Conference, 3 June 1995, p. 13.

[5] Gunter,L.(1999).End campaign spending limits.*Policy Options, September*.

[6] Ibid.

[7] The political establishment digs in.(1993).*Alberta Report,22 February.*

[8] Ibid.

[9] Royal Commission proposes new"voter-friendly"election law for Canada.(1992).*Main Communiqué from the Royal Commission on Electoral Reform and Party Financing*,13 February,Ottawa.

[10] Notes from National Citizens' Coalition. *NCC battles gag laws*. Retrieved 7 September, 2002 from www.morefreedom.org.

[11] Boyer,P.(1992).*Direct Democracy in Canada*.Toronto:Dundurn Press,p.76.

[12] Ads don't buy votes.(1994).*Globe and Mail,* 30 April.

[13] Mitchell,A.(1995).Election-ad gag law has difficulty in court.*Globe and Mail*,9 May.

[14] Ibid.

[15] Ottawa's gag law struck down.(1996).*Globe and Mail*,7 June.

[16] Ibid.

[17] Elections are not for parties alone.(1996).*Globe and Mail*,9 October.

[18] National Citizens' Coalition news release,10 May 2001,based on *Access to Information* requests.

[19] The unnamed parliamentarian was taken from Hansard.October 25,1983,28-29,and quoted in Stanbury, W.T.(1995).*Reforming the regulation of the financing of federal parties and candidates*.Vancouver: Faculty of Commerce and Business Administration,University of British Columbia.Prepared for the 2nd Annual BC Taxpayers Conference,3 June 1995,p.13.

[20] Why does Harvie Andre really want to stifle your freedom of speech during elections? (1991).National Citizens' Coalition campaign ad.

[21] Broadbent,E.(2000).Let's deodorize political influence.*Globe and Mail*,22 June.

[22] Ibid.

[23] Brenner,Honourable Mr.Justice.(2002).Pacific Press & Garry B.Nixon *v.* Attorney General of British Columbia. *Reasons for judgement*,9 February,para.167.

[24] Harper,S.(1999).Dear Jean,you're gagging us.*National Post*,19 November.

[25] Ibid.

Notes to Chapter 6

[1] Burke, E. (1987). *Reflection on the Revolution in France*. Harmondsworth, Middlesex: Penguin Books Ltd. First published 1790, p. 356.

[2] Yergin,D. & Stanislaw,J.(2002).*The Commanding Heights:The Battle for the World Economy.* New York: Touchstone / Simon & Schuster,New York,p.189.Original quote in Goodman,D.S.G.(1994).*Deng Xiaoping and the Chinese Revolution*. London: Routledge.

[3] Gordon,C.(1999).The myth of Canada's 'tax hell.' *Maclean's, 26 April.*

[4] Quoted in:Submit joyfully to taxes.*National Post, 20 April, 1999.*

[5] Quoted in:Crusade for caring economy heads to Ottawa.*National Post, undated*,1999.

[6] Nystrom, L.(2002) Building a better way for Canada.Politics Canada website,Retrieved 7 August,2002 from www.canadawebpages.com.

[7] Finlayson,J.(2002)."A look at income in British Columbia."Policy Perspectives.Vancouver:Business Council of British Columbia.

[8] Maddison,A. (2001). *The world economy—a millennial perspective*. Development Centre Studies, Organization for Economic Development and Co-operation and Development. All figures adjusted for inflation to 1990 Geary-Khamis dollars,pp.289,304,323.

[9] Emes,J. & Walker,M.(2001).*Tax facts 12*.Vancouver:The Fraser Institute,pp.59-60.

Notes to Chapter 7

[1] Retrieved 30 June,2002 from http://caselaw.lp.findlaw.com/data/constitution/amendment16/

[2] Ibid

[3] Tax opponent's unique argument buys him time for his day in court.(2000). *Vancouver Sun,* 17 February.

[4] Hendley,N.(2000).Try paying your taxes in pesos.10 February.Retrieved 30 June,2002 from www.eye.net

[5] Smith,M.H.Q.C.(1999).Are income taxes illegal? *The Taxpayer Magazine*.Canadian Taxpayers Federation, 1995 and reprinted in 1999.Also available at www.taxpayer.com.

[6] Perry,J.H.(1989).Provincial taxation:Constitutional limits," *Taxation in Canada (Fifth Edition), Canadian*

*tax paper No. 89.*Toronto: Canadian Tax Foundation, p. 150.

[7] Winnipeg family loses fight against taxman. (1999). *Edmonton Journal, 14 September.*

[8] 'Sir Daniel's' going to jail. (2001). *National Post, 28 August.*

[9] At war with the taxman. (1999). *Kelowna Capital News, 8 August.*

[10] Retrieved from Canada Customs and Revenue website, Non-filer prosecutions, April 18, 2002, www.ccra-adrc.gc.ca/

[11] Smith, M.H.Q.C. (1999). Are income taxes illegal? *The Taxpayer Magazine.* Canadian Taxpayers Federation, 1995 and reprinted in 1999. Also available at www.taxpayer.com.

[12] Can't pay tax in pesos, court rules. (2000). *National Post, 23 March.*

[13] 'Detaxation' movement takes hit in court. (2000). *National Post, 15 September.*

Notes to Chapter 8

[1] Computer chip plant won't get aid—Klein. (1999). *Edmonton Journal, 28 May.*

[2] Canada's top business associations unite in call for tax cuts. (1999). The Canadian Chamber of Commerce, the Alliance of Canadian Exporters Canada, and the Business Council on National Issues, joint media release, 28 September.

[3] Bliss, M. (2001). The company that built a country. *Report on business magazine, September.*

[4] Alberta public accounts, Compiled by the Canadian Taxpayers Federation, 1994.

[5] $377 million in lost opportunities—A study of commercial loans and guarantees in employment and investment, Small Business Tourism and Culture, Forest Renewal B.C. (2000). Victoria: Canadian Taxpayers Federation, British Columbia Division, p. 23.

[6] Canadian Bankers Association. (2001). Business credit to small, medium and large customers. Retrieved July 2001 from http://www.cba.ca/eng/statistics/stats/loan_loss.htm

[7] See Moore, S. & Stansel, D. (1995). Ending corporate welfare as we know it. Policy analysis No. 225. Washington, D.C.: Cato Institute; Moore S. (1999). Welfare for the well-off: How business subsidies fleece taxpayers. *Essays in Public Policy, May.* Stanford: Hoover Institution; Mihlar, F. (1998). The government of British Columbia, 1991-1998: An assessment of performance and a blueprint for economic recovery, *Critical Issues Bulletin No. 47.* Vancouver: Fraser Institute; McMahon, F. (1996). Looking the gift horse in the mouth: The impact of federal transfers on Atlantic Canada. Halifax: The Atlantic Institute for Market Studies.

[8] Office of the Auditor General of Canada. (1995). Report of the Auditor General to the House of Commons, Chapters 18-21, Ottawa.

[9] See: Bachelor, L. (1997). Business participation in economic development programs: Lessons from six Ohio cities. *Urban Affairs Review, Vol. 32 (5),* p. 704-23; Bartik, T.J. (1994). Better evaluation is needed for economic development programs to thrive. *Economic Quarterly, Vol. 8 (2),* pp. 99-107; Dewar, M.E. Why state and local economic development programs cause so little economic development. *Economic Development Quarterly, Vol. 9 (2),* 1998, pp. 134-146; Grant, I. & Sherman, D. (1995). Measuring state-level economic development programs, *Economic Development Quarterly, Vol. 9 (2),* pp. 134-136.

[10] Buss, T.F. (1999). The case against targeted industry strategies. *Economic Development Quarterly, Vol. 13 (4),* pp. 339-357.

[11] Buss, T.F. (1999). To target or not to target, that's the question: A response to Weiwel and Finkle. *Economic Development Quarterly, Vol. 13 (4),* pp. 365-371.

[12] See Dewar, M.E. (1998). Why state and local economic development programs cause so little economic development. *Economic Development Quarterly, Vol. 9 (2),* pp. 134-146; Buss T.F. (1999). The case against targeted industry strategies. *Economic Development Quarterly, Vol. 13 (4),* pp. 339-357.

[13] Thomas, K.P. (2000). *Competing for capital: Europe and North America in a global era.* Washington, D.C.: Georgetown University Press.

Notes to Chapter 9

[1] Backgrounder on pay equity—Chronology, Treasury Board of Canada Secretariat, 31 May 1999. A conservative estimate of the $317 million paid out in 1990, and the extra $76 million in wage costs annually between 1990 and 2002 inclusive, would yield a figure of $1.3 billion, not adjusted for inflation (which would make it higher) and this estimate also does not factor in additional federal government employees employed at the pay equity-boosted levels which would further increase the estimate.

[2] Perspectives on labour and income. (2001). *Statistics Canada, Vol. 2 (12).*

[3] Ibid.

[4] Ministry of Attorney General, Province of British Columbia. (2001). Pay equity in British Columbia—A discussion paper, Victoria: Ministry of Attorney General, Province of British Columbia.

[5] Ottawa exaggerating costs of pay-equity ruling, union says. (1998). *Globe and Mail, 31 July.*

[6] Backgrounder on pay equity—Chronology, Treasury Board of Canada Secretariat, 31 May.

[7] Ottawa exaggerating costs of pay-equity ruling, union says. (1998). *Globe and Mail, 31 July.*

[8] Public Accounts of Canada, Receiver General of Canada, Volume II, Part II, Ottawa, Canada, p. 10.29.

[9] Pay equity pricey. (1995). *Edmonton Sun, March 10.*

[10] RCMP employees newest recipients of pay-equity deal, 13 July 2000, *Vancouver Sun.*

[11] Ibid.

[12] Pay equity program puts points over jobs. (2000). *Vancouver Sun, 4 July.*

[13] Federal pay equity deal gives some up to $60,000. (1999). *National Post, 28 October.*

[14] *Fact Sheet, Negotiations with the Public Service Alliance of Canada, 17 September 2001.* Ottawa: Treasury Board of Canada Secretariat.

[15] Government moves ahead with classification reform. Treasury Board news release, 8 May 2002, Ottawa.

[16] Bean was quoted in "Federal pay equity deal gives some up to $60,000," 29 October 1999, *National Post.*

[17] PSAC Pay Equity Bulletin No. 50, 4 February 2002.

Notes to Chapter 10

[1] Quoted in Keating, R.J. (1999). Sports pork: The costly relationship between major league sports and government, *The CATO Institute Policy Analysis, 5 April.* Retrieved 30 May , 2002, from www.cato.org

[2] Plan afloat to help NHL teams with proceeds from sports lotteries. (1999). *Canadian Press* and *Victoria Times Colonist, 6 December.*

[3] Small-market teams can't skate with NHL's rich, says U.S. investment bank. (1999). *National Post, 29 June.*

[4] Ibid.

[5] NHL awash in red ink, Bettman says. (1999). *Ottawa Citizen, 10 June.*

[6] NHL payrolls. (199). *National Post, 28 June.* Averages are taken from top 20 players in 1989 and top 24 players in 1999 as listed by the *Post.*

[7] Team payroll estimates. Retrieved 15 August, 2002, from www.HockeyZonePlus.Com

[8] Players aren't the only ones seeing mega-cheques. (1999). *Vancouver Province, 15 December.*

[9] Burke sees NBA sale as a warning. (1999). *Vancouver Sun, 24 September.*

[10] Manley backs NHL rescue plan. (1999). *National Post, 13 October.*

[11] Senators' subsidies would just fuel NHL salaries: Harris. (1999). *National Post, 29 October.*

[12] Ontario offers tax break to NHL arenas. (1999). *CNews, 28 October.*

[13] Ottawa could reject aid for Canucks. (2000). *Vancouver Sun, 15 January.*

[14] Big bucks to Canucks: Poll. (1999). *Vancouver Province, 29 December.*

[15] Residents won't support bailout minister says. (2000). *Vancouver Sun, 19 January.*

[16] Mayor: City's hands tied on Canucks' property tax. (2002). *Vancouver Province, 2 June.*

[17] Canucks brass, players encouraged by B.C. poll result. (1999). *Vancouver Province, 30 December.*

[18] NHL asks for lottery cash help. (1999). *Vancouver Sun, 18 September.*

[19] Ibid.

[20] Jeers from the crowd kill NHL bailout. (2000). *National Post, 22 January.*

[21] "Burke insists NHL deserves lottery funds," *Vancouver Sun,* 14 April 2000.

[22] Losses number NHL's days in Canada. (2000). *Vancouver Sun, 4 January.*

[23] Canucks brass, players, encouraged by B.C. poll results. (1999). *Vancouver Province, 30 December.*

[24] Canucks bottom line: They don't want a subsidy. (2002). *Vancouver Province, 2 June.*

[25] Burke insists NHL deserves lottery funds. (2000). *Vancouver Sun, 14 April.*

[26] Flames, Oilers get their lottery. (2001). *National Post, 21 November.*

[27] Burke insists NHL deserves lottery funds. (2000). *Vancouver Sun, 14 April.*

[28] Flames, Oilers get their lottery. (2001). *National Post, 21 November.*

[29] Statistics Canada, Total business bankruptcies reported in the calendar year 2001.

[30] Canadians unwilling to bail out NHL: poll. (1999). *National Post, 16 July.*

[31] Keating, R.J. (1999). Sports pork: The costly relationship between major league sports and government, *The CATO Institute Policy Analysis, 5 April.* Retrieved 15 May, 2002, from www.cato.org, p. 15.

[32] Mintz, Jack. (2002). Why taxes tax productivity. *Vancouver Sun, 20 August.*

[33] Keating, R.J. (1999). Sports pork: The costly relationship between major league sports and government, *The CATO Institute Policy Analysis, 5 April.* Retrieved 15 May, 2002, from www.cato.org

[34] Quoted in Keating, R.J. (1999). Sports pork: The costly relationship between major league sports and

government, *The CATO Institute Policy Analysis.* Originally from Staudoher, P.D. & Mangan, J.A. [Eds.] (1991). The blue line and the bottom line: Entrepreneurs and the business of hockey 1927-90. In *The business of professional sports.* (1991). Chicago: University of Illinois Press, pp. 181-82.

Notes to Chapter 11

[1] Morton, F.L. & Knopff, R. (2000). *The charter revolution and the court party.* Peterborough: Broadview Press, p. 97.

[2] News release from John Bryden, Member of Parliament, "Memo to charities: Pipe down and get back to work," 27 March 2002.

[3] Public accounts of the province of British Columbia, Ministry of Finance, fiscal years 1992-2001.

[4] Results from *Access to Information* request from the Canadian Taxpayers Federation to the federal department of Canadian Heritage, Multiculturalism Program, Ottawa, fulfilled January 11, 2002.

[5] Results from *Access to Information* request from the Canadian Taxpayers Federation to the federal department of Canadian Heritage, Multiculturalism Program and Environment Canada, Ottawa, 2002, and fulfilled January 11, 2002.

[6] Results from *Access to Information* request from the Canadian Taxpayers Federation to the federal department of Environment, Ottawa, 2002, fulfilled January 11, 2002.

[7] Ibid.

[8] Ibid.

[9] Ibid.

[10] Data on grants and contributions and other suppliers, money from the public accounts of British Columbia 1992-2002. Details from *freedom of information* requests filed by the Canadian Taxpayers Federation 2002. Fulfilled on various dates.

[11] Ministry of Finance, Estimates 2002-2003, Part III, Ottawa.

[12] Data provided by REAL Women, interview by author, 27 September 2002.

[13] Morton, F.L. & Knopff, R. (2000). *The charter revolution and the court party.* Peterborough: Broadview Press, p. 99.

[14] Ibid., p. 97.

[15] Ibid.

[16] Ibid., pp. 98-99.

[17] The left's secret slush fund. (2001). *The Report, 14 April.*

[18] Morton, F.L. & Knopff, R. (2000). *The charter revolution and the court party.* Peterborough: Broadview Press, p. 97. The original sources: McCartney, P.A. (1991). Government sponsorship of voluntary associations in Canada: Research and reflections. *Annual meeting of the Canadian Political Science Association,* Kingston, Ontario; Pal, L. (1993). *Interests of state: The politics of language, multiculturalism and feminism in Canada.* Montreal/Kingston: McGill-Queen's Press.

[19] Cut grants to lobby groups with axes to grind, MP says. (1994). *Canadian Press, 30 November.*

[20] Bryden, J. (1994). MPs report, special interest group funding. Retrieved 3 June, 2002, from www.johnbrydenmp.com/reports1994.html, p. 18.

[21] Elections Canada, Contributions to political parties, various years. Retrieved 15 June, 2002, from www.elections.ca

[22] Robinson, W. (2000). *Atlantic Canada Opportunities Agency: The lost decade, a 10-year quantitative analysis.* Ottawa: Canadian Taxpayers Federation, 9 May.

[23] Robinson, W. (2000). *WED: Wasted effort and tax dollars? A 13-year quantitative analysis of Western Economic Diversification.* Ottawa: Canadian Taxpayers Federation, 2 November.

Notes to Chapter 12

[1] Gylfason, T. (2001). Natural resources and economic growth: What is the connection. CESifo *Working Paper No. 530.* Munich: Center for Economic Studies and Ifo Institute for Economic Research. Retrieved 17 August, 2002, from www.CESifo.com

[2] Moore, A.M. & Perry, J.H. (1953). Financing Canadian Federation, *Canadian tax papers, 6.* Toronto: Canadian Tax Foundation, p. 5.

[3] Ibid.

[4] Perry, J.H. (1955). *Taxes, tariffs, and subsidies.* Toronto: University of Toronto Press, p. 619.

[5] Ibid.

[6] Moore,A.M. & Perry,J.H.(1953).Financing Canadian Federation,*Canadian tax papers, No. 6.*Toronto: CanadianTax Foundation,p.6.

[7] Ibid.

[8] Perry,J.H.(1955).*Taxes, tariffs, and subsidies.*Toronto:University ofToronto Press,p.621.

[9] Moore,A.M. & Perry,J.H.(1953).Financing Canadian Federation,*Canadian tax papers, No. 6.*Toronto: CanadianTax Foundation,p.16.

[10] From *Equalization Program,* FederalTransfers to the Provinces andTerritories.Ottawa:Department of Finance.Retrieved February 2001 from www.fin.gc.ca

[11] Major federal transfers to the Provinces andTerritories.Ottawa:Department of Finance,4April 2002. Retrieved 14August,2002,200? from www.fin.gc.ca

[12] Major federal transfers to the Province andTerritories.Ottawa:Department of Finance,4April 2002. Retrieved 15August 2002,from www.fin.gc.ca

[13] Statistics Canada, Financial Management System (FMS) Basis, Provincial and territorial government revenue and expenditures,2001-02 data.Calculations by the author.

[14] Mella, Honourable P.J.(2001).Presentation to the Senate committee on national finance concerning the equalization program.ProvincialTreasurer,Prince Edward Island, 24 October 2001.

[15] For more on this, see Maddison,A. (2001). *The world economy—A millennial perspective.* Development centre studies, Organisation for Economic Development and Cooperation.

[16] Gylfason,T.Natural resources and economic growth:What is the connection,CESifo *Working Paper No. 530.* Munich:Center for Economic Studies and Ifo Institute for Economic Research.RetrievedAugust 2001 from www.CESifo.com

[17] Brison,S.(2002).An Irish model for growth inAtlantic Canada.*National Post*,17August.

[18] Murray,L. & Cools,A.C.(2002).*The effectiveness of and possible improvements to the present equalization policy.* Ottawa:Standing Committee on National Finance,The Senate of Canada.

Notes to Chapter 13

[1] $50,000 federal grant to examine strippers.(2000).*National Post, 12 June.*

[2] McMahon, F. (1998)."Close Cape Breton's coal industry," *Moncton Times and Transcript, 24 April.*

[3] Devco:What price loyalty. (2000).CBC News Review.Retrieved March 20, 2000,from www.cbc.ca/newswire

[4] Ibid.

[5] Author interview with Fred McMahon,Fraser Institute, 15August 2002.

[6] "Agreement reached to sell Skeena Cellulose,"Ministry of Competition,Science and Enterprise news release, Government of British Columbia, 20 February 2002.

[7] Something is rotten inWinnipeg.(1999).*Alberta Report, 4 October.*

[8] Ottawa loans to bikers bombs out.(1995).*Canadian Press/Vancouver Sun, 22 March.*

[9] Outrage spreads over federal $750,000 loan for'Party Central.'(2002).*National Post, 15 July.*

[10] Defence tab estimated at $1 million a month.(2002). *Victoria Times Colonist, 6 July.*

[11] 'Bored'lawyer agrees to settlement.(1995).*Vancouver Sun, 27 May.*

[12] Truscott, R. (2000). Half-baked potato plan costs taxpayers. *Let's Talks Taxes* commentary from the Saskatchewan division of the CanadianTaxpayers Federation,1 June.

[13] Williams,J.(1999).*Waste report,*(media release) from JohnWilliams,Member of Parliament,June.

[14] Federal grant fundedWTO protest film.(2000).*Southam News/Reuters, 16 February.*

[15] Ibid.

[16] Liberals paid firm $615,000 to evaluate own work.(2001).*Globe and Mail, 7 May.*

[17] Liberals to promote'Canada' as a brand.(1999).*Globe and Mail, 12 July.*

[18] Taxpayer taken for a $2.5 million ride.(1995).*Vancouver Sun, 7 December.*

[19] Empire of waste.(2001).*National Post, 1 June.*

[20] Chretien admits:Perhaps a few million dollars was stolen.(2002).*Vancouver Sun, 1 June.*

[21] Helicopter cancellations prove costly.(1996).*Canadian Press/Southam News, 24 January.*

[22] "Alberta government boondoggles since 1980."Alberta division of the Canadian Taxpayers Federation, undated research. Compiled from the Alberta public accounts 1980-1994. $55 million figure from: Gainers loss hits $209 million. (1994). *Globe and Mail, 24 March.*

[23] Author interview with Fred McMahon,Fraser Institute, 15August 2002.

[24] Office of the Auditor General of British Columbia.(2000).*Report 5:A review of the fast ferry project: Governance and risk management*.(1999/2000).Victoria:Office of the Auditor General of British Columbia.

Notes to Chapter 14

[1] Hayek,F.(1994).*The Road to Serfdom*.Chicago:The University of Chicago Press,1944 (renewed 1972), p.114.

[2] Gibson, G.(2001). *Testimony to Select Standing Committee on Aboriginal Affairs*. 2002 Legislative Session: 2nd Session, 37th Parliament. Hansard. September 26, 2001.

[3] Coon Come,M.(2001).Speech to the United Nations conference on racism in Durban,South Africa,30 August.

[4] Government of Canada, Public accounts 2001, various charts, Ottawa. Per capita figures arrived at by measuring on-reserve population in each year and total federal funding and then adjusted for inflation. Calculations by author.

[5] Comparison of social conditions, 1991 and 1996.(2000). Ottawa:Indian Affairs and Northern Affairs Canada.Also, see *Some fast facts on the funding of Aboriginal programs*. (2002). Indian Affairs and Northern Affairs Canada, 1 August.

[6] Department of Indian Affairs and Northern Development,Ottawa.

[7] Statistical data from Basic Departmental Data 2001 and from Comparison of social conditions, 1991 and 1996.(2000).Ottawa:Indian Affairs and Northern Affairs Canada.

[8] Results from *Access to Information* request by the Saskatchewan division of the Canadian Taxpayers Federation.Released by Indian and Northern Affairs Canada, 1 June 2001.

[9] Truscott,R.(1999).Native bands:Where has all the money gone? *Let's Talk Taxes*,Canadian Taxpayers Federation,Saskatchewan division,9 February.Retrieved from www.taxpayer.com

[10] Results from *Access to information* request by the Saskatchewan division of the Canadian Taxpayers Federation.Released by Indian and Northern Affairs Canada, 1 June 2001.Tax equivalent calculations by R. Truscott,Saskatchewan director.

[11] Truscott,R.(2002).Complaints,allegations and superstar salaries.*Let's Talk Taxes*,Canadian Taxpayers Federation,Saskatchewan division,15 January.

[12] Number of native politicians from CTF *Access to Information* request 2001.Released by Indian and Northern Affairs Canada.

[13] Allard,J.R.(2002).*The rebirth of Big Bear's people—A new foundation for status Indian rights in the 21st century*,CD Howe Institute.Page number omitted here as quotation is from advance unpublished copy.

[14] Ibid.

[15] Flanagan,T.&Alcantara,C.(2002).Individual property rights on Canadian Indian reserves.*Public policy sources No.60*.Vancouver:Fraser Institute.

Notes to Chapter 15

[1] Taxes and society.United States Department of the Treasury.Retrieved 2 June,2002,from www.ustreas.gov/education/faq/taxes/taxes-society.html

[2] Bird,R.M.(1970).The growth of government spending in Canada,*Canadian tax papers No.51, July*.Canadian Tax Foundation,Table 25,p.266.

[3] Fukuyama,F.(1992).*The end of history and the last man*,New York:The Free Press.

[4] Klein, N. (2001). Signs of the times. *The Nation, 4 October.* Retrieved date, 2 August 2002, from www.thenation.com See Courtois,S.et al.(1999).*The black book of communism:Crimes terror, repression.* Boston: Harvard University Press.

[6] Crook,C.(1997).The world economy,a survey.*The Economist, 20 September.*

[7] Perry,J.H.(1989).A fiscal history of Canada—The postwar years, *Canadian tax paper No.85*.Canadian Tax Foundation,Table 17.21,p.419.

[8] Ibid., p. 416.

[9] Ibid., p. 611.

[10] Statistics Canada, Canadians statistics, life expectancy at birth, catalogue no. 82F0065XCB.

[11] Original World Health Organization data presented in Robinson,W.(2001).*The patient, the condition, the treatment*,11 September,Canadian Taxpayers Federation.The study is available at www.taxpayer.com

[12] Thomas, K. (2000). *Competing for capital: Europe and North America in a global era.* Washington D.C.: Georgetown University Press.

[13] *Total federal subsidies to business from the Public Accounts of Canada, 2001.* (2001). Ottawa: Receiver General of Canada, Ottawa.

[14] "Subsidies to business as much as 29% higher in Atlantic Canada than in the rest of the country," news release from Atlantic Institute for Market Studies, 13 March 2001.

[15] Flanagan, W.G. (1997). Thanks for the subsidies. *Forbes, 7 July.*

[16] Mitchener, B. (1997). Europe looks askance at auto subsidies as overproduction looms as problem. *Wall Street Journal, 3 November.*

[17] OECD in figures, statistics on the member countries. (2002). *OECD Observer*, pp. 26-27.

[18] Tanzi, V. & Schuknecht, L. (1996). Reforming government in industrial countries. In *Finance and Development.* Washington, D.C.: International Monetary Fund, pp. 2-5.

[19] PM hints tax hike on offing. (2002). *National Post, 2 October.*

[20] Perry, J.H. (1989). A fiscal history of Canada—The postwar years, *Canadian tax paper No. 85.* Canadian Tax Foundation, pp. 653-655.

Index

Barbarians in the Garden City

Barbarians in the Garden City – The BC NDP in Power
provides an grim overview of the patronage, abuses, waste and
repression of free speech, that the province of BC went through
during the NDP's 10-year reign of terror. By Mark Milke.

1-4 books

Quantity _____ x $19.95 = ... _____

(BULK: 5 or more books)

Quantity _____ x 16.95 = ... _____
Discount price only applies to orders of 5 or more

Postage: $5.00 first copy .... _____

(+ .50 per each additional copy) .... _____

Sub-total .... _____

G.S.T. (7%) (on books and postage) .... _____

P.S.T. (6% Sask Residents only) .... _____

Total .... _____

Ship to:

Name: _____

Address:_____

_____Postal Code _____

Payment:
❑ **Cheque /** ❑ **Money Order /** ❑ **VISA /** ❑ **Mastercard**

(No C.O.D. or cash orders)

Card Number:_____Exp Date:_____

Name on Card: _____

Signature: _____

Fax orders: 1-800-465-4464   **Phone orders:** 1-800-667-7933

Postal orders: Canadian Taxpayers Federation, 105-438 Victoria Ave E.,
Regina, SK   S4N 0N7

Tired of High Taxes and Government Waste?
So Are We!

The Canadian Taxpayers Federation is Canada's leading taxpayer advocacy organization. From coast to coast we are 65,000 Canadians working to lower taxes, reduce waste and hold politicians accountable.

We are a non-profit & non-partisan citizen advocacy group.

For more information or to support the Canadian Taxpayers Federation call:

1-800-667-7933

or visit us on-line at www.taxpayer.com

CANADIAN
Taxpayers
F E D E R A T I O N
Fighting for taxpayers